I0554835

Home At The Edge

Ronald Schulz

Tumbleweed Books
Tumble through the pages of our books

HOME AT THE EDGE
RONALD J SCHULZ

Tumbleweed Books
Tumble through the pages of our books

Tumbleweed Books
HTTP://TUMBLEWEEDBOOKS.CA
An imprint of DAOwen Publications

Copyright © 2023 by Ronald J Schulz
All rights reserved

DAOwen Publications supports copyright. Copyright fuels creativity, encourages diverse voices, promotes free speech, and creates a vibrant culture. Thank you for buying an authorized edition of this book and for complying with copyright laws by not reproducing, scanning, or distributing any part of it in any form without permission. You are supporting writers and allowing DAOwen Publications to continue to publish books for every reader.

Chicago Rage / Ronald J Schulz
ISBN 978-1-998029-05-1
EISBN 978-1-998029-06-8

This is a memoir. Names, characters, places, and incidents are the product of the author's memory and recorded to the best of his ability to be actual persons, living or dead, businesses, companies, events, or locales recreated to the best of his ability. Permission to use legal names were obtained when possible. If permission was not received, the individual(s) name was changed.

Cover art by MMT Productions
Edited by Douglas Owen

10 9 8 7 6 5 4 3 2 1

To all those trapped on the edge, the unbalanced, who slip deep into the crevasse of despair, into suicidal longing, and to those who with bloody fingers climb back out, laughing with victorious glee at a grim society that doesn't get the joke. To all of you companions in the darkest night I send this love letter, like a bullet, straight to your heart.

Editor's Note

This work contains actual excerpts from doctor and nurse hospital logs. To stay true to their observations, no editing or grammatical corrections were performed on the hospital notes.

Red October 1969

Time had run out. The napalm horror of the Southeast Asia war blasted into our conscience on the evening news. Smiling generals stood proudly over piles of enemy corpses. *Gooks*, they called them, insisting Asian mothers didn't feel the same grief American mothers did for the lost fruit of their wombs. We watched GI's torching *hootches*, the homes of civilians, with their handy Zippo lighters, burned along with village rice supplies, forcing the occupants into government *hamlets*, a euphemism for concentration camps.

The political establishment of the United States, tainted by the racism that had flavored the dispossession of the American Indians, called it a *just war* to halt Communism from toppling over Third World countries like dominoes. But we, the errant children of the Cold War machine, saw it as a People's War of Liberation from neo-colonialism. Our teachers had instilled in us the democratic ideals of equality and the pursuit of happiness espoused by our nation's founders. We'd learned these were the birthright of all Americans, but the news cameras showed us black Americans beaten, fire-hosed, and murdered for demanding those same equal rights.

As a well-read teenager with an abiding interest in world events, I saw through the lies and my conscience wouldn't allow me to turn off my brain and conform to the demands of our racist, warmongering, dysfunctional society. We needed to build a more humane social structure. I identified as a yippee, a hippie who'd moved beyond passive resistance to the status quo to active resistance and revolution. To achieve that, we needed to *up the ante*, demand radical change in society and stop the mindless carnage in Vietnam before that tropical land became nothing more than a parking lot for the War Machine's Apache helicopters.

The Prisoner

Busted

The cop stood me against the wall facing the camera and hung a placard around my neck – CHICAGO P. D., followed by a number and the date, 11 OCT 1969. I peered under the bandages that swathed my head and covered my left eye. The police photographer yanked them above my forehead.

"Hey, I'm still bleeding!"

"We need to see your ugly mug, kid. Stand up straight." He left the small patch encrusted on the wound above my left eye, from which a trail of fresh blood trickled. The other cop got back behind the tripod camera.

"Face front. Look up!" *Snap* went the strobe. "Face right." *Snap.* "Face left." *Snap.* My mug shots were complete. They'd already taken my fingerprints. My attempts to resist smudged the first card, earning me a smack upside my head and the cop's vice-like grip on each finger as he inked and pressed them. I had nothing more to hide and answered his questions.

Full name – Ronald James Schulz. *Age* – seventeen. *Birthdate* – March 26, 1952. *Address* – Wood Dale, Illinois. The cop paused and looked up from his form.

"So, you're a local hoodlum, huh? Not one of those outside agitators, imported to wreck our fair city."

"Nope, I'm home grown."

His questions resumed. *Occupation* – Stockman. His lips curled into a grimace. "You don't look like you wrangle cattle in the Chicago stockyards."

"Well, no." I felt myself blushing. *Stock boy* felt too demeaning. I was a man, dammit. "My last job was stocking warehouse shelves. Just put down laborer."

He didn't bother changing what he'd already written, but dumped my paltry possessions onto the counter: a buck and a half in change and two scraps of paper – the scribbled addresses of Bonnie's folks back in New York and the Big Purple commune in New Jersey, friends, I hoped to see again.

"Sign here." He put his finger on a space at the bottom of the list. "You'll get this shit back when, I mean *if,* you're released."

The rest of my possessions rested in my duffle bag, which I'd dropped, along with Karen's backpack, in the trunk of our new friends' car. The car belonged to students who'd driven in from Grinnell, Iowa, for the DAYS OF RAGE demonstration. They intended to split back to Grinnell later that day. It looked like I wouldn't get out in time to ride with them. My stuff should end up safe at Grinnell college. When and *if* I got bailed out, I'd have to hitchhike out there and find them. Then, together with my dear Karen, I'd resume my glorious, free life. This stint in jail, I assumed, should only be a brief bump on the rocky road I traveled.

Active 1: The last time I, Ron Schulz of Wood Dale, got arrested, I was a fifteen-year-old runaway in New Orleans with no rights. This time, even though I was still underage for voting or legal drinking, I was a ripe seventeen-year-old legal dropout and considered myself an adult with human rights, so I spoke up.

"Don't I get a phone call?"

The cop snickered and glanced at his watch. "You've got the gall, kid. I'm pulling overtime thanks to you goddamn punks and haven't slept in two days."

"Well, no one knows where I am. See? Don't political prisoners have rights under the Geneva Convention?" I'd come to the grandiose conclusion that the international rules of war protected me and my fellow arrestees.

"Fuck your rights." He glanced at his sheet of paper. "Jesus, kid, your goose is cooked. Your bail will be higher than some of these other scumbags." He cleared his throat. "You're charged with aiding an escapee, aggravated battery – on a police officer for god's sake, resisting arrest, and mob action. You'll be goddamn lucky to get out anytime soon." He snorted, turned away from me and shouted, "Next!"

They dragged the next long-haired youth up to the counter as another cop grabbed my arm and hustled me along to my next station of the cross. My life had sure taken a nosedive. Only hours before I'd woken up between two groovy chicks. The three of us had talked long into the night of a rosy future together in one of the communes I'd visited out west. The snap decision to pull a comrade free cost me my freedom and my lovers. If only I'd skipped that last wild charge into police lines, I'd still be free with my ladies at my side, marching into the glorious future we envisioned.

Beautiful, brown-eyed Karen, a sixteen-year-old runaway, had been my lover ever since we'd met in New York's Greenwich Village thirteen days before. Our journey to join the Days of Rage in Chicago was a grueling hitchhiker's hell, but we saw the real America up close that most people, breezing along the Interstate, missed. She'd stood by me through each crazy situation we found ourselves in, and my love for her had grown with the miles we traveled.

Blond, blue-eyed Kay had only joined us in the wee hours of that morning. She was at least two years older than me, a freshman at Grinnell College in Iowa and a self-proclaimed feminist, who had come to Chicago with fifteen fellow students in a three-car convoy. Students and dropouts like me had come from all over the US, even

Canada, to bring the Vietnam war home to the American heartland. Ending the war was only part of our agenda. Our nation needed revolutionary social change, true People Power in place of the Piggy Corporate rule that made a lie of our supposed democracy.

The Days of Rage, sponsored by the Weatherman, the most militant faction of SDS, the Students for a Democratic Society, was supposed to kick off a wider youth rebellion against the establishment. The Weathermen said we needed to be *Vandals in the mother country*, to wake up our smug nation to the crimes we were doing in Southeast Asia. I'd met Kay at a planning session where her pacifist views incurred the wrath of a militant cadre, who I understood was himself a Vietnamese on a student visa. He screamed at her.

"You are a nationalist chauvinist, racist, sheltering behind your white skin privilege!" He swiveled around to take in the approval of his audience. "She can just sit there and say the Vietnamese should fight, but *she* doesn't have to. The Vietcong would kill her. She shouldn't even be here. We should kick her out."

The girl's mouth popped open as she cowered in shock under his attack. Angered, I stood up to defend her.

"We're more intent on fighting each other than the real enemy. We should save our anger for the pigs tomorrow."

That defused the tension, and the girl crawled over to sit beside me at the back of the crowd. Her trembling hand grasped mine. "Thanks for speaking up for me," she whispered. "I'm Kay, by the way."

I gave her hand a reassuring squeeze. "I'm Ron. It's crazy to attack everyone who disagrees with their tactics. We need a common front. People's War is waged with more than bullets." I stood up. "I've got to take a piss and will be right back."

As I passed the back door on my way back the guy on the watch ran past me. Something was up. *Crash*, a cop in riot gear smashed his baton through the full-length glass door and stepped through the broken shards to run up to me. I grabbed a football helmet from the pile on the floor to parry his blow, and he froze, but with his backup following through the shattered door, it was futile to resist so I backed into the meeting room.

"Up against the wall!" The cops lined up a couple hundred of us, minus the few who escaped out a window. I stood beside Kay with my hand over hers to give her courage as they frisked us from behind. They arrested a few of our leaders, disappeared into the night and Kay and I found Karen at another church that hosted us, zonked out in her sleeping bag.

She blinked and sat up but didn't say a word as I introduced her to Kay. "What do you think, Karen? Let's bring Kay into our affinity group. We'd make a nice threesome."

To avoid infiltration by undercover agents, the Weathermen recommended we stick together with those we knew and trusted in tight squads they called affinity groups. Until then, Karen and I only had each other. Her eyes searched mine, but her blank face didn't clue me into her feelings. Her sleepy voice was flat as she spoke.

"The Weatherwomen say Monogamy is counter-revolutionary, and we need to smash it."

"Right on, Karen!" I squeezed her knee. "Jealousy be damned, limiting our love to a single person damages our unity. Our love will grow deeper, if more inclusive."

We three curled up together under our unzipped sleeping bags and, too exhausted to put theory into immediate practice, we dropped into a few short hours of sleep. It was already tomorrow, the climax to the *Days of Rage*.

The Haymarket

We rendezvoused at the empty concrete pedestal where days before the statue of a nineteenth century cop had stood. I watched a curly headed guy in a brown leather jacket climb up on the empty pedestal where he began an energetic war dance. As he gyrated like a go-go dancer on his small stage, the foot-long fringe that hung from his jacket swirled around him. Fate would soon throw me together with this wild man to become fast friends.

The Haymarket was sacred ground to the working-class movement. In 1887, the police attacked a peaceful worker's demonstration there, and in the resulting mayhem several cops got killed. The authorities blamed the labor leaders for the death of the officers, and after a farce of a kangaroo court, hung several who had spoken at the event. To show solidarity with the working class, the Weathermen blew up the statue as a prelude to the Rage. The Trial of the Chicago Eight for Conspiracy to disrupt the 1968 Democratic Convention was front page news. History was repeating itself in our lifetime. The Government wanted to fix the blame on leaders of the Anti-war movement, although journalists on the scene described it as a "Police

Riot," a heavy-handed response by Mayor Daily's political machine to crush free speech. The Days of Rage was as much our revenge for that trumped up justice as our goal of bringing the war home from Southeast Asia.

Black Panther Bobby Seale was one of the Chicago Eight defendants. He insisted on having his own lawyer, but Judge Hoffman refused to consider that motion. On October 29, it would reach a crisis when judge Hoffman ordered Bobby gagged and chained to his chair. That image would become an icon of the unjust proceedings. Finally, on November 5th, the judge severed Bobby Seale's trial from the others, and the Chicago Eight became the Chicago Seven.

YIPPEE founders Jerry Rubin and Abbie Hoffman, no relation to judge Hoffman, were leaders of the Youth International Party, or YIPPIES, which, of course, included radical hippies like us. We didn't only want to elect a candidate or change a law; we wanted sweeping cultural change to revamp what we saw as a culture of DEATH into a LIFE affirming one. Members of our Hippie-Yippie youth culture took up where the older Beatniks left off. We saw ourselves as part of a continuum, an evolution, a holistic mind-body-spirit transformation, the dawning of an enlightened Age of Aquarius. But the realists among us knew that creating a world of peace and love required more than singing songs and holding hands, it required aggressive actions. Although Kay, Karen, and I didn't buy some of the more doctrinaire Weatherman dogma, we went along for the ride.

A guy in a red football helmet stood before the pedestal, called for attention, and began a rousing speech. Someone nearby whispered. "That's John Jacobs from the National Office."

Let the revolution begin! We linked arms, forming a phalanx with the others, and rolled into history. The massive police force surrounding us discouraged many of our comrades, who melted away. Fearing for the safety of my ladies, I considered pulling out too, but I wanted to see it through.

The grandiose words of Thomas Paine popped out of my school days' memory. "Summer soldiers and sunshine patriots will shrink from the service to their country." The spirit of 1776 seemed to infuse 1969, intoxicating me with the promise of our new American Revolution. The old one hadn't gone far enough. They had proclaimed that "All men are created equal," but that equality didn't include women, their black slaves, or the Native Americans, Indians like the Oneida tribe, who'd broken with the pro-British Iroquois confederation to join the Rebels, but the land hungry white rebels refused to grant American Indians the same rights that white men demanded and they lost their land to the very Revolutionaries they'd fought and died with. Our new, all-inclusive revolution would fix those omissions.

We surged south from the Haymarket, to turn east on Randolph Street. A tight cordon of well-armed police encircled our outnumbered band of three hundred stalwarts. It would be an unequal struggle at best, but we had to show we meant it. When we reached the Chicago River, the bridge vibrated under our tramping feet and our full-throated chants gave us a sense of power.

Che, Che, Viva Che!

Ho, Ho, Ho Chi Minh, NLF is gonna win.

Ho, Ho, Ho Chi Minh! Dare to struggle, dare to win!

The sight of Kay laughing as her voice rang out filled me with joy. To the other side of me, misty-eyed Karen also was caught up in the mood. Both of my heaven-sent dream girls looked ever so beautiful. Monogamy was too narrow for our love and didn't belong in the new society we were creating. I, too, had to overcome my selfish, possessive instincts if either of them bedded another guy. There should be plenty of time for all of us to get better acquainted and organize our relationship, our whole life lay before us.

At Lasalle, we turned south. One, two blocks farther, we marched without incident before we heard an animalistic roar.

"Break!" Those in the lead charged off the approved route to the left and smashed through the startled police cordon. Our little affinity group, exhilarated with the invincible arrogance of youth, erupting onto Madison Street through the hole they'd made, to the racket of

thuds and smashing windows. Scattered cops tried to grab and subdue individual comrades.

A guy on our left in a long green coat and a top hat stuffed with rags struggled with a blue helmeted cop who held his arms. The green man reminded me of a Charles Dickens character. Here was my opportunity to do something meaningful.

"I'll go help that guy and catch up with you," I shouted above the noise. Their momentum carried my girls away as I ran back to find that the green man had pulled his left arm free and was flailing the cop. I grabbed him and, with a couple of good yanks, wrenched him loose. He took off after our vanishing parade as I ducked, and the cop's club swung past my ear. But before I could run off, he grabbed my coat and pulled me up against his chest with his shiny silver badge in my face. It would make a great souvenir; I thought as pulled it. Fastened only by a thin pin, it came off easier than I expected. But as I wrenched myself free, a second cop closed in behind me.

Crack! Twinkling stars danced before my eyes, like in the cartoons. Then more blows, *wham-bam*, rained down on the back of my head. My ears rang, muffling sound as everything turned into a slow-motion movie. I found myself on my knees, still clutching the badge, as another blow slammed into my left forehead. I rolled into a ball on the pavement to protect my head. Trapped between the cops, I hoped in vain for someone to come to my rescue.

"Let go of it, you *fucking bastard!*" Through the stars in my head, I realized he must be talking about the badge, which I'd already forgotten about. I'd never get away with that symbol of their authority. One cop kneeled on my back, pinning me on the street, as the other's booted foot crunched my right hand into the tarmac.

"Let go of it, you goddamn hippie scum!" The edge of the badge cut into my fingers and palm. I couldn't release it even if I tried. One finger at a time, the cop pried my trophy loose and snatched it up. Pulling my arms behind me, they slapped on handcuffs. The first cop pinned his badge back on, laughing in relief as his partner kept me pinned under his knees. Both cops looked to be in their mid-twenties, no older than many of the Weathermen. Other cops ran up.

"What have you guys got here?"

"That son of a bitch let another punk get away and tried to steal my badge."

They pulled me to my feet, dragged me to an unmarked car, and slammed me facedown onto the hood. My left eye was blind, covered in blood, my ears rang, and my head throbbed. For a moment I was alone, then other disheveled, bloodied, and handcuffed long-hairs with bruised and sullen faces were dragged over to join me face down on the car as the muffled din of battle grew distant.

The speech by Black Panther Fred Hampton I'd listened to outside Cook County Jail two days before echoed in my brain, a warning I should have heeded. He called the Weatherman strategy "Custeristic." Custer's forlorn attack against a larger enemy force had been a stupid mistake, one I hadn't learned from.

"Idiot," I hissed at myself, realizing that I may have lost the best love of my life. Karen was my real responsibility, and I'd blown it. The pain in my head couldn't distract me from the bigger pain in my heart. Frantic self-destructive thoughts erupted from the deep, empty well within me. Like a defeated samurai I should commit hari-kari and redeem myself with macho honor. But no, I had to stay positive. *Where there's life, there's hope.*

Sure, I'd fucked up, but I had to remain calm and think. Karen and Kay were tough, smart women. SDS lawyers should bail me out of jail soon and I'd get back to them. Some of those arrested on Wednesday had gotten out by Friday. Once out, I'd hitchhike to Grinnell, where Karen and Kay would be waiting for me. Together again, we'd join a commune, create a tribe, have babies, a loving revolutionary family. Our forever after utopia would last for *as long as the grass shall grow, and the rivers flow,* to fulfill the broken treaties made with Native Americans.

My role models sprang from the history I'd read. Surrounded by the madness and despair of the Auschwitz concentration camp, Rudi

Vrba had steeled his nerves to remain calm and disciplined. He'd escaped that hell and his book had given me, as a fifteen-year-old runaway, the courage to plan and escape my high school nightmare. David Sterling, the founder of the British SAS Commandos, had a motto that I'd made my own. As they threw another bound prisoner onto the car hood beside me, I whispered, "Who dares wins, man. We'll live to fight another day."

The Angel of Mercy and The Bullpen

Through the blood in my eyes, I saw a black helmeted guy with a Red Cross armband run up to where I lay on the hood of the car.

"Are you all right, mate?" In his strong Australian accent, he shouted at the cop standing over me, "This man needs medical attention." The cop, busy restraining other prisoners, ignored him.

The Aussie bent over and whispered to me, "These coppers really laid it on you. You're covered in blood, mate, the worst case I've seen here. Let's hope it's not as bad as it looks."

I couldn't believe the cops were letting this hippie medic run around free to work on their prisoners and wondered if he was an undercover agent. As he opened his medical pouch and fished out supplies, he explained, "I'm with the Medical Cadre. So far, they're allowing me to treat the injured." He wiped the congealed blood from my left eye. To my great relief, I could see again.

"That's some nasty head wound." He took out scissors and snipped away a patch of hair over the wound on top of my head. Then he shaved it with a razor before sponging the tender areas. "Well, mate, you have a deep gash above your left eye and two more nasty cuts on top of your head." He applied gauze and covered my head and left eye with bandages. "You look like a mummy that your mommy wouldn't recognize." I had to laugh at that little joke.

A blue and white paddy wagon backed up to us. "Alright," bellowed a cop. "Let's load 'em up." With our hands still cuffed behind our backs, they began dragging us over and shoving us into the van.

The cop called the Aussie. "You too, get in!"

"Yes, I should tend to the wounded. Lord knows they won't get any help in jail." When they tried to confiscate his First Aid kit, he pulled away. "I'm a medic and need my kit and hands free." Still wrapping my head, he followed me into the wagon and plunked beside me on the bench. He was the only uncuffed prisoner in the paddy wagon. Maybe the cops were as impressed as I was by this dedicated medic's courage. They let him keep his kit.

We rode a long, bumpy ride to a precinct station. There we unloaded, and the medic disappeared before I could ask his name, leaving me to wonder what became of this angel of mercy. It would be nice if the cops released him without charge. With my hands still cuffed behind my back, a cop pulled me and two other captives into an elevator.

"Hold the elevator!" A couple of middle-aged uniformed police-women ran up and squeezed in after us. *Ew*, the women scrunched their faces and held their noses in theatrical disgust. "They stink like the animals in the zoo. Don't these hippies ever bathe?"

All I could smell was blood. I held my head up to peer under the bandages at them before answering. "We've been too busy to shower the past few days."

The officer gripping my arm jerked it. "These are the big, bad Weathermen," his voice boomed. "Not so tough now, are they?"

The ladies giggled like naughty schoolgirls as the elevator dinged open. The cops pulled us up to a counter and uncuffed our hands to get our prints and mugshots. Then they re-cuffed me to a bench and ignored me while they led out all the other prisoners. All alone I sat and waited for some time until another group of over twenty prisoners came in and sat on either side of me. These were all black men unconnected to the Weatherman, and I was the only white prisoner among them.

The cops dropped a long chain on the floor before us and shackled our feet to it. Then they manacled our hands in front of us, linked to the chain between each of our legs. We'd become a human centipede that had to move in tandem with the prisoner shuffling in front and behind or get jerked off balance.

The man in front scowled back at me with undisguised hatred. He made sudden, erratic movements, which jerked me one way or the other. It seemed to be his way of fucking *with whitey,* meaning me. I had to keep sharp to prevent him from yanking me off balance, which could get me in trouble with the even bigger, though calmer, black guy behind me.

Our chains jangled as the cops led us on a meandering walk outside around the building to a blue and white paddy wagon parked at the back of the station. My tormentor seated beside me continued to jerk my hands around. Apart from a few mumbled words passed between men who seemed to know each other, a wary silence reigned. After a long, bumpy ride, we arrived at our destination.

Under the baleful eyes of our guards, we filed out in the same lumbering procession into a building I recognized, the Cook County Criminal Courthouse on California Avenue. Karen and I had joined the big demonstration there where I'd heard Fred Hampton's speech.

One by one, the cops unshackled and shoved us into a large windowless room painted a dark industrial green. We stood crammed shoulder to shoulder with of a mixture of both white and black prisoners, who sorted themselves into companionable groups. I recognized some of the whites from the Weatherman action, but I hadn't gotten familiar enough to know any of their names. One of them remarked to his companion, "We're back in the Bull-Pen again." That seemed a fitting name for our corral.

"Hey," I called out to no one in particular. "I didn't get my telephone call yet. Isn't that our right when we get arrested?" They ignored me, a stranger, so I slunk through the crowd to the wall and collapsed on the bench that encircled the room.

From time to time, the door opened, and the cops called out names. Those prisoners went out to face a judge in the adjoining courtroom, giving the rest of us more breathing room, but not for long. Soon another large group of white Weathermen came in.

Among them was the flamboyant, larger-than-life fellow I'd seen dancing on the Haymarket pedestal before we marched off into the downtown Loop. With dark curly hair and long sideburns, he wore an American Indian style brown leather jacket, decorated with colorful beadwork and foot long leather fringe that hung from his arms and across his shoulders at the back. He flew about the room, enacting his animated tale of his struggle with the pigs, and the long leather strips swirled and snapped, *ka-crack*, each time he spun about. His confident antics made tougher looking guys step back to give room to his dramatic performance.

Then he noticed me, stopped, and squatted before me. "Wow, man, they really did a number on you. Didn't they?"

"Yeah, banged me up good. Some Australian medic patched me up, though. It was one crazy scene, huh? Did you get a phone call? I didn't get one yet."

"Phone call?" He laughed from deep in his belly. "This is Pig City Chicago, my man. You ain't got no rights here. I bet none of these other Weathermen got one either." He shook his head. "Did you give the Weather people your name and home phone number?" I nodded. "Good, their legal committee should arrange our bail. It shouldn't take but a couple of days at most."

"Great, but I'm not a member of SDS, and I bet there aren't enough funds for everyone."

"Neither am I. We're probably a lower priority." With tender caution, he touched the top of my head. "Does that hurt?"

"It throbs a bit. The pigs took most of the bandages off for my mug shot. I don't see the medic here. Maybe they let him go?"

"You need to get some stitches on that when you get out. Blood is still seeping through the bandages." He held out his hand. "I'm Pete Fischetti, by the way."

"I'm Ron Schulz." We did the usual up-down double-slap of our palms and then interlaced our thumbs and shook on it.

"My dad's pretty famous," he said. "He's a Pulitzer Prize-winning cartoonist for the Chicago Daily News."

"Wow, Pete, I dig the Daily's cartoons. Pulitzer Prize, huh? That's cool."

Pete's flamboyant personality cheered me up, but the cops soon called his name, and he was gone. One by one they called the rest of the white prisoners out, including those who'd arrived long after I did, leaving me once again the lone white in a crowd of black men. Although my skin color marked me as an outsider, only a few of them seemed hostile, and I was grateful to be ignored rather than harassed.

The crowd in the Bull Pen thinned down to just a few before they called my name. With a cop on either side of me, I stood before the weary judge slumped over his high desk in the adjacent court-room. He gave me a disinterested glance as the bailiff read my charges: aiding an escape, assault, resisting arrest, and mob action, followed by some legalistic mumbo-jumbo. The judge banged his gavel, and the officers led me away.

Deep into the subterranean corridors of the building they hauled me, until we reached a series of holding cells filled with the Weathermen I'd seen earlier, but my escort shoved me into an adjacent cell with only one lone black kid. He looked to be about sixteen, shorter than me, but just as thin as I was.

He held out his hands. "Gimme some skin, *maaaan!*" I ran my palms over his in the popular greeting ritual. "My name's Ice Cube. Where you busted in the Loop too?"

"Yeah, I'm Ron. Are you with the Weathermen?"

He nodded with vigor. Ice Cube was the only black Weatherman I met. Too bad I never learned his real name. As a minor, he expected the cops to release him to the custody of his mother and avoid serious jail.

"It's sure been a wild week, Ice Cube. Only a couple of days ago, I stood right outside these jail walls and listened to Fred Hampton's speech. He called the Weather action 'Custeristic.' It surprised me, him being a revolutionary and all."

Ice Cube grinned. "That's politics, man. Fred knows how to win over people. Know what I mean? Like, in April he marched right over to Uptown, to confront those hillbillies in the Patriot Party."

"The Patriot Party? I never heard of it."

"You probably will soon. Some of them crackers are raciest motherfuckers, but as broke-ass poor as any of us Blacks. But you know what?"

"No, what?"

"Fred got them to join his Rainbow coalition!"

"Really?"

"Yeah, man, those white trash refugees from Appalachia joined along with the Puerto Rican Young Lords and those wild Indians in AIM. You heard about the American Indian Movement, right? Thousands of Indians are coming off the reservations to find jobs in the cities."

I nodded and raised my fist. "Power to the People! It's about time all races joined in that Rainbow coalition. Black, Red, and Brown power, man! Some Cheyanne guy told me about AIM last year when I hung out at the American Indian Center in Chicago. Seems we're getting together in the common cause."

"Right on, Ron. That's what Fred said. He's against all this factionalism, like the Weatherman bullshit that split up SDS. Fred's trying to keep the Labor Unions and the middle-class liberals all on the same side." He started laughing. "Too bad you and I didn't listen to Chairman Fred."

"You're right, Ice Cube. This suicidal Weatherman thing today could have cost me my old lady. I've got no way to get in touch with her now that I'm in the clink."

Cook County Jail

The cops opened all the cells, lined us up in the corridor before we filed through an assembly line, to endure rites of passage for our admission as inmates of Cook County Jail. All the officers involved in this process were Black, and they hustled us along without sympathy.

In the barbershop, a few trusties, inmate employees, half of whom were white, wielded electric clippers to shear off our long hair with a few quick strokes. More than one long-haired Freak balked.

"You've got no goddamn right to cut my hair!"

"Shut up, asshole," came the response. "You've got no more say here than I do."

Without bothering to fuss, I plunked into the swivel chair when my turn came.

"Oh, Jesus," sighed the white barber as he tried to peel off the remaining bandages on the back of my head. "This'll hurt." The layers, cemented together by congealed blood, took a while as he pried them loose with more care than the cop. He, too, left the small patch over my eyebrow.

It had taken all year for my wavy locks to reach my shoulders, but they came off in seconds, along with my identity. All of us looked identical, like Marine recruits, adding to our confusion in recognizing each other.

In the next room, a thick-muscled, bullet-headed black officer screamed, "Strip down, everything off. No modesty here! Shuck your goddamn briefs too!" He held his head high with his chin jutted up like a black Mussolini reveling in his power as he paced before us.

"Face the goddamn wall. Bend over, grab your ass cheeks and spread 'em. We need to shed light where the sun doesn't shine."

A chorus of giggles erupted, and I couldn't help joining in. Mussolini smiled, proud of the appreciation his quip received. A team of two black cops wearing thick rubber gloves up to their elbows took over. One held a long flashlight as the other probed deep inside the anus of each of us, making certain that we carried no hidden weapon or other contraband in our nether regions. Other officers, also wearing thick rubber gloves, went through our clothes, piled on the long table behind us, feeling along the seams for hidden contraband. With a satisfied smirk, Mussolini called out, "Okay, men. Get your stinking asses to the showers!"

Six at a time, we entered a communal washroom with an equal number of showerheads. I looked forward to a refreshing, hot wash, but turning the creaky valve all the way, I got no blasting jet of hot water, just a disappointing trickle of rusty lukewarm liquid. There was no soap, and I had to scoop up a handful of water to wet myself all over.

After every murmured complaint, a smirking black guard yelled, "You think you're at the fucking Ritz? You assholes are enjoying the free hospitality of Cook County Jail, at taxpayer expense." Before I'd gotten more than a superficial rinse, he yelled, "Get out! You guys are done! Next six men in!"

Rather than the bright orange garb worn by other prisoners, us radicals had to put on the same clothing we'd been arrested in. After another trek along a labyrinth of corridors, a heavy metal door opened, and we entered a dayroom with large picnic tables anchored to the floor, around which sat more of our comrades. Throughout our incarceration, we congregated there for meals and to hang out when not in our cells. As I took in my new home, I recognized some of the Weathermen I'd seen speaking at rallies.

Someone clapped me on the shoulder. "Welcome home, Ron." I turned to spot the smiling face of Pete, my pal from the Bullpen. I grabbed his outstretched hand like a lifeline.

"Pete Fischetti! So good to see you, man. Looks like we're back together." The throbbing in my head vanished. In Pete's magic presence, I could only be cheerful.

"This place ain't bad," he said, slapping my back. "I've been busted for possession of dope, but this time we're among righteous people." He waved his hand at the somber faces around us. Our hardcore leaders were all deep in the eternal discussion of revolutionary theory and practice. Words like *dialectical materialism, thesis,* and *antithesis* floated up from the buzzing monotone. Pete giggled as if it was all a big joke. "Come on, man, I'll show you around."

The jail was divided into tiers that radiated off a central command-and-control area. Through the bars, I could see another tier directly opposite ours. It looked something like the spokes of a wheel.

Pete smiled. "We're interlopers here. The pigs moved all the black and Hispanic prisoners out to other tiers. Before us, these cells had become their home away from home, and they blame us for kicking them out. The pigs want to isolate us dangerous radicals from the other inmates. We're quarantined like an infection. They're afraid we'll radicalize those thieves, murderers, and rapists." He winked at me. "Come on I've got something to show you."

Pete was my tour guide exploring a strange new country whose inhabitants were exiled. Two long rows of cages with an aisle around them led from the dayroom. "At night, we're locked in the cells, and a guard patrols this corridor. The rest of the time, they ignore us, letting us run our own affairs on the tier pretty much as we want. Check this out."

He pulled me into a cell. They walls were decorated with exquisite sexy sketches of provocative women. One stood out. The black woman's face bore a striking resemblance to Angela Davis, haloed by her massive trademark Afro.

She stood, spread-legged and proud, a black Aphrodite, a fierce warrior holding an automatic rifle above her navel, nude except for the bandoliers of ammunition slung from her shoulders that criss-crossed between her large, pert breasts and framed her taut belly. Her haughty, defiant, conquering smile seemed to mock weaker men, while welcoming true Bravehearts as her worthy consorts. Where was the model for this superheroine, if not an idealized snapshot in the hopeful heart of the lovelorn artist, who rendered his lost angel with mythic, impossible power.

The other guys huddled around that exquisite masterpiece with me in sincerest admiration. We all missed our own flesh and blood heroines. This naked Amazonian icon of black womanhood was an artist's labor of love and for me, and all my jailed companions, she became an object of veneration.

"Pete, what became of our women?"

Pete put his ear to the ventilation grate. "Listen, they're on another floor." Indistinct feminine voices punctuated with banging on the metal screen filled me with hope. I added my shout to the mix.

"Is Karen Blake there? I'm Ron."

A muffled voice shouted what sounded like, "Yeah, she's here."

My heart skipped a beat. "Can I talk to her?"

Several women talking over each other answered until one shushed the others for me to be heard.

"I'm Ron Schulz. We came in together from New York. Anyone know her?"

It was hard to make out, but the voice seemed to say, *there is no*

Karen here. I got the same result asking for Kay. Banging and shouting through the ventilation ducts made for uncertain communication. I tried to remain optimistic, if Karen and Kay weren't there, they'd be free, out on their own or with our Iowa friends. Maybe another guy had glommed onto them, I had no proprietary rights and believed in the virtue of shared love, but destiny had put us together and, I hoped with all my heart, would reunite us in due time.

My head wounds would have to heal on their own without stitches. The long day was over, and I was exhausted. Pete showed me to an empty bunk in a cell and I collapsed on the iron bed, bolted to the wall. The guards slammed the barred cage doors shut, locking us in two to a cell. Throughout the night, blue uniformed guards patrolled the corridor, peering at our sleeping forms with flashlights.

In the dawn's early light, the doors popped open one at a time, a jarring series of *bang-bang-bang* sounds that repeated all the way down our row of cells as the guard in the control center flipped the switch. During the day, they allowed us out of the cells, but there was no outside exercise yard for us. We remained confined to the tier as black trustees, our only contact with other prisoners, ran errands and brought our meals into the dayroom.

A persistent rumor claimed that they laced prisoner food with saltpeter, to keep our sex drive in check. This was refuted by a guy who'd had some college education. "Naw, man, saltpeter is just potassium nitrate, there's no proof it makes your dick soft."

"Aw, man," someone beside me at the table whined. "Fucking reconstituted eggs and stale toast again."

"Looks good to me." I winked at Pete. "I've been flat broke and starving the past week, hitching back to Chicago with my girlfriend."

"Really?" The whiner took an interest. "Where from?"

"Greenwich Village in New York. We had some crazy adventures, got picked up by this hillbilly who said he'd take us for a drink at every bar in West Virginia, but he got shit-faced and ran over a whole row of fence posts before we got too far. Destroyed his car, but that was one of our better rides. Ohio got worse, left us stuck for days with no rides."

We had time to share our stories. Jail, with three feeds a day, gave me a chance to fill my belly and rest up. I gobbled up the food others turned down. It was mostly pork stew and potatoes, with baloney sandwiches for lunch.

Critical Thinking

The next morning and for several mornings thereafter, my hand reached out for Karen as it had so many times before, only to fumble across the empty space to the edge of the iron cot. Baffled, my brain awoke to take in my new reality. She was gone, but the memory of her warm body and fervent kisses haunted my thoughts.

One early morning, somewhere in Pennsylvania, she'd risen on her elbow to stare down at me with a furrowed brow. "Do you love me, Ron? I mean, really love me?"

"Of course, I do, babe. You've been right beside me through thick and thin, all the way from New York. After Chicago, we'll set out west to a commune, somewhere we can relax and breathe like free spirits. I'll make all this up to you, I promise."

She needed more than words to cheer her, and promises weren't all I gave her. Hugging her tight, I kissed her pouting lips and gazed into her dreamy eyes. "Want some more, baby?" She nodded, expectant, so I nibbled her ear, making her giggle. "I'm crazy about you, Karen."

Those memories tore at my conscience as I laid sleepless on my iron cot in jail. If only I hadn't released her hand to help that guy. I should have stayed beside her all the way to the end, but it was too late, I'd blown it. An empty hole filled my chest, where satisfied love had been. I could manage jail, but losing the best girl I'd ever known crushed my spirit. She should have been with me through all my future adventures, my comfort and encouragement, maybe even the mother of my future children. Someday, somehow, I *had* to find Karen. Convincing myself of that kept me from falling into suicidal despair. I couldn't let that happen. Life had to be about more than just me, facing the world alone.

Bang-bang-bang... the cell doors slammed open on a new day like any other. When mine rolled open, I joined the crowd heading to the dayroom. I'd eat my fill, do some sit-ups, jumping jacks, push-ups and a few Hatha Yoga stretches to keep up my health, then I'd meditate in my cell. Sticking to a routine was important to keep my mind clear and focused to get through this.

Isolated from the other prisoners, our Weathermen leaders ran our internal affairs with little interference from the jail staff. They broke us into small groups for political consciousness-raising sessions in the cells. Much of it sounded like mumbo-jumbo to me. I struggled to make sense of the rhetorical language, including cliche quotes from Marx and Mao along with harsh criticism of their former comrades in RYM Two, slamming them as running dogs, whatever that meant, but the overall pep talk message was clear.

We Weathermen are the Vanguards of the Revolution, leading the charge of white youth into the larger struggle of the oppressed black and brown People for liberation. We must be tough and attack the pig within us. White Skin Privilege protects us from the oppression that people of color receive. The pigs murder them with impunity but are less likely to kill us because of our color and status. We can afford to raise the "ante," be more combative, which will take some of the heat off our Third World allies and create a crisis of conscience within the power structure. They have to confront us, their own children, as the enemy. That must fuck with their heads.

Self-criticism seemed healthy at first. We needed to take an honest look at ourselves, analyze our individual motives to make ourselves into committed revolutionaries. Sitting in a circle on the cell floor, they began.

"Brothers, we must struggle to destroy the pig within ourselves. We must crush our individuality into the collective body for the good of all." Then, one at a time, a speaker rose to lash into their first victim, one of our own. "You haven't respected the fighting spirit of our female comrades." Another one added, "You belittled other comrades, calling our sisters *chicks* who need to stay protected in the rear."

The accused blanched and nodded in humble agreement, one outdid himself, admitting his sexist, male chauvinist faults, his doubts about the fighting capabilities of our sisters and lovers, castigating himself for a lack of wholesome communist spirit. But his accusers weren't satisfied. They piled on more accusations of White Skin Privilege and Defeatism. He accepted their criticism in a sort of masochistic frenzy until they tired of him and turned their wrath on the next victim.

As in some Catholic confessional, or self-destructive auto-da-fe, guys accused themselves and each other of all 'counter-revolutionary' sins. White Skin Privilege, Male Chauvinism and Sexism were the original faults that we had to flagellate from our souls, but the definitions became broad enough to include almost everything we said or did. Whatever beneficial advice there might be for the recipient became canceled out in an obsession to break down his *pig-ego*. I tried to sympathize with the lofty goal of rebuilding ourselves into the new socialist man and woman, to purge ourselves of the harmful, anti-social traits that held us back from true revolutionary selflessness, but it seemed to go too far.

As Pete and I were new, outsiders to the SDS cadre, they didn't subject us to this. We could only watch, wide eyed with a combination of bemused wonder and shock, as one after another of the experienced members and leaders of Weatherman passed through the ordeal. The French Revolution popped into my head. Revolutions devour their own children. Stalin, too, purged and slaughtered too many of his erstwhile comrades in the aftermath of his rise to power. I hoped the Weathermen evolved out of that before it was too late.

Very few non-whites became members of the Weatherman. However, one of the most outspoken members in our jailed group was Japanese. I'd first noticed Shinja Ono at meetings before my arrest and overheard someone whisper: "He's Yoko Ono's brother." That was only a wild guess based on his surname, but I later learned that he was her cousin.

Shinja Ono was twenty-eight-years-old, a graduate of Columbia University and accredited as a teacher by New York City's board of education. He'd injured his leg during his battle with the police, and like me, he didn't get any medical attention in jail. He limped about the tier, grimacing in obvious pain, but his strident voice rang out, encouraging us to struggle on.

After one of our jail-house meetings broke up, a short, muscular guy walked up. His hair was so beachboy-surfer blond as to be almost white. A tiny green jade Buddha hung from a leather thong around his neck, which intrigued me.

"Hey, man, how did they let you keep that charm in here? They took all my personal stuff away."

He smiled and held it out for me to examine. "I told them it has religious significance to me. I'm a Vietnam vet, see? While on *R and R* in Thailand, a Buddhist priest taught me to meditate, blessed me and gave me this. He told me it would channel buddha's blessings and keep me safe."

"I'm a meditator too," I told him, eager to connect with my new soul brother. "I've never been out of the country, but I read a lot and practice Tantric meditation."

One of our Weather leaders stood nearby, stern-faced listening in. "Religion is the opiate of the people," he said, quoting Marx, and stepped between me and the blond guy, drilling me with disapproving eyes.

"But, but..." I tried to get a word in, to explain my concept of blending spirituality with political action, but with no Marxist-Leninist scripture on the tip of my tongue, I had nothing to fire back that could make rhetorical sense to him.

With a shrug, he turned his back, blocking me out of the conversation, and faced the vet. His strident tone became gentle, as if he was talking to a child.

"Wow, that's a nice talisman you've got there. Can I touch it?"

The vet nodded, and he lifted it up to the light. "The Thai priest said it would bring me good luck and maybe it worked, because I went through some hairy firefights after they rotated me back to the bush in Nam."

All I could do was watch with growing disgust as our leader buttered up the guy, fawning over him as if his succumbing to the opiate of the masses didn't equate with mine. Despite his serving the imperialist side in the war, this veteran had more propaganda potential than I did. But I'd soon be draft age and needed to hear as much as I could about Vietnam and the war from those who'd been there, so I stood by like a jilted lover, listening in as the vet continued.

"The more I got to know the people of Vietnam, the more I grew to support the Vietcong. The Saigon Government is totally corrupt. Dig? The morally wrong side. That's why I joined you guys. Being Catholic, the regime persecutes Buddhists. Also, our body-counts of enemy killed in action include too many women and children, civilians, to pad the number of enemies killed. They either get caught in the crossfire or blasted by our trigger-happy guys who don't give a fuck about these people they call gooks."

Listening to him convinced me that we were right to oppose the war. We were on the same side, but my dour Weatherman comrades continued to disappoint me, so I'd keep my unpopular opinions to myself. Kay had been right to call them bombastic and intolerant. They took themselves and their dry materialism too seriously and needed a sense of humor. I expected the Weatherman views to mellow out over time. We needed to be like Fred Hampton with his inclusive Rainbow Coalition and join forces in the common struggle.

To pass the time, I continued meditating in my cell, but whenever that pompous Weather leader saw me sitting on my bunk in the Lotus position, he made a disgusted face that reminded me of my father and said, "Come join our self-criticism meeting in five minutes."

The Barn Boss

T he cop banged his stick along the bars. "Everybody out! Assemble in the dayroom, on the double-quick assholes!"

It wasn't dinnertime, and I wondered what all the fuss was about. Blue uniformed officers came inside and stood facing us along the bars of our dayroom, their truncheons at the ready. As I sat at one table, one of them shouted, "The Warden wants to talk to you."

Warden? That title seemed proper for a penitentiary but too grandiose for the administrator of a county jail, but Cook County Jail was not some Mayberry village lock-up. An angry looking, bald, compact, and well-muscled black man with the face of a bulldog strode into the dayroom, obviously the guy in charge, and began to harangue us.

"This is *my* goddamn jail! I run it, and I will not tolerate anyone contradicting my authority. Hear me? I won't have any goddamn Barn Bosses in here."

Barn Boss was a new term to me. His fiery gaze drilled into of each of us, lingering longer on those hard-core Weathermen who'd assumed the leadership that he felt was rightfully his. "Do you moth-

34

erfuckers understand me?" Our leaders sat meek and unresponsive, enduring the tirade directed at them without a murmur.

"Some of you think you are hot shit. Huh? Maybe you were big wheels on the outside, but in here your ass belongs to me, so don't you forget it. I don't care who the fuck you are, I won't stand for any Barn Bosses on any tier in *my* jail. Is that understood? If not, you will find yourself down in the Hole."

I'd seen movies and read about tough cons or Allied POWs locked in the sensory deprivation of an isolated black hole, but that was the first time I heard that Cook County Jail had a hole. Our warden wanted to impress us with his authority and his theatrics broke up the monotony of our day and gave us a look at the man in charge, not that it changed anything, our leaders still ran our daily affairs.

One day, a guard chose me to help a cheerful young black trustee carry in the chow from a distant kitchen. It was a welcome crack in our isolation and my chance to see more of the jail. As I passed along the cells, black prisoners blurted out questions.

"What all you white boys in here for, anyway?"

The trustee raised his fist high and spoke for me. "They're revolutionaries. You dig, my man? Power to the People!"

A warm feeling of interracial solidarity engulfed me. We were on the same side, fighting together against intolerance.

The Chicago cops arrested over one hundred and eighty of us on the last day of the Weatherman Rage, bringing the total arrested during the four-day event to two-hundred-eighty-four. Later I learned that the SDS National office assisted radical attorneys at the People's Law Office on Halstead to raise bail for our release. Contributions came in from all over the country, mostly from relatives, but the $19,892.93 raised fell far short of the $2,145,820.70 needed for everyone's bail bond. I was never an actual member of SDS and too low on the totem pole for the lawyers to take my case.

Day after day, our numbers dwindled as my cellmates were bailed out. One afternoon, Pete hurried up to me on his way to the dayroom. "See you around, Ron. My father made bail and I'm out of here." He clapped my shoulder and whispered, "Don't sweat it, man, you'll be out of here in no time." Losing his excellent company weighed heavy on me. None of the other doctrinaire comrades with no sense of humor, could fill the void.

One day, trying to meditate on my bunk, someone ran along the tier shouting, "Ron Schulz, you have a visitor." Maybe it was an SDS lawyer. No one else knew where I was because I hadn't gotten my telephone call.

Whenever a visitor came, whether family member or lawyer, they'd stand before the barred entry where they could talk through the pinholes at face level on the gate. To my surprise, I saw my father's face looking confused and uneasy.

"Hi Dad. How is Mom and the girls?" I tried to sound cheerful, in control of my situation. I didn't need to hear his humiliating *I told you so* sermon.

"Well, Ronnie, I suppose you need me to bail you out."

"You don't have to, Dad. The SDS legal team will manage my case with all the others."

"Ah, no, the People's Law Office called and told me they don't have the funds for your bail and asked me to do it."

"Well, Dad, I'm getting plenty to eat here. You don't need to waste money on me." I had to hold my head high, prove to him and myself that I was no wimp, but a dedicated revolutionary who could handle a stint in jail.

Dad didn't seem to know what else to say, and neither did I. His sad eyes darted everywhere but avoided looking at me. I swallowed hard to suppress a sudden feeling of guilt at the trouble I'd caused him.

"Goodbye," he mumbled, and left.

I felt dizzy as I stumbled back to my cell. Despite my show of confidence, I couldn't help wondering whether, without Dad's bail, I might have to stay in jail until my court date. The wheels of justice turned slow, and a court date could be months away. If convicted, I might remain there, to serve my stretch however long that could be.

Facing the wall with my legs locked in the lotus position, I reminded myself who I was or was trying to be. *I am a Revolutionary warrior with an indomitable spirit. They won't break me.* Jail was an opportunity to focus on my spiritual journey, to build a psychic connection to the Tantric gurus who would aid my spiritual development. Earlier that year, I had some success with Dream Yoga, lucid dreaming, becoming conscious that I was in a dream, without waking up. This was supposed to be a step toward navigating the psychic plane. I had to ignore the occasional snickers from comrades passing my cell and continue trying to achieve results.

Right after breakfast the next day, they called my name again. Without a word of explanation, a guard led me out to a busy office, where they spilled the envelope of my possessions onto the counter.

"Sign here," the desk officer said. Only then did it hit me. After nine days in jail, I was going back into the world.

Life at the Edge

Homecoming

A wave of euphoria washed over me as I realized I was getting out of jail. My first order of business would be to go looking for Karen. As a runaway and a stranger in town, she might not be easy to find. I'd ask around the hippie ghetto of Old Town. If not there, she'd probably have gone to Iowa with Kay. Grinnell is much smaller than Chicago. It should be easy to find her there.

With bubbling elation, I told the guard, "Looks like I'm finally free!"

He snorted. "Well, not exactly free, kid. You're underage, so you'll be released to the custody of your parents until trial." That torpedoed my initial euphoria. I'd have to mollify my folks for at least a couple of days before I could go seeking Karen.

I found Dad waiting in the next room. "Thanks Dad." I tried to show my appreciation while retaining some dignity.

Dad didn't answer and led me to the car. As we got in, he said, "We have an appointment with a lawyer this afternoon."

"A lawyer?" Lawyers cost money, I hadn't expected my frugal folks to shell out for that. "But, Dad, we could use the SDS defense team or a public defender. That's gotta be cheaper."

He didn't day more, but I knew he didn't like my idea. The Chicago Eight Conspiracy Trial, still winding its way through Judge Hoffman's courtroom, was making national headlines. Jerry Rubin and Abbie Hoffman of the YIPPIES made a mockery of the proceedings and the Weatherman promised to make their event as much of a Show Trial. As a staunch conservative, leery of hippies or any alternative philosophy, Dad couldn't understand how I and so many of my generation had turned their backs on everything he accepted at face value. It galled him that I, his only son, had chosen the other side. However, he restrained himself much better than I expected under the circumstances, and it behooved me to do the same.

Neither of us knew what to say to each other on the long ride home. I hadn't belonged there since I was fourteen and became an alien species in Dad's eyes. Family and school always felt like a simmering pressure cooker that I endured until I exploded. The street battle in Chicago only brought things out into the open.

My five sisters stared at me as if I was a Martian when I walked in, which drove home the fact that I didn't belong under my parents' roof, but I'd screwed up by getting busted, and pay the price for failure until I could get away and find my people, my tribe, my lovers.

Mom gave me a restrained hug, then put her palm to my forehead. "Jesus, Ronnie, you're burning up."

"Yeah," I croaked. "My throat's bothering me, it hurts to talk. I felt okay this morning until I got out of jail."

"Let's take you to the clinic." Mom graduated as a Registered Nurse the same week she married Dad, but she didn't work long, raising kids, six in total, took all her time.

"Looks like a case of strep throat," the doctor said after a brief examination. He gave me a shot of penicillin and wrote a prescription. We got back home in time to meet the lawyer, dressed in a blue suit and red tie. He looked younger than Dad, but I felt sure he held the same conservative views.

With a forced smile, he said, "I live nearby in Itasca. Your Dad chose me to represent you on this case." He laid a stack of papers on the kitchen table. "Mr. Schulz, take a look at these, then you can sign where I've marked." As an underage minor, I had little to say in the matter. Legal fiction took over my life. Although I was guilty as hell and proud of it, he insisted that I plead not guilty under some still to be figured out legal strategy.

I could feel my parents' tension. They had brought me into this world, I was flesh of their flesh, and yet I had no idea how to have a day-to-day relationship with them under the same roof. Dad mocked my values, lecturing me on how American big business and the free enterprise system were the answer to all the world's problems. We'd always ended up shouting at each other, and my voice was no longer in shape for that.

My parents were simple people, unconcerned with world events. The war in Indochina had to be a just cause, because we were the good guys in white hats who, like Superman, fought for "Truth, Justice and the American Way." It must have shocked them that I'd rejected the status quo and they must think I'm crazy. I could almost see Dad shaking his head and asking Mom, "Why on earth would Ronnie have gotten involved in all this?"

After dinner, Darlene, my year younger sister, pulled me aside. "Ronnie, tonight we are going to bring you to see a different doctor, ah, about your sore throat." Her bubbly, upbeat voice sounded phony and manipulative, as if she was talking to a child or a crazy person. I'd learned years before not to trust her.

"Another doctor? You mean a shrink, don't you, Dar?"

She looked startled, then recovered. "Whatever gave you that idea?"

"Come on, Dar. You don't have to lie to me. Tell me the truth for once. They're probably taking me to a shrink, so we can plead *innocent by reason of insanity*."

"Don't be silly, Ronnie. We're family, and ah, even if you have, ah, problems, you can always feel safe here. Everything is going to be all right. You'll see."

It was the twentieth of October. By the time we arrived at the clinic, it was dark as a winter evening. We pulled up to a small office on Irving Park in Bensenville. A sign by the door read:

Doctor Suhail Ghattas, Psychiatrist/Neurologist.

Mom and Dad went in first to speak privately with the doctor while I waited in the anteroom. Once again, I was a bug under the microscope. It was a familiar circumstance that harkened back to my grammar school days and their fear that I was so different from what they thought a normal boy was supposed to be. They took me to a series of psychologists who couldn't find anything wrong with me, no reason I couldn't fit in to be a *normal* boy, like Beaver Cleaver on TV. My folks had never known what to do with their oddball son, especially after I'd run away to New Orleans at fifteen, then officially dropped out of school at seventeen, to wander the country where I felt that I belonged. Everything was going so well until I got arrested, but I couldn't keep kicking myself over that. I'd keep my cool, bide my time until I could get away again.

Finally, the door opened. My parents came out bringing with them the sweet smell of cherry flavored tobacco and ushered me into the august chambers of Dr. Ghattas, who sat swathed in pipe smoke like a mystery man behind a large wooden desk. I wondered if I could turn this shrink into an ally.

A desk lamp gave dim illumination to the dark wood paneled office, giving the room a relaxed, homy feel as befitted the office of a psychiatrist. Several diplomas and a few tasteful pictures hung on the wall. Under the subdued light, Dr. Ghattas wore an expensive dark suit and had a slight build, a thin mustache, and an olive complexion.

"Please have a seat, Mr. Schulz." He spoke with an accent I couldn't place, causing me to wonder where he was from. "Why don't you tell me about your problems?"

"Problems?" I rose to the challenge. "Our Nation's problems are much larger than petty crap each one of us faces in life. I'm not alone. My whole generation" –I waved my arms wide as if to embrace the world– "have become revolutionaries fighting to save our democracy before it slips deeper into totalitarianism."

Dr. Ghattas leaned back in his swivel chair and listened without comment. My rant must have seemed insane to such a well ordered and all too conventional man as he appeared, but convinced of my powers of persuasion, I rambled on, expecting to sway the good doctor to the righteous cause.

He reached inside his suit jacket and took out the tools of his trade. Not a pen and notebook, but his pipe and smoking accessories. Freud was a cigar man, so I already knew these to be symbols of the psychoanalyst. With slow deliberation, like a witch doctor performing a sacred ritual, he laid open a pouch of tobacco on his desk. I caught a whiff of the sweet cherry smell as he filled the bowl of his pipe, tapped it down, lit and puffed it alive to cheery red sparks with a lazy, urbane detachment.

He leaned back and blew a couple of smoke rings at the ceiling without addressing any of the issues I'd raised, as if invoking the shades of Freud, waiting for me to say more, but I'd said my piece, and sat mum. There must be a tome written on the psychological impact of smoking to induce a father figure link, a paternal hold over the subject by the analyst. Although I wasn't a smoker, I enjoyed the wispy smoke that filled the room with its sweet aroma, but I was determined not to be seduced by head games. When his pipe burned out, he slowly tapped out the residue into the ashtray and took a white pipe cleaner from the medicine bundle of ritual objects laid before him on the desk. Carefully, he cleaned out every crevice before refilling the pipe with fresh reddish-brown leaves, and with as much fetishism and dignity as a pot smoking hippie, he lit and sat back to savor it, reminding me of the caterpillar savant smoking the hookah in *Alice in Wonderland*.

Finally, he straightened up and looked directly at me. "How would you feel about getting away to a nice, quiet place for a while?"

I laughed. "Are you sending me to the funny farm?" Funny farm was slang for an asylum or mental hospital. The comedy song, *They're Coming to Take me Away, Ha-haaaa*, by Napoleon XIV, AKA Jerry Samuels, popped into my head. The song was a hit in 1966, and it always got a laugh out of me, but some radio stations banned it for poking fun at the insane.

The good doctor coughed and cleared his throat. "Your parents paid a very steep bail and you've been released under their supervision. They cannot just let you wander around on your own. We have this nice, quiet facility in a natural setting beside the Des Plaines River. I'm sure you'll enjoy it. You will make friends, meet other young people like yourself."

"How long will I have to be there? I need to get out as soon as possible to look for my friends."

He raised an eyebrow. "Friends?"

"Yes, I got separated from my girlfriend when I got busted, and I'm worried about her."

"Let's try it for three weeks or so and see how it goes."

"Okay, I'm not in a position to refuse. Anyway, it sounds like a good place for me to resume my meditation. I'm a yogi, you see."

Dr. Ghattas sighed. It was the end of a long day for him. He pulled something out of a drawer and handed it to me. "Here is a book I think you would enjoy reading." On the cover was the sketch of a mustachioed man, with several similar sketches throughout the book, entitled *The Prophet* by Khalil Gibran.

"Have you heard of him?"

"Yes, sort of." It was popular among many of the dreamy eyed hippie chicks I'd met.

"Khalil Gibran was Lebanese like me." He chuckled. "And that comedian, Danny Thomas." There was the answer to my unspoken question of his origin.

Pretending interest, I leafed through the book, but I fed on sterner stuff and had no time for the airy sentiments expressed in poems. He was the author of the too often repeated line about love. "If you love somebody, let them go, for if they return, they were always yours. If they don't, they never were."

On that bland assurance, I'd let my most promising love interests slip away to the arms of other guys. But who was I to complain? The loss of Karen, my dearest and best, was entirely my fault.

"Take the book with you," he said. "Read it at your leisure."

With that, he opened the door for my parents to join us. They'd already agreed I should go. Dad said, "There's no time like the present. Why bother to wait for morning?" Mom, in her fake cheery voice, added, "I suppose it wouldn't hurt for Ronnie to stay there a few days while we figure things out."

Despite the lateness of the hour, I would go to this pleasant facility that very night. It felt rushed, but I couldn't go back to being the twelve-year-old kid I once was. Jail would be preferable to staying at home.

The River's Edge

NURSES NOTES

Date, 10. 20. 1969. Time, 10:45 PM. Remarks:
Admitted to room 202 adolescent male ambulatory
and accompanied by orderly. HT 6' 2" WT 150 B/P
130/80. Pt cooperative during admission procedure
but cannot understand why he is. Went straight to bed.
Dr. Ghattas called and orders received. -----M
Schulz RN

The admitting nurse had my rare last name spelled without the "t," which I took as an omen. She stuck me with needles for a routine lab work up, then an orderly led me and my parents into the elevator to the second floor, where he unlocked a heavy door with a tiny window at the top. The ominous thud as the door slammed behind us reminded me that I was still a prisoner.

We approached the nurses' station on our right along a faded yellow corridor. Coming our way, at that late hour, I saw an old, white-haired man and woman in pajamas clinging onto handrails to keep from stumbling as they walked down the hall. Still feverish, I mulled over escaping from that dreary place as soon as I felt better.

A white uniformed nurse stood like a grim sentinel behind the waist-high counter going over charts. She glanced up and forced a smile. "Why don't you take our new guest to his room?"

The orderly nodded and turned to us. "This is Two North, a locked ward. Some of these patients are on suicide watch." Noticing my parent's apprehension, he added, "Don't worry, after a few days they should put him on the adolescent or young adult unit."

The door to room 202 sat open. On the left was a private bathroom with a tub and showerhead, an amenity I'd missed in jail. On the second of two beds, farthest from the door by the window, a short, pudgy youth lay fully dressed over the still made bed, his innocent face resembled a cartoonish Pinocchio before his nose got longer. He wore a suit coat and tie, as if ready to go to church, with his feet encased in black patent leather shoes, which he hung over the side of the bed, so as not to muss the bedding. He jumped up when we came in.

"Are my parents here yet?" His head bobbed up and down, jittery. "I'm not supposed to be here, you know. This is all a big mistake. I'm a good boy, really, I am."

"They've gone long ago," the orderly said. "You'll be alright a few days until they visit." Pointing to me, he said, "This is your roommate. Maybe you could tell him something about yourself?"

"No," Pinocchio shouted. "I don't want to talk to anyone. My parents are coming right back to bring me home. I don't want to be here. I'm a good boy, really, I am."

The orderly winked at my parents and turned back to Pinocchio. "We'll leave you alone for a few minutes to settle in. Why don't you take your shoes off and get ready for bed? You'll feel better after a good night's rest."

The corridor ended two doors down by a large window, above a brown plastic couch, but it was too dark to see outside. A heavy metal door, locked, I assumed, was on our right.

The orderly smiled. "You can sit here a few minutes until your roommate settles in." He walked back to the nurses' station. Dad and Mom sat nearest the door on my left and we faced the long empty hall. A heavy silence of mutual embarrassment hung over us. Then the side door opened and a smiling couple holding hands slipped in, saving us from ourselves.

"Hello!" The bearded young man extended his hand to Dad, then me. "I'm Rick."

"And I'm Marjorie Weiselman," his dazzling yellow-blond partner chimed in. She wore shimmering bangles and a colorful, flowing dress. Putting her hand over her mouth, she suppressed a giggle and gave me a wink. "If you like, you can call me Marge." Her flamboyant charm and curvy assets captivated me. Speaking in unison, like Munchkins from Oz, they recited a greeting they must have practiced.

"As the official Riveredge welcoming committee, we sincerely hope you will enjoy your stay with us here on Two North. It shouldn't be long, and you will soon be transferred to the open ward on Two South."

Dad sighed, visibly relaxed by their cheerful skit, and Mom smiled. "Thank you very much."

The hippie looking couple sat down, like bookends on either side of us. Maybe it wouldn't be so bad, with them around I could get used to the place. While Rick made small talk with my folks, Marge focused on me. "Have you ever attended any group therapy sessions?"

"No, but I look forward to it. Will you be there?"

She smiled and patted my knee. "Maybe. We'll be glad to have you join us." I enjoyed basking in the glow of her attention, but then a loud shriek sounded from down the hall. I looked up to see the orderly running toward us.

"You kids! You've been warned to stay off this unit!" Our welcoming couple jumped to their feet.

"Nice meeting you folks," Marge said. "But we really have to go now!" They opened the side door, removed a piece of tape over the latch, and disappeared into the stairwell. The heavy door thudded shut behind them.

The orderly arrived, out of breath. "Damn kids," he snarled and resumed wheezing. "They're not allowed on this restricted ward. That Marge is too clever by far. She always finds ways to sneak around and break the rules."

Mom blinked. "Do you mean they're not the staff welcoming committee?"

"I'm afraid so," the orderly said. "Sorry about that. I'll see that it won't happen again."

"Well, okay," Mom said, before giving me a peck on the cheek. "Guess it's time for us to go now." The nurse buzzed them out the way we came in, and I retired to my room with Rick and Marge very much on my mind. The bravado of these imposters cheered me with hopes of seeing them again. They were my kind of people, incorrigible pranksters who could make life bearable. Marge was a perky beauty from every angle, and I envied Rick's good fortune.

Back in my room, Pinocchio was as I'd left him, dressed, whining for his parents to take him home. I felt sorry for the pathetic little guy and tried to cheer him up, but the more I talked to him, the more his depth of naïveté shocked me. Although he was about my age, he'd never been away from home, not even overnight, and possessed no ambitions, friends, or wants beyond hiding in the safe bosom of his overprotective family.

It was long after midnight and my throat ached. I needed sleep, so I undressed and went to bed, but Pinocchio kept turning the lights back on as many times as I got up to turn them off. Then he'd pace around our small room, his shiny leather shoes squeaking with each step from his bed to the door. He'd peek into the dim hallway as if expecting the triumphant return of his parents and repeat his loud wail of longing for what could never be. Then he'd lie back over the covers in bed, jerking his legs, which set his shoes and the bedsprings to squeaking like so many mice.

At my breaking point, I yelled, "Stop the racket! You're driving me crazy!"

"Stop what?" He looked at me with a stupid, wide-eyed innocence that angered me even more. I begged this pudgy little mouse to at least take off his noisy shoes, but he refused and went on squeaking through the night.

I pulled the covers over my head and flopped around in bed, trying to drown out the noise, but it was no use. Only my revolutionary discipline restrained me from choking him to silence. As if that wasn't enough, throughout the night and for every night thereafter, the door would creak open as the night staff popped in on their rounds to shine their flashlights directly into my eyes.

"Jesus," I screamed. "Get that goddamn light out of my face. I'd almost gotten to sleep."

"Well, ah," they stammered, as if surprised at my reaction. "We need to keep you under observation."

My lost freedom haunted me. The events that led up to my arrest and took Karen from my side played out in my harried mind, but I had to shake off despair. I considered myself a political prisoner fighting the People's War in the mother-country. The movies and books about prisoners enduring sleep deprivation came to my aid. They'd survived and so would I. Fred Hampton, my new hero said, "If you dare to struggle, you dare to win." He added a critical point, "If you dare not struggle, then damn it, you don't deserve to win."

Despite Pinocchio and the snooping orderlies, I snatched a few moments of sleep before the knocking at our door summoned us to breakfast. Opening the curtain facing east, I beheld an orange sky over the dim view of a river with what appeared to be a cemetery on the far side.

Stepping into the hall, I saw more cemetery through the back window and wondered how the view affected my suicidal fellow patients.

Pudgy little Pinocchio's elderly, sad-looking parents arrived, disappointed that he wasn't adapting to life without them. Challenged as he was, he'd never grow up enough to launch into independence, not if they kept rescuing him. Their plight saddened me, as they'd soon be too feeble to care for him.

I called out, "Good luck, man!" But basking in his parent's weary love, he ignored me as he followed them out. Fine. I looked forward to getting more sleep without him.

A line of patients formed along the hall awaiting escort to the cafeteria. As I joined it, a voice called, "Hey, Ron!" Surprised, I turned to see the pretty blond from the night before.

"Marge! What are you doing here?"

"Oh, man, I got in so much trouble last night," she said, taking her place behind me. "Rick and I got busted for coming up to meet you. They left him on South, where they put all us hippies and moved me here to separate us, but I'll see him in the dining room."

"Mr. Schulz." A male orderly came over. "I'm sorry, but you're restricted to the unit. Go wait in the Dayroom for your tray. The cart will arrive soon."

Marge grabbed my sleeve as I turned to leave and whispered. "Don't worry, dude, new people are always restricted. After a couple of days, they'll lift it unless you're suicidal or something. You'll love it when you get off North."

Marge restored my spirits. This wouldn't be such a bad place in her company.

The Panther and the Mummy

A few bent and mumbling geriatrics slumped at tables in the dayroom across from the nurses' station. I felt lost and depressed among them. Then I spotted a guy with long sideburns and a paisley shirt. A short, dark-haired woman in a polka dot dress sat beside him. They seemed to be about thirty.

"You must be new here," he said, waving me over. He half-stood and gave my hand a vigorous shake. "I'm Carl, a former Marine and longshoreman."

"I'm rambling, Ron, a wandering dropout."

The woman pointed to the chair across from them. "Sit down, Ron. It's nice to talk to someone close to our age."

"This is my old lady, Clara," Carl said. "She's just visiting. Aren't you Hun?"

She nodded and held out her hand. "Pleased to meet you. What are ya in for?"

"Oh, I got busted fighting with a cop in a riot."

Carl snorted. "Well, I've done my share of fighting with the Shore Patrol in Yokosuka. Some goddamn misunderstanding got me sent here this time." He threw his arm around the woman. "Let me tell you about life in the Corps…"

Clara cut him off with a wave of her hand. "Don't get started on that, Carl. Tell him about your arm." She turned to me. "He sliced up his arm pretty gosh darn good. That's why he got sent here the first time."

"*Aww*," Carl scoffed. "Ron probably don't want to hear about that shit."

"Come on, Carl." She punched his shoulder. "Tell him about your arm."

"Oh, all right." He shot me a broad grin as he rolled up his right sleeve to the elbow. Mottled scar tissue covered half of his forearm from the back of his wrist. Above that appeared the tattooed tail and hindquarters of a sleek black cat.

"The back of the cat looks nice," I said. "What happened to the front?"

"I had this Black Panther put on my arm years ago, before they started that *son-of-a-bitchen* Black Panther party. It's one of those things you do when you're drunk on the waterfront." He grinned with macho pride and slammed his fist on the table for emphasis. "I didn't want to be associated with those black rascals, so I downed a bottle of Scotch and took a buck-knife to it."

"He's some crazy guy, ain't he?" Clara said, her eyes gleaming with admiration.

Carl chuckled, happy to be the center of attention. "I peeled half of it off before I passed out, so drunk it didn't hurt much. But when I came to, it hurt like a motherfucker."

Clara interrupted, "I heard him screaming and called the ambulance. There was a bloody mess all over the place." Carl nodded. "Sure was, and after they patched me up, they sent me here. Shit, they said only a crazy motherfucker would do this to himself."

"They're goddamn right," Clara said. "You are one lean, mean, crazy Marine, but you're my guy and I love you, anyway." She leaned over and planted a noisy kiss on his lips.

"Those Black Panthers will pay for making me do this to my arm." He glared at me to show he meant every word.

He was a working-class dude with all the usual prejudices. Like so many others I'd grown up with in Chicagoland, braggarts focused on showing off their brawn and bluster. I was at home in this enemy country and knew I had to keep my admiration for the Panthers to myself. Arguing wouldn't do any good, but with a little prodding, this guy might wake up someday and join the class struggle.

An aluminum cart arrived. The staff passed out thick plastic trays with indentations to separate the foods. Although the eggs and oatmeal weren't as hot as we wanted, we dug into our chow until a weird voice startled us.

Hua-gaha-ha. An icy hand seemed to grip my heart as I beheld a ghastly apparition looming over our table. It looked like one of the demonic beings I'd encountered during my most recent LSD vision quest, and it took a moment before I could recognize the creature as a rotund woman, still dressed in a pink flannel bathrobe. Her neck and face were swathed in bandages like a mummy, her forehead and eyes were visible above a gaping black hole where her mouth should be, reminding me of *The Scream,* the famous painting by Edvard Munch. A charcoal-black mass half wrapped in bloody white bandages protruded three inches from the gruesome hole in her face. It had to be her tongue but appeared more like a burned tree branch with linen bandages streaked with blood hanging from it. Unable to form words with her mouth wired open, she spoke unintelligible sounds. "*Hauuo, ha ah wa-hu...*"

The sight shocked me, but I reminded myself to be compassionate toward all creatures tormented by karma.

Carl responded with fury. "You damn bitch! I've told you to stay the fuck away from our table. Now get!" His vehemence shocked me almost as much as this unholy wraith of a woman. She stepped back, but then closed in again, muttering mournful gibberish through her bandaged mouth.

"Hey!" Carl called to the orderlies. "Get her the hell out of here!"

Then to me he said, "That stupid bitch has been pulling off her bandages again. She does it on purpose just for attention, trying to spoil our breakfast. She can't eat normal food anyway, so they ought to keep her in restraints, locked up in her room, where she can't bother anybody."

I tried to overcome my disgust and sympathize with her. "Poor thing," I began, but Carl cut me off.

"Don't you dare feel sorry for that bitch. *Arh!*" He exhaled in disgust. "She did this to herself, drank a full bottle of Draino. You know, the acid that unclogs drains?"

His eyes bugged out for emphasis. "You can't chug-a-lug something like that, not like you'd down a bottle of liquor. The acid burns all the way down from your first sip. *Good to the last drop.*" He laughed at his reference to the Maxwell House coffee commercial slogan, but then got serious. "Just imagine what that shit did to the inside of her throat. It wasn't her first suicide attempt. She should have the decency to jump off a building and spare us this shit."

I wondered what could inspire someone to attempt such a painful, horrifying death. As she closed in on us, I became mesmerized by her bloated, extended tongue, barbecued crisp. Even though fresh blood oozed from it, I doubted they could save it.

The orderlies had their hands full serving trays and feeding some of the feeble-minded patients, but one finally responded to Carl's demands and took the mummy to a table on the far side of the room. He forced her into a chair and stood over her.

"Hi Ronnie!" The cheerful greeting seemed out of place. I looked up to see my parents walk in. I hadn't unexpected them, and it took me a moment to clear my head. Mom pulled up a chair and sat beside me. "We came to have breakfast with you. Who are your new friends?"

We only had time enough to introduce each other and ask the proforma *how do you dos*, before the living mummy returned. Her orderly had run to help a patient choking on his oatmeal, and the mummy, like a vengeful evil spirit, zeroed back in on us.

A ghoulish laugh came from deep in her chest, *Hua-hua-hua-ho*, as if she relished her chance to treat my parents to her awful spectacle. Their faces blanched, and they squirmed, unsure how to respond.

The mummy picked off bits of her barbecued tongue to shove them in our faces like gory trophies until only one last crispy chunk remained. With a mighty jerk, she wrenched it off. Only then did two orderlies race up and grab the tongue-less ghoul. She kicked and shrieked in her muffled way, as they held her on the floor, cuffed her arms and legs, and a nurse administered a shot in her hip to sedate her. Then they hauled her away, never to be seen by us again.

Carl shook his head. "What the fuck good is it to keep someone alive who only wants to die?"

Mom let out a long sigh. "I've heard that attempting suicide is a cry for help."

With a sudden look of concern, Carl glanced at my parents. "I'm so sorry you nice folks had to see that display."

"Jeez!" Clara shook her head. "We're sympathetic to those more deserving, but this bitch is mean and nasty. Right Carl?"

"Sure thing, kiddo. She only wants to fuck with our minds. Ah, I mean upset us. For God sakes, if you're going to kill yourself, do it right the first time or don't even try!"

Clara grabbed his shoulder. "Whoa, there, man!" She giggled to take the edge off and turned to my folks. "You see, Carl's a realist, not a bleeding heart, but he usually has a kind word for almost everyone, even for those with suicidal tendencies, as long as they behave decently."

I never heard more of the mummy's backstory. The Draino drinking girl got shipped to a State Mental hospital, the proverbial end of the line, a big step down from the amenities and care one received at a private hospital like Riveredge.

A few hours later, I was watching TV in the rec room when Marge came and sat beside me on the couch. "Mind if I hang out with you until lunch? Rick is in a conference with his shrink."

"Not at all." I was in awe of this wild, beautiful gal and if I could steal her away from Rick, I would.

"Look at this." She giggled and pulled up her billowing sleeves to show me white scars crisscrossing both her wrists. "They're from trying to do myself in a couple years ago." She sounded boastful.

"Shit, Marge, you have too much to offer this world. Don't go out like that."

She laughed, giving me hope that she wasn't serious about carrying it through. Then a pretty, olive complexioned girl with stringy black hair walked in. Marge waved her over.

"Louise, remember me?" Louise's face gave no sign of recognition, and Marge continued, "It's a good thing they transferred you back here with us."

I said *hello* and patted the space beside me for her to join us, but she only stared at me. Marge elbowed my side. "She's kind of shy, Ron. Give her time. Right, Louise?" She got up and took Louise's arm. "Come on, it's time for us chicks to go down for lunch and catch up on stuff. Ron is still restricted to the ward."

She turned to me and whispered, "She's a little spacy from all the meds they give her." Then, in a louder voice, she said, "We'll be back soon."

Marge intrigued me far more than this too thin, introverted Louise, but she was hooked up with Rick. Louise could be a nice consolation prize. I needed somebody to help fill the void in my life.

Minutes after they left, I heard a commotion outside and ran to the window overlooking the parking lot. I saw Louise strapped to a gurney, her forearms swathed in white bandages, as they rolled her across the parking lot to the West Wing. When Marge got back, she filled me in.

"I knew that chick from the other joint we were in before here. She's been bouncing around mental hospitals all her life." She pulled me to a quiet corner and whispered with excitement.

"Down in the cafeteria, Louise stood behind me in line with her tray. Suddenly, she grabbed a glass off the serving line, surprised the fuck out of me how fast she was. She dropped to her knees and smashed it on the floor. Before any of the staff could do anything, she curled into a ball and began sawing at her wrists with it."

Marge squinted into my eyes. "That chick was always kind of depressing. She's nothing like me, Ron. I mean, I can't figure her out. She's pretty, the dudes love her, but she doesn't care. It took several orderlies to pin her down. They tied her onto a gurney in four-point restraints and took her to the ITU."

"Four-point restraints, ITU, what's that? I'm new to the lingo around here."

Marge nodded sage-like. "Each point means a limb. Two points is just your arms, so four points means having your arms and legs strapped down." She demonstrated, stretching her arms and legs out in an X configuration, and laughed. "It's like doing jumping jacks." She pulled me close and whispered. "The ITU or the Intensive Treatment Unit, is like a fortress, man. You're under constant surveillance, one staff to each patient. Whoever flips, or *acts out*, as they call it, gets sent there."

The legendary ITU was across the parking lot on the West wing, where I'd seen them wheeling Louise. These severe measures were negative reinforcements. Positive reinforcements included earned privileges, like cigarettes or going down to the cafeteria to eat and earning passes to leave the grounds. These concepts stemmed from B. F. Skinners Behaviorist School of Psychology, which Marge studied and expounded upon in her jovial, sarcastic manner.

Carl, my opinionated friend, had a theory about the dark-haired girl. "She's more of a masochist than suicidal, just looking for attention. I mean, if she'd been serious, she wouldn't have tried it in a crowded cafeteria. She knew she'd be stopped." He clicked his tongue and sat up straight, continuing in a professorial tone.

"The stupid bitch cut her wrists crosswise, like an amateur, the way people who know nothing about suicide attempt it. With her experience, she knew better. There are strong tendons that you really can't cut through without a hacksaw." He ran his finger down his forearm. "To get right down to the blood vessels underneath, you've got to cut long-ways, down the groove between the tendons."

Carl implied she wanted attention, not death. But with so many suicide attempts under her belt, she took on a lot of pain for her trouble. Some patients used drugs or poisons, hoping to slip away with less pain from their present reality, but there seemed to be a strange kind of romance, a masochistic pleasure, for those who chose to cut or burn themselves.

Over the next few weeks, new patients transferred in. Some had roadmaps of failed suicide attempts on their wrists. The wounds terrified me. From knives to glass and razor blades, even a jagged tin can, some took a bizarre, twisted pleasure in boasting of their deeds. But sometimes, once their bandages came off, the scars looked superficial, disappointing Carl. Anyone who arrived after a failed attempt could soon learn the best techniques or die trying.

"Shit," he whispered when we were alone. "Their will to live must have been stronger than their half-hearted will to die."

I tried to wrap my head around what would make someone even try such a desperate act of self-destruction. "Maybe they hadn't thought it through beforehand. It must have seemed like a game before they felt cold metal or glass slice into their own flesh. The shock of sudden pain would be more than they anticipated."

"Yeah," Carl said, smiling wide as he pulled his sleeve back to show off his mottled scar. "I know something about that, but one of these days, I'll finish the job and get this big pussy off my arm."

Soul Food

At the end of another night locked up on Two North, I arose sleepless before dawn and ventured out of my room. A beautiful, coal black woman in a trim white nurse's uniform sat on the couch at the end of the hall, where I'd first met Marge and Rick. She beamed a welcoming smile as I approached.

"Can't sleep?"

"No." I smiled back. "I'm an early riser. It's nice to meditate before everyone gets up in the morning. Have you ever tried it?"

"Can't say that I have." She moved some papers off the space beside her. "Come sit and tell me about it. I'm just finishing my charting while I watch for the pretty dawn colors at the end of my shift." Her musky sweet fragrance pulled me in to sit as close as I dared to this angel.

"How'd your night go?" I asked.

"Oh, this NOC shift takes some time getting used to. Sitting here, this view sure makes it bearable, and I like to call it the graveyard shift." She chuckled and gestured at the still dark cemetery outside the window.

NOC was the abbreviation for nocturnal, the official designation of the overnight shift, but calling it the graveyard shift made just as much sense to me.

"You must be Mr. Schulz, the new patient in room 202?"

"Call me Ron." I gave her my hand.

"I'm Rochelle." Her hand felt warm and inviting.

Our chat roamed beyond meditation basics to current events. I mentioned my admiration for the Black Panthers, Bobby Seale and especially Fred Hampton, whose speech had so resonated with me. She glanced around to be sure we were alone, leaned close and whispered, "I'm not supposed to discuss politics or race with patients, but you seem to understand a lot for a white boy."

She could have been in her mid-twenties, an intoxicating *older* woman to me, but at seventeen, all my girlfriends had been two or more years my senior. All except fifteen-year-old runaway Karen, gone from my life since my arrest. Much as I missed her, I had to accept the impossibility of getting out in time to find her and we had no choice but to move on.

Rochelle blew me away. Besides her great vibes, the buttons holding the front of her uniform threatened to burst from the pressure of her bosom. She was the full package of everything I yearned for.

An orange glow began washing over the gray cemetery below us. We half turned to enjoy our vista of the day's resurrection and our knees touched, sending a thrill through my nervous system. Neither of us moved away.

"This is the best part of my job," she said, turning her warm brown eyes on me. "Watching the world light up while it's still so quiet and still, feels like God's loving arms around me."

"I know what you mean." I wanted to say that I'd put my arms around her too if I knew we wouldn't get in trouble. A black male orderly, her no-nonsense work partner who'd told me innumerable times to *get back to sleep* after he flashed his light in my face, patrolled back and forth at the far end of the hall, grimacing our way as he went about his rounds.

Rochelle leaned closer to me. "That boy never seems to smile."

She shook her head in disapproval and her hand fell on my knee where it lingered, communicating what words dare not, sending another charge between us. We remained hovering on the edge of overt flirtation, neither of us daring to cross the line. She had to appear *professional,* adhere to the artificial social conventions or lose her job.

My heart pounded, my brain raging to express my desire to flirt with her in an open and honest way. For too short a time, we gazed at the somber view below, only the light touch of our hands and knees expressing our body's desire for union. The warm comfort of our timid touching weakened my knees, making me delirious.

"This is *soooo* nice." Rochelle's languid words oozed out like warm lotion. She jotted a few lines and a signature to finish her report and closed the folder. "We must do this again when I'm back at work in a couple of days."

"I hope so." I grinned and chuckled. "You know where to find me. I'm your prisoner here."

"Too bad." She took her hand off my knee to look at her watch. "I have to get back to the nurse's station for the cross-shift." Her voice got low and husky. "See you later, Ron-honey."

Honey! I took that sweet endearment to heart, my eyes glued to her round butt as her swinging gait carried her down the hall. Her smile and musky sweet fragrance remained heavy on my mind for the rest of that day and the next in anticipation of her return.

Several days passed with no sign of her. I even wondered if she'd been a mirage, the product of my fevered imagination. She was way out of my league, too good looking for some down on his luck guy like me to hope for. It proved difficult for me to push her out of my head to focus on the here and now. My meditations visualized her as my shakti, my sky-dancing dakini, as if I could join her in the spirit world.

My parents arrived every other day. One morning we were standing at the nurses' station, about to head for the dayroom, when the phone rang. Mr. Doaty, a dour thirty-something orderly, picked up the receiver and listened. Then, with a puzzled look on his face, he beckoned me over.

"Just a minute." He held out the receiver. "Mr. Schulz, you have a phone call."

My first thought was Dr. Ghattas, but the surprised look on Doaty's face indicated it was someone unexpected. My mind raced over the possibilities. Could Karen or Kay have tracked me down?

"Hello Ron," a sultry voice purred in my ear. "Do you know who this is?"

"Yeah. Of course, I do," I lied, as much for my audience as the caller. My stunned mind drew a blank, but I didn't want to disappoint whoever it was. She didn't sound like Karen or Kay, or Marge playing a prank.

"Oh, I bet you don't remember me. Do ya, Ron?" She sounded petulant and a bit drunk. "I met you on the NOC shift. Remember now?"

"I sure do." Rochelle's image exploded back into my brain. I wanted to put more emotion into my words, but Doaty and my parents leaned in, trying to hear our conversation, so I walked as far from the nurses' counter as the telephone cord reached, but even then, we had no real privacy.

"Ya know, Ron, I've been thinking of you and our nice little, ah, *talk* the other day."

With furrowed brows, my parents and Mr. Doaty, joined by the duty nurse, stared at me, scrutinizing my facial expressions. I hid my emotions as best I could, unsure what kind of trouble Rochelle and I could get into, but they would try to keep us apart.

"Honey," she purred. "Have you been thinking of me?"

"Yes, of course I have." The recollection of her warm presence flooded my mind, but I couldn't express my feelings as loud and clear as she needed to hear. Doaty may have recognized her voice, more reason for me to be careful, as her boozy voice grew louder.

"What music do you like, Ron-honey? Blues and Jazz, or Rock and Roll?"

"I dig all kinds of music. Whatever you've got suits me just fine."

"Ever had soul food?"

"Ah, no, but I'd sure like to try it." All I knew about soul food was that chitlins were supposed to be greasy hog intestines, but I was adventurous enough, so long as it was with her. Maybe I could turn her on to healthier food, like brown rice and vegetables.

"Well, honey, I wanna cook you a really nice meal at my house. You don't belong in there, with all of them old crazy folks, but your restriction should end real soon. Then I could sign you out and bring you over here. Would you like that?"

"Yeah, sure. I'm looking forward to it."

I covered the receiver tight against my ear to muffle her voice. No two ways about it. She was drunk or high. It would have taken a bit of Dutch courage for her to make that call. To think that I turned her on enough to risk her job. Wow, that flattered me, but if the secret got out, it could derail our relationship before we even had a chance to kiss.

"Oh, honey, we could have such a wonderful time hanging out together. Don't ya think?"

It had been only about two weeks since losing Karen, and I didn't want to lose Rochelle too. Everything about her, her buxom looks, her sweet sultry voice, her mere touch that promised so much, intoxicated me. As a patient on a locked ward, I could only place my fate in her hands and hope that she would come through. I had to hold my anticipation in check or go crazy.

"My apartment is in, you know, a Black neighborhood and all. Would that bother you?"

"Not at all," I blurted too loud, then lowered my voice to a whisper, hoping she'd get the hint to lower hers too. "I'd love that, really I would." But her voice grew even louder, as she repeated her promise to sign me out and take me home, hinting at delights beyond mere food, music, and wine, maybe some grass, that we would soon enjoy at her home.

The lascivious edge to her voice turned me on, fueling my hope that this sweet, soon to be lover, reciprocated my feelings. Maybe we could run away together, go underground before I had to face the judge, or even escape to Canada before I turned eighteen in a few months to evade the draft. Otherwise, I'd have to get a fake draft card with a big "4F" stamped on it, making me ineligible for the military, but I was getting way ahead of myself.

Sure, yeah, uh-huh, I kept my responses muted using words that didn't arouse suspicion on my end while trying not to disappoint her and praying that she wouldn't change her mind after she sobered up. I couldn't bear the thought of losing her before we even had a chance to make it. To keep my dancing heart still, I focused on my breathing.

We said our goodbyes. The wide-eyed look of astonishment remained on Doaty's face as I handed back the phone. Beside him, the duty nurse sat tight-lipped, oozing hostility.

"Was that a girl?" Mom asked. "She sounded kind of, ah, mature."

"Oh, she's a friend, that's all. She heard I was here and just called to say hi."

That must have sounded as improbable to them as it did to me. I still didn't have permission to make telephone calls, so how could someone outside the hospital get news of my whereabouts? My parents kept pestering me, wanting to know more, but I brushed them off.

"Come on, you guys, let's go sit by the window in the dayroom. How's Grandpa and Grandma? Are the girls happy with classes?"

Throughout that week and into the next, I waited for Rochelle to call or come back, but she never again appeared on the ward. My discreet inquires met a wall of silence. As a mere patient, they had no obligation to tell me anything. Whether she got cold feet, was fired, or transferred out stayed a mystery. Paranoia set in as I wondered if this whole episode had been a set-up, some psychological game by Dr. Ghattas to manipulate me. No, that would be *too* crazy. Such a *Big Brother is watching* scenario would be too complicated for them to pull off, at least I hoped so.

The Riveredge Neighborhood

Nurses Notes

10.21.1969. Pt said he was sent here because he wanted to change the thing that was going on in the world. Pt. came here from jail. S. Waters, NA. (*Nurses Aid*)

PHYSICAL EXAMINATION

Schulz, Ronald Age: 17. Admitted: 10/20/69. Examined: 10/22/69.

The patient is a 17-year-old white single male student who has no complaints... No history of diabetes, heart, or contagious diseases... Does not smoke or drink. Has not been taking any medication prior to admission... Denies headaches, chills or fever. No loss of weight or appetite... a well-developed, well-nourished white male in no acute distress.

BP 130/80, Pulse rate 80 regular.

Riveredge was on Roosevelt Road in Forest Park, across from Miller's Meadow, a large park consisting of a giant field with thick woods along the riverside, a favorite stomping ground for patients on pass, and I heard that Rock concerts had even played there in the summer. Much as I wanted to go out for exercise and enjoy nature, I'd have to wait for permission from Dr. Ghattas. The long hallway was all the range permitted me for exercise.

True to my calling as a revolutionary, I attempted to radicalize patients and staff at every opportunity. Blacks made up half of all the nurses and orderlies at Riveredge, while all the patients I'd seen were white. There may even have been an unwritten color code, such as affected the housing and rental market in Chicago. Black patients would be expected to go to a more affordable state hospital. Almost all the NOC, or graveyard staff, who worked from eleven at night to seven in the morning were black, while most of the daytime staff were white. I attributed this to the racial and income disparity. Riveredge was an expensive private hospital that most people paid for with insurance.

From my room's east-facing window, I saw the tree shaded Des Plaines River, and beyond it stretched a cemetery. The large window at the north end of the hall, where I'd sat with my parents and Rochelle, presented even more cemetery, which gave me inspiration for my meditations on death and impermanence. Although I considered myself well disciplined, immune from depression, I wondered how the view affected patients with suicidal tendencies. The dayroom window gave me a clear view to the west of the hospital parking lot and the building housing the West ward. Beyond it, I could see a car dealership.

Marge told me the whole first floor held administration offices, conference rooms, the cafeteria and the PT, or physical therapy clinic. The second floor housed three wards, each named by the cardinal direction in which it lay. Two North stuck out like a finger in that direction and Two South pointed opposite, overlooking Roosevelt. Two West's open ward for adults was across the parking lot. Patients there could sign themself in and out with more liberty than on the other wards. It was a smaller unit because the ITU took up a section of it.

Chronological and sometimes mental or emotional age classified patients as Adolescents or Young Adults for participation in programs. There seemed to be some confusion about how to classify me and I managed to get included in both groups. Many patients considered themselves hippies, and drug use and lifestyles were the usual reason for their admission to Riveredge, whether they were signed in by parents or by a court order, attempting to change or *rehabilitate* them into "normal" members of straight society.

The ITU, Intensive Therapy Unit, sometimes called ICU for intensive care, was a restricted, forbidden world of its own. Suicidal patients or those deemed a danger to self or others could be locked up there, depending on their doctor's decision, for a few hours to several weeks. The heavily locked, almost soundproof doors were more formidable than elsewhere. The elevator didn't even stop there, unless activated by a special key. Few of my informants had gotten a glimpse of it, unless they'd been sent there hog-tied and sedated with Thorazine. Rarely was another patient allowed to visit that secure ward. Anyone entering had to be frisked to prevent all sharp objects from getting in.

Beyond several car dealerships to the west, Roosevelt intersected First Ave., where a large Zayre's supermarket stood. To the southeast, across the river and Roosevelt Road, which marked our southern boundary, was Sambo's pancake restaurant, another favored haunt of patients out on a pass.

The Weathermen were going underground to wage guerilla war on America's military industrial complex. Even though I disagreed with their factionalism, the thought of living on the run sounded like a romantic adventure. Maybe I should join them. But without money in my pocket and with the police on my trail for jumping bond, I'd get saddled with an even longer list of charges and might spend years in the slammer. No, it would be better to bide my time to see how my court case went before I made any rash move, but I kept looking for opportunities.

The Des Plaines River lay below my second-floor window. If I got out, I could follow the stream north to Lake Street, then a few blocks west to Fisher's Woods, where I could count on friends to help me get farther away. Rather than panting with temptation to run off, I had to keep my emotions in control and weigh my options before I tried anything rash that could backfire on me and spoil my future chances to escape.

Life on Riveredge took on a semblance of normalcy. I looked forward to chatting with Marge and the others. I'd never wasted my time playing cards before, but with them I relaxed and had fun. Marge taught me an easy game called War, which frittered away our time together until they sent Marge back to South, and released Carl back into the community, leaving me no one to talk to but demented geriatrics.

Stir Crazy

NURSES NOTES

10.22.69. Wednesday 2 N. Prescribe Thorazine 50 mgm if patient becomes very upset.

3-11 pm. Pt. very talkative all evening, spent most of time talking in German to other adolescents and playing cards.

10.23. 7-3:30. Pt very quiet and likes the young ladies we have on the ward; he seems to be friendly with all the patients. Eats well, cooperative.

10.24. Pt must be getting used to this place because he is now getting smart. Someone says he is the leader of a gang that is starting on this ward. Pt says he has a sore throat, gets angry when he does not get anything for it, pt. spends a lot of time trying to make personnel think he is bad, walking with a grimace or frown on his face, looking mean or thinks he is anyway. Eats good keeps clean---R.T. Williams

It's fascinating to read how different members of the staff perceived me as either friendly or mean, cooperative or bad. The different opinions may be due to their respective ages and whether they identified with aspects of the counterculture. Our common denominator was our lifestyle. Some activity workers had long hair and admitted to smoking *weed* and some of the older staff seemed to be *lackeys of the power structure*. Ms. Williams didn't believe that I was sick, however, the next day my temperature rose to over a hundred, and they finally prescribed penicillin for five days. As for being a gang leader, I'm flattered that they gave me that much credit. With a lot on my mind, I must have had a serious face at times.

Most of the younger patients didn't seem any crazier than my friends on the outside. Many patients had conservative parents who wanted them to become clean cut and get out of the hippie culture. The only reason we were on the inside and our peers remained on the outside was that we'd gotten caught. They were my people, and I identified with them.

To keep fit, I exercised in my room and walked the halls before meditating. The Beatle's song *Blackbird* held just the right amount of pathos to express my moments of despair, which I sang and whistled as I paced the halls.

Blackbird singing in the dead of night. Take these sunken eyes and learn to see. All your life. You were only waiting for this moment to be free...

Those dark lyrics gave me grim solace. Tears welled in my eyes as I thought of my missing loves. Karen, Kay, and finally Rochelle, who'd been stolen from me before we'd had a chance to become better acquainted. It wasn't fair, but as a revolutionary, I knew life was never fair unless you took charge and made it so.

Into the light of the dark black night went the song, and yes, damn it, I'd fly into the light of the dark black night, whatever that meant. Another Beatles song, *Hey Jude,* told me I could *take a sad song and make it better*, because I was *made to go out and get her,* which meant Marge, of course. These songs encouraged my will to persevere, but my choice of music did not enthrall some of the older staff, and they didn't appreciate my efforts to stay active.

"Your pacing is bothering the other patients."

"But the hall is empty!" My protests were in vain, so I withdrew to sulk in my room. I tried to be a model prisoner, but I was young, bursting with energy and I craved society and inspiration.

With Marge and Carl off the ward, only geriatrics in various stages of dementia remained. These oldsters awaited the grim reaper to usher them into the next life and I sympathized with them. Their well-earned *golden years* were spent in a less than idyllic setting.

The more lucid of them chatted with me during our long, boring days. One old Polish man made an impression on me. He'd forgotten whatever English he'd learned and reverted to his native Polish, spending his time chatting with another old Polish woman who still remembered some English. She told me that the Nazis had put him in a concentration camp during the War, which sparked my desire to learn more of his story, but he only shook his head when I tried to talk to him through her. I tried some of my high school German on him, presuming that he'd picked up some of that during his imprisonment.

At first, he looked bewildered and stared at me through ancient rheumy eyes, but then they lit up as a sort of recognition kicked in. His face hardened, and he began shrieking at me in Polish.

The woman laughed. "He say you stupid German pig, stop telling me what to do!"

My attempts to reassure him I wasn't a Nazi failed. The staff came running up, shouting, "Stop pestering the old man," so I retreated to my room.

Then there was Ancy, the one genuinely crazy patient. Her name sounded like Antsy, which fit her nervous demeanor. Although only in her thirties, her short black hair had pronounced steaks of gray. She was a former housewife and mother who simply went over the bend with a serious breakdown. Deep in her world of delusion, her rapid, non-stop flow of words prattled on without punctuation. An amazing stream of consciousness, word associations, and random plays on words poured out of her.

One of her favorite spiels was a rambling lecture about the "Ants from Antarctica" who took the shape of people, even masquerading as people she knew.

They are coming again, you know. Did you see them here? Maybe you are one too and I thought I knew you yesterday but today I just can't be sure, because you knew you can never know now can you when they look just like you and me and did you see me over there, but I'm here and I don't want to go to Antarctica, and they said I don't have to, but I know better – they want me to go – I don't know when and again the ants are coming...

She rambled on with seeming indifference to events going on around her. Although we hadn't been introduced and I didn't think she knew who I was, she ran up to me one day, face etched with concern as she peered deep into my eyes.

"Ron? Ron? Is that really you in there, Ron?" This was the first and only time I heard her call someone by name, which startled me. "Because you could be him, you know. You look so much like his face, but you never know about the eyes. You could be a replacement. I was so worried about you, because I haven't seen you in so long and I hope you weren't replaced by an ant. They come from Antarctica; you see..."

She may have been crazy, but her concern gave me new respect for her as a human being. Dr. Ghattas happened to be her doctor too. Once I saw him standing, head bowed in concentration, as he listened to her avalanche of words. It looked as if he was trying to snatch a pattern from it that he could use to find a cure, but it proved beyond him.

"Stop talking that nonsense!" he snapped in an unprofessional yet emotionally honest outburst.

Ancy drew back, blinking, as if he'd slapped her. I assumed the good doctor was trying to shock her out of her delusion, but it didn't work. She shook her head and carried on as if nothing had happened.

Ancy remained crazy, wandering the halls, chattering incessantly, upsetting her husband, and grown children who were unable to locate the wife and mother they had once known.

Drugs and Recreation

A nurse handed me a couple of little red pills and stood by, waiting for me to swallow them. "Open your mouth," she commanded. "Raise your tongue." She glanced in, didn't see them, and moved on to the next patient.

Our shrinks prescribed psychotropic drugs as a matter of routine administered in regular doses to keep us docile. I considered it a nefarious plot to crush our spirits and remold us into compliant zombies. While I didn't notice any special effects, I decided against these chemical controls. When the nurse handed me another dose that evening, I pretended to swallow it, but flipped it between my cheek and gums.

They'd moved Marge back on the South ward with Rick, but she used her stealthy skills to sneak over to visit me. Her visits kept me sane, no matter what I looked like on the outside. I showed the pill to Marge, my nearest drug expert.

"That's Mellaril," she said. "It's a brand of Thioridazine."

"What does it do?"

"Oh, it's a common antipsychotic. They give it for schizophrenia or depression. Did you tell Dr. Ghattas that you took LSD?"

"Ah, yeah."

"See? Join the club, man! They think all of us LSD tripping freaks are schizophrenic. The definition is vague enough for a diagnosis of the psychedelic experience."

"Wow, I asked Ghattas what my diagnosis was, but he wouldn't say. Schizophrenia, huh?"

"Hey." Marge's voice lowered to a whisper. "Want to give away your pills?"

"Do you want them?"

She hesitated and glanced around. "Not me, but plenty of my friends do. They save up a bunch of them to take all at once and get a real rush."

"I hope they don't overdose on this stuff."

"Don't worry, they know what they're doing."

"Okay, here you are."

"Cool, man. Someone will thank you for this!"

I'd smoked my share of marijuana and found merit in using psychedelics, but, as *The Pusher*, by Steppenwolf, put it: *I never touched nothing that my spirit could kill.*

The next day, as I walked the hall, Marge popped the back door open a crack, stuck her head in, and waved me over.

"Shh, Ron, follow me, quick." As I slipped into the stairwell behind her, she added, "A girl on South wants to meet you, man." She wedged the door latch to stay unlocked, then she waved a skinny blond girl up from below.

"Ron, this is Stephanie Hopkins. I'll be right back."

Stephanie shot me a bashful smile. "Marge tells me you're a fire sign, like her."

"Sure am. Do you know much about astrology?"

"Well, I'm learning to make charts. Maybe I'll do yours when I'm ready." She leaned close and whispered, "I've got a present for you, Ron. Hope you like it."

She handed me a kind of flashy tin belt that women wore,

consisting of shiny clasps hooked together. It looked something like a decorative Navajo breastplate.

"Nice, thanks, Stephanie." I supposed this meant that she liked me. It flattered me, but I wasn't sure what to do with her gift. Hippie fashion blurred the line between male and female attire, so I hung it around my neck as a kind of low hanging necklace.

"Those pills you gave us were killer, Ron. I just want to show my appreciation and welcome you into our world."

"Glad you liked 'em, I've got more. Here." I handed her my morning meds.

Stephanie was a pretty, dishwater blond, but nowhere near as voluptuous as Marge. Maybe introducing me to Stephanie was Marge's way of pushing me away, and I had to roll with it. I didn't believe in monogamy anyway, so like the song says, *If you can't be with the one you love, love the one you're with.*

Marge called up from below. "Stephanie, quick, we'd better get back." I leaned in to kiss Stephanie goodbye, but she ducked and ran downstairs. Maybe she just wanted a friendship that precluded sex.,

There was no sense pouting away on the sidelines, waiting for some idealistic, impossible love, so I shrugged it off. There's nothing noble in such a foolish waste of life's vitality, I needed a real woman like Marge or Nurse Rochelle, hungry for wild, fulfilling action. Without that, I could only focus on meditation, and slip into a monastic shell to make the best use of my time and until a goddess smiled to free me from my enforced celibacy.

Group Therapy

D r. Ghattas leaned back in his swivel chair, smiling at me through a haze of sweet-smelling pipe smoke. "Tell me about you father... your mother..."

He insisted on focusing on my relationship with my parents and family rather than the real problems I saw in our society and culture. From my reading and discussions with Stephanie and Marge, I knew that was the Freudian way, but I'd read some Carl Jung, which better fit my spiritual approach to life and death.

"I don't blame my parents for who I am, Doc. They brought me into this world and raised me as best they knew how, but that's behind me. We're part of a larger society. See? I look beyond myself at how our materialistic culture forces us into a rat-race with insufficient reward. Life ought to be more than grinding away at some job. We need to see ourselves as citizens of the vast cosmos beyond our mere family and nation. We're thinking creatures, not robots. We can choose what's important to keep or throw away from the culture we're born into."

Dr. Ghattas took me downstairs into the dark corridor below North. It was my first time off the ward, and I felt happy as a puppy to be in a fresh environment. We passed a door where I'd noticed a bearded rail thin little man, almost a leprechaun, sitting on a couch in a perfect lotus position, a rare sight. It had taken me months of stretching to be able to twist my legs into that position for any length of time.

"Wait here a moment," Dr. Ghattas told me. "I have to check if the conference room is ready and will be right back." It seemed odd that he hadn't turned on the lights and left me in the dark hall by myself.

Then a voice loud as a thunderclap shouted. "You are as a woman of India!" I stepped back to where the grizzled little man sat. He looked dark complexioned enough to be from India, but his accent didn't fit. Curious, I approached him.

"Who's the woman of India you speak of?"

He fixed me with sharp black eyes in a hostile stare, his back still ramrod straight, his legs immobile in what the Tibetan yogis call the Vajra position. "What are you talking about? I said no such thing."

His denial made me wonder whether he was coming down off a heavy acid trip, or even an actual manifestation of my Tantric Guru come to shock me into enlightenment. I took a deep breath and looked at my hands, as my study of Dream yoga advised to assure myself that I was in the waking state, not dreaming, so I asked the obvious questions.

"Are you meditating?"

"I don't meditate – ever!"

"Who are you?"

"Please go, leave me alone."

I never saw the little man again, and wish I'd learned more about him. When the doctor came back, I asked, "Who is the guy in that room?"

"What guy?"

"The one two doors down, he shouted, 'You are as a woman of India,' as soon as you left me. Didn't you hear him?"

He shrugged his shoulders. "I don't know. I'm not his doctor." He didn't seem curious, which struck me as suspicious. Then he led me down the hall to an empty room where he conducted a standard session, asking about my family, but couldn't help wondering if Dr. Ghattas had set up that scene to play a mind game on me, if only to convince me that I was crazy. His job was to mold me back into a compliant cog in the straight world. My duty was to remain true to my ideals.

Dr. Ghattas finally gave me permission to join group therapy sessions, and I was glad for any activity to interrupt my boredom. An orderly escorted me to a small room on the first floor where several well-dressed white participants gathered, all middle-aged adults except for me. Most of them seemed to be outpatients. Dr. Ghattas wasn't there. A younger man functioned as moderator, asking each of us round robin fashion to share something with the group.

An odd couple sat across from me. A noticeably short average looking guy with a severe crew cut sat holding hands with a statuesque, fashionably dressed woman who towered over him. Sexy as she looked, she could have been a model. I soon realized that he was the patient, and she was his wife. When it came his turn, she coaxed her man to speak up.

"Ah, well, I, ah, you see I guess I'm doing better now..." His whiney hesitant voice stammered out too few words, interrupted by long pauses.

It hurt me to listen to him. He took so long in his delivery that I lost the gist of whatever he was talking about before he finished. Despite my best efforts to arouse sympathy for him, my compassion failed me. He was a sad bundle of nerves, so self-absorbed that he couldn't appreciate the wonder of his life. He had a knock-out chick beside him who gave every indication of her devotion, and all he could do was whine about the petty insecurities bugging him.

The moderator broke into my thoughts. "Ron, do you have anything to say?"

"Sorry." I cleared my throat. "Ah, I'm not sure what I'm supposed to talk about. I don't have any problems. My mind is on my upcoming court date and whether the trial will become a media sensation. You know, like the YIPPIE Conspiracy Trial with Judge Hoffman."

They stared at me, waiting for more, so I gave them my blend of mysticism and *smash the state* political rhetoric. "Do any of you pay attention to what's going on in this country? Bombs fall on Southeast Asia while we sit in comfort listening to crybaby crap. We need to stand up to racism and the capitalist War Machine. Dig it?"

The little man's woman glanced at me with what I thought was furtive interest before she turned away. She sighed and squeezed his hand tighter, as if to deny to herself that she was unhappy and living a lie with him. There were more important things happening beyond the little picket fence of their privileged world, and they too needed to expand their horizons.

The meeting broke up. Some of them had other therapies to attend, including electric shock, one of the blessings of modern technology. An orderly explained to me how they sent high voltage shocks into the patient's brain, meant to destroy traumatic memories. Side effects, however, included confusion and memory loss affecting a patient's personality. It sounded barbaric to me. At the next meeting, I saw the little man again. He seemed even more remote and disjointed than before, and I overheard patients whispering about him.

"Shorty is getting his shock treatment again. Look at him. He's out of it."

He seemed to be living proof of what went wrong when you break down a person's mind. Following that meeting, they gave him another shock session before sending him home with his wife. We never saw him again, but I heard whispered rumors from the others.

"As soon as he got home from shock therapy, Shorty took a kitchen knife and castrated himself."

They whisked the poor fellow to a state hospital, just another basket case whose insurance ran out. I regretted my harsh appraisal of Shorty. Each of us has his own dark valley to cross and we're more alike than not. I vowed to work on my compassion.

Fresh-Air

PROGRESS NOTES

10.25.69. Patient can now eat in cafeteria.

Nurses Notes

10.27.69. Dr. Ghattas in this a.m. pt. sitting on floor at end of corroder with his legs folded over and his hands resting on knees, palms up. Socializing in dayroom with adolescent pts. Meals on the unit.

10.28.69. retired 1:00 AM, up @ 5. AM EEG to be done... Very hostile seems angry @ everyone. Sitting in hall on floor, told to set in day room, became angry, cooperative...

3-11 pm. pt. is pleasant & cooperative when approached, up and about. Seem to be distraught over the way society is handling things in the country.

In the cafeteria, I could finally join Marge and Stephanie for meals, but then it was back to North, where meditation remained my principal outlet. Gallows humor entertained me. On October twenty-nine, a nurse quoted me as saying, "I've been contemplating doing something to be put in restraints and if I scream, I'll get something to dope me up." She didn't appreciate my sarcasm.

On Thursday, October thirtieth, I sat gazing out the window when a twenty-year-old dark-haired woman with twinkling brown eyes breezed into the dayroom. After scanning the blank, unresponsive expressions of several oldsters, her eyes fell on me.

"Hi, there." She smiled, glanced at the chart in her hand, and sat across the table from me. "You must be Ron. I'm Paula, a student nurse."

After a brief chat, I told her I hadn't been outside the building since being admitted.

"Really?" She put her warm hand on my wrist. "Well, then, let's take a nice stroll in the sunshine."

She led me up to the unattended desk and signed me out. As far as I knew, they still restricted me to the unit, but I didn't want to jinx this chance to get out and kept my mouth shut. We crossed Roosevelt Road to Miller's Meadow. My sense of wellbeing in the company of this pretty lady shot up to the expansive blue sky overhead. We circled clockwise around the field, chatting away like old friends. She told me about her dreams of a nursing career and her student trip to Yugoslavia, where her family came from. I shared what I knew about that country from my extensive reading.

"President Tito seems to have fixed the rift between the Croats and Serbs. They fought each other more than they did the Germans in World War Two."

Her teeth sparkled as she threw her head back, laughing. "Your understanding of history surprises me, Ron. You're too young to be a college student."

"True, I'm a high school dropout, but I read a lot. This world is a fascinating place to me. We should get to know its dramatic history because it's all part of our story too."

We came to a tree at the edge of the meadow. I grabbed a branch and swung up to pump out a set of pullups, then did somersaults as she giggled like a schoolgirl below. Dropping back down, she grabbed my elbow as I caught my breath.

"Man alive, Paula. It feels so good to be back outside. Do you like to climb trees?"

"My brothers do. Looks like getting outside perks you up. Maybe we can do this again on my next visit."

"Thanks, I'll look forward to it."

She wrinkled her brow and looked me up and down, appraising me. "Why did they send you here, Ron?"

"I quit school and rambled out west where I took a big dose of LSD and lived in a commune in Taos, then I went to New York before coming back to Chicago, where I got busted in the Weatherman action and spent a few days in Cook County Jail."

I didn't want to scare her off, so I left out the details of my love life. Nonetheless, I noticed that her body stiffened, and her lips tightened. I paused for her feedback, but never expected her earsplitting explosion.

"Stop lying to me, Ron! If you think you're going to impress me with this impossible tale, you are sadly mistaken, mister." I stood in open-mouthed shock as she raged at me. "I cannot believe a single word of this crap you're peddling. You're only seventeen, a suburban kid, for gosh sakes. It really upsets me that you feel you must embellish the truth instead of just being honest with me."

"It's all true, I swear." I'd ruined a perfect date and wasn't sure how to salvage it. "Everything I said is the honest truth, and I haven't even told you the half of it, Paula."

"No way could you have done all the things you say."

"If you don't believe me, look in my chart." I assumed they'd written something there to back up my story.

"I certainly will." She pressed her lips together as if she'd bitten a sour lemon. "You can be assured that your lying carries a penalty with me, Buster. I won't take you off the ward anymore. We're finished."

She continued to huff at me until we got back into the building. All my attempts to calm her down backfired, sending me into a funk. The RN on duty glared across the counter at Paula. "You should have asked me before you took this patient off the ward. Dr. Ghattas hasn't lifted his restriction yet."

Paula's self-righteous demeanor wilted under the RN's curt reprimand. Despite the tongue lashing she'd given me, I tried to put in a good word for her.

"It was all my fault. Since I've been eating in the cafeteria, I assumed that all my restrictions were lifted."

"That's no excuse. She needs to learn to follow procedure. Paula, come with me."

She followed the RN around the counter and through the sliding glass door to the back office where, after more scolding, I watched her sit down to flip through clipboards and binders with a determined look on her face. I assumed she was checking my bona fides.

My opportunities with women always seemed to turn sour. I was paying for losing Karen, my best love. Maybe I'd never find another love like hers. Sitting in my room, I attempted to turn my disappointment into positive meditation, but I left the door ajar just in case Paula came looking for me. Even her anger was sweeter than the loneliness I felt. Before my closed eyes, like a slideshow, passed the smiling faces of Karen, Kay, Rochelle, Marge, Stephanie, and finally Paula. Each of them had raised my hopes for happiness, only to flit away like an elusive bird.

"Knock-knock!" I looked up to see Paula at the open door with an unexpected grin. "Can I come in?"

"Of course." I unlocked my legs from the lotus position and moved to give her space to sit beside me on the bed.

She sat down with a sigh. "Alright, Ron. I went through the charts and checked up on you."

I sucked in a deep breath, readying myself for another tirade, but she only stared at me with a puzzled expression. "I'm really sorry for doubting you, Ron. Although there's not a lot of detail, it does look like you were being truthful. Young as you are, I never expected you had such an eventful life."

My muscles relaxed. "That's cool, Paula. People tell me I'm too serious, but I kid around sometimes, just not about stuff that matters. Maybe I'll be off restriction in a few days. We can take more walks. I really had a fun time with you. I mean it."

She brushed her hand along the side of my face in a much-appreciated show of affection. "Well, I'll try to put in a good word and see what I can do about getting you off restriction." She patted my knee as she got up and I had to restrain myself from grabbing her hand as she rose, if only to hold on to her for at least one more precious moment.

"My shift is over, Ron. Got to go, but I'll see you next time, I promise."

She walked to the door, turned, and opened her mouth to say something, but only blinked and walked out, leaving me in my solitude.

I wondered if I'd remain locked up on North until my court date. Then I might go straight to jail to serve my time. With no idea how much time I'd get, I had to make the most of every little perk that came my way. A hungry black hole of self-pity gaped below me. To counter falling into it, I forced a grim smile on my face, reminding myself that I was a warrior, fighting for truth and justice, and I was not alone in my struggle. Somewhere out there, I had true comrades and lovers waiting for me.

NURSES NOTES

10-30-69. 7-3 pm. Pt. taken on walk through Miller's Meadow. Seemed to enjoy being out. Pt. tried to climb tree, did somersaults in tree, afterwards stated he feels better, not so tense...

Paula had written nothing about our misunderstanding, or the scolding she gave me and the one she received from the RN. Too bad, I never saw her again.

Dueling with the Dark Side

NURSES NOTES

11/2/69. Sunday.

11-7 AM. Slept.

7.30 AM. pt came into the dayroom appear(s) very hyper. I asked what was wrong and he said he had just heard some news about the conspiracy trial which made him very angry.

About 10 am he became extremely anxious. He walked very rapidly up and down the hall whistling the "death march." He said, "I feel like I'm going to explode." He got up on his soapbox becoming loud, making statements which were contradictory to his usual political views. He stated, "I feel so happy and I shouldn't feel this way." He appeared very euphoric.

5 pm. Approached desk and requested "Thorazine or something to stop the nerves before my head flies off." Stated he had been pacing & upset all day, but

**when asked the precipitating factor he said he didn't
exactly know. Given Thorazine 50 mgm.**

The Conspiracy Trial was in full swing, and the antics of
Judge Julius Hoffman continued to make a farce of the
justice system. On October 29th, he gagged and bound
Black Panther, Bobby Seale, to a chair after he demanded his own
lawyer to defend him. That and the rest of the preposterous legal
circus made the inadequacies of our justice system clear. The lack of
outrage at this miscarriage of justice in the news and popular media
turned my stomach. I needed catharsis and to do more than cry out in
protest. Like a one-man guerilla theater, I ranted and raved, trying to
shake people awake.

On November 2nd, as I paced the hall, I saw the back door crack
open an inch. Marge's grinning face peered in. She'd become an
expert at jimmying the door.

"Fuck Ron, get over here quick. I've been caught too many
times."

I ran over, blocking her from the view of the nurses' station at the
other end of the hall. She whispered through the inch wide crack.
"Goddamn it, I can't stay long. They'll miss me."

Her profanity laced conversation jump-started my flagging heart
as if they were sweet endearments. If I knew I wouldn't blow it by
rushing things, I would have dived in for a kiss.

"I just wanted to see how you're doing, Ron. Have you heard
anything about moving to South yet?"

"No, they don't tell me anything. Guess they think I'm a
dangerous felon."

She laughed. "Yeah, dude, you're a fucking killer, man! That's
what I love about you."

The lump in my chest did a somersault. She started to turn away.

"Wait, Marge." My mind scrambled for something to say. "I've
been thinking about trying Thorazine. Tell me about it."

"You're bullshitting, right? That shit will knock you on your ass. Fuck, man, I know from personal experience."

"You've done it. Right?"

She gave me a vigorous nod. "Fuck yeah. It'll wipe out your energy and willpower."

"Well, I'm curious to see if I can control it with my willpower. I mean..."

"Hey!" the muscular black orderly yelled from down the hall and came running. "Get away from that door."

Marge took off before the orderly got there. "Who was that?" I wouldn't squeal, but he knew who it had to be. "Them two chicks are gonna get put in restraints if they keep this up." He glared at me. "You better watch yourself too, if know what's good for you."

Ever since Marge introduced us, Stephanie had come back with her a few times on surreptitious visits. Although friendly, she continued to push away my amorous advances. Marge gave me just enough attention to stay on my radar, although Rick remained her steady guy, and I didn't know what I could or should do about it.

By five o'clock I'd made up my mind and marched up to the nurses' station. "Give me some Thorazine or something to stop the nerves before my head flies off."

The good-looking blond nurse squinted at me. "Are you sure?" It was not the way that drama usually went down. The staff didn't have to hold me down to shoot me up as I'd seen them do to other patients. She told me to lower my pants. To give her a jolt, I dropped them down to my ankles.

"Hey," she shouted. "I only need the top of your hip."

With a chuckle, I said, "Let it all hang out is my motto." It wasn't a big deal to me after living with nudist hippies out west, and I had a duty to blow her straight little mind. If it turned her on, that would be a bonus. To express her animus, she stabbed her needle into me with much more force than I anticipated.

"You should lay down in your room now before it takes effect."

"We'll see about that," I said and resumed pacing the hall. My macho goal was to see if I could master its effects.

Although woozy, I continued my *march of death,* as they called it. My raving Aries' intensity proved victorious against their repressive Thorazine drugs. That was a morale booster, even if a hollow one, for they could always up the dose if necessary.

NURSES NOTES

11/2/69. 6:30 p. Came to desk, appeared less agitated. His eyes were red. Said for a while he had some difficulty breathing. Continues to pace the hallway.

3-11:30. Patient saw a young adolescent female that came up the back stairway through the back door and this may be the reason for the above behavior. He seemed to have gotten upset because he couldn't see her. After the medication took effect pt became calm able to sit down in dayroom and socialize with his peer group. Has been pleasant and cooperative.

Two South

11/4/69 11-7. Quiet a.m. socializing with other youth on ward. Went to 2 South with group this afternoon. Pt. joins adolescent group therapy.

11/5/69. Wednesday. Wt. 152. Seen by Dr. Pendarsky. Transfer pt. to 2 South tonight as a temporary transfer. Observe pt. on 2 S – his reaction to ward. Transferred to 2 South, to room 287 at 8:30 p.m. Can make phone call.

3-8:30 Transferred to 2 S ambulatory, accompanied by staff with belongings. Pt received on 2 S & admitted to 287.

9-11. Pt socialized with adolescents for remainder of evening.

11-6-69. 11-7. Apprehensive about flashlights at bed check times, but by 2 AM relaxed & pleasant to orderly question if all were ok with him...

7-3:30. Attended ward meeting – adjusting to ward,

socializes with peers. "It's better to be here instead of jail."

Only a couple of days after demanding Thorazine, they'd let out of my cage, which seemed to be proof that making a fuss got faster results than complacent waiting. The South's daily ward meetings appeared to be like group therapy, but with more proactive emphasis on organizing social activities. It was a nice change from pacing the hall on North. I had fun with arts and crafts, modeling clay figurines, and even painting messy watercolors. The Adolescent program directors told me that if I minded my manners, I'd even get overnight passes. If only Rochelle was still around, maybe I could visit her as she promised.

The temporary transfer went well, so the next day they sent me back over with my stuff as a permanent transfer. After dropping my clothes in my room, Marge popped in. "Welcome to the Ward, Ron! Rick's out with his folks on pass. Come on, I'll show you around."

She grabbed my hand, pulling me down the hall to another room. My heart raced in expectation of spending some time alone with her, but instead I found a bearded, long-haired guy sitting up in bed with a book on his lap.

"Ron, this is Mike Williams, the sage of Two South. He talks about mystical stuff just like you. His room is a great hang-out for us."

Mike winked at me. "Marge and Stephanie have been yakking about you for days. You're a reader, huh?" He gestured to the dresser at the foot of his bed. "Take a look at my books. Borrow anything you like." He had a full selection of books by Allen Watts. I'd already read *The Way of Zen*, so I picked up *Psychotherapy East and West.*

"Guess I'll start with this. Thanks Mike."

"Knock yourself out, man. We can discuss it when you're done." A smile crept over his face. "You smoke weed?" I nodded. Stephanie popped in the room and Mike wiggled his finger at her, mouthing, "Close the door." He pulled a baggie out from under the covers, withdrew a ready-made joint, struck a match, and lit it. Marge lit a stick of sandalwood incense and waved it around to mask the smell.

Mike coughed, exhaling his smoke as he passed it to Stephanie. "I'm counting on you, Ron, to be cool about this. Remember, if you ever get caught with anything, it didn't come from me."

Steph took a hit and elbowed me. "Mike always has some dynamite shit stashed away." She exhaled smoke and let it escape with her words. "Sometimes he gets quality psychedelics. Did you ever try mescaline?" She passed the joint to me.

"Not yet, Steph, but I've tripped on some pretty heavy acid."

I passed the joint to Marge. She winked, filled her lungs, leaned over, and blew the smoke back in my face. Then she laughed. "I bet I've tripped way more than you, Ron. I was in Ann Arbor, next to Detroit, when the Revolution hit last summer. Man, that was *far fucking out!*"

My esteem for this rebel girl rose to new heights. "Wow, Marge, tell me about it."

"John Sinclair, manager of MC-5, a band that plays some heavy jams, started the White Panther Party in Ann Arbor to support the Black Panthers. They have a ten-point program, too, but a little different." The joint circled back, and she sucked in the sacramental herb, held it a moment and with her eyes locked on mine, she again blew it my way.

"Go on, Marge," I begged, as she passed me the joint.

She blinked. "Uh, where was I? Oh, yeah, Sinclair's program. It goes, 'A total assault on the culture by any means necessary, including rock and roll, dope and fucking in the streets.' Can you dig that shit, or what? Sinclair is a heavy dude!"

"Keep it down to a whisper, will ya?" Mike said. Marge giggled, crossed her eyes at him and went on in a lower volume.

"We took over the whole fucking city, and the pigs came down hard. This damned good-looking chick I know fought back like she was one of the dudes until the pigs grabbed and cuffed her. The bastards dragged her into the back of a paddy wagon. They yelled,

'Give us some of your free love, bitch,' and took turns humping her in the wagon. She yelled, 'Fuck for Peace and Love, give it to me, I can take on all of you pigs.'"

"Wow," I coughed, choking on the smoke. "That's some story, Marge. I've heard about Chicago pigs fucking women they arrested, mostly hookers, but I imagined Ann Arbor, as a college town, was some kind of rural oasis."

Marge grinned defiance at me. "I was *there*, man." She melted into nervous laughter before continuing, her voice subdued, yet assertive. "I've been raped too. Dig? It's not always such a big deal as some of them prissy broads say."

She held her hands up over her face and mimicked a crying girl. "*Boo-ho*! I lost my virginity, Mama. I'm nothing but a whore." She put her hands back down and pinned me with an intense gaze. "Fuck that crybaby shit! I mean, it's just sex. You can pretend it's your goddam boyfriend, let 'em get it over with, maybe you'll even enjoy it."

Marge was about a year younger than me, yet her gritty stories indicated a wide life experience. She was more to my taste than the anemic, self-absorbed fashion models strutting the runways or the too perfect Playboy centerfolds. Despite her *Shiksha* blond hair, she was Jewish, just like my ex-lover Bonnie back in Greenwich Village.

She took a last long drag, consumed the joint, winked, and passed the stubby roach to Mike, who slipped it back in the baggie. Marge leered glassy eyed at me. "Man, I'm stoned outta my freaking gourd on this shit. Where was I?"

"You were talking about being raped," I said, blushing despite myself. I swallowed to hide my embarrassment and went on. "How did you handle it? I mean, lots of chicks won't even talk about sex and pretend that it didn't even happen."

She put her hand on mine, sending a hot thrill through me. "I'm not like most chicks, Ron. Can you dig that?"

Stephanie giggled. "That's for damn sure, Marge. You're a fire sign and I'm gonna do your astrological chart."

Marge continued. "One time a bunch of Puerto Rican dudes in

New York–"

I broke in. "You've been to New York? So was I." I wanted to climb into her head and see how much we had in common. She grinned and winked at me. "I lived on the streets for a whole week before my fucking parents dragged me back here."

"Maybe it's our karma to be together here," I said. "I feel like I'm on the same path with you guys."

"Like I was saying," she continued in a low dreamy voice, her hypnotic eyes locked on mine. "Some PR guys cornered me and pushed me into an alley. 'We got you now, you little hippie slut.' But I used mental judo on 'em. See? I laid down on the ground, spread my legs and pulled down my jeans. That surprised the hell out of 'em! I said, 'Come on boys, I'm ready. It's been hard to get laid ever since I got VD.' You should have seen their faces! Those dudes took off like a devil was after 'em! That's reverse psychology, the best way to handle punks like that."

I didn't know whether to believe all her stories, but Paula hadn't believed me and, true or not, I could listen to Marge all day.

Knock-knock! Steph got up, peeked out the door, and let Rick in. He sat between me and Marge, holding her hand. Even with him beside her, Marge aimed her flirtatious vibe at me. Stoned as I was, I saw Rick as my mirror image, a brother in love with the same girl. I didn't want to offend him by stealing her away. She'd have to choose between us. But why must one of us lose for the other to win? Possessive love is a merciless battle of *winner take all,* but if she was willing, I'd share her affection with him.

Mellow Mike spent most of his free time sitting up in bed. Like a king holding court on his throne. We chatted over books and topics ranging from Revolutionary politics to the Prophesies of Edgar Cayce, reincarnation, and our expectation that Atlantis would rise from the ocean *any day now.* Our frolicking and serious discussions in Mike's room didn't always involve getting high. We had to be cautious, only including people we trusted and only when the staff was busy with charting or cross-shift meetings.

Open Ward

At two in the afternoon on November 12th, I got my first hour of unaccompanied open ward, but they insisted that if I came back a minute late, I'd lose the privilege. All my new friends were already out on pass by that time, so I debated how to spend it alone. The bright sun took the winter chill from the air as I trekked a circuit around the expansive Miller's Meadow, mulling over the temptation to run off to look for Karen in Old Town. There'd be no turning back if I did. I'd have to go on the run, underground, but with only two dollars and the clothes on my back, it would be a rough start. I had to be realistic. There was only a slim chance that Karen was still in Chicago, or that I'd find her somehow. If caught, I'd be back in jail or stuck back in a locked ward.

Like a coyote on the prowl, I jogged west along Roosevelt. At the intersection of First Avenue, I turned north, thinking to make a wide exploratory swing around the cemetery. Without a watch, I couldn't be sure of the time and had to keep shaking the urge to run away. I hadn't gone far up First Avenue when a car pulled over in front of me. Someone was offering me a ride. Maybe this was an omen that I *should* take off and link up with my destiny back in the real world. As

I reached the open passenger side window, my fantasy exploded. Dr. Ghattas sat in the driver's seat.

"Hi, Doc," I said with an air of nonchalance. "I'm taking a walk on open ward."

"Get in!" The edge to his voice made me wonder if he'd been keeping an eye on me the whole time, but I pretended nothing was amiss.

"Nice weather today. I love the crisp fall weather. Don't you?" He didn't answer, so I continued. "Gee, it's so nice to breathe fresh air again."

"Where were you going?" His voice was low and even. Dangerous.

"Just stretching my legs, Doc."

"You only had one hour, and the pass does not entitle you to roam far. If I hadn't come along, you'd never get back before three o'clock."

"Oh, I didn't realize it was that far."

He turned right on Harrison. He was right, it was much farther around the cemetery than I'd thought. We crossed the bridge and made a right turn on DesPlaines Avenue. The cemetery continued along Roosevelt until we reached Riveredge. Ghattas shot me a serious look.

"If you were late, I'd have to revoke your privileges. Promise me that you won't overstay your time off the ward."

"Well, okay, Doctor." I laughed to keep it light. "Sure, I'll give my word. I don't want the court to give me a stiffer sentence." I presumed that he or his diagnosis had some influence on how my trial went.

He pulled into the parking lot and dropped me off. "This is only a warning, young man."

With only a few minutes left, I entered the lobby, where I found Marge chatting with the receptionist. She broke into an angelic smile when she saw me.

"Good timing, Ron. I just got back, too. How was your pass? The rest of the gang should be back soon, so let's go up." Marge gave me enough reason to stick around. The Revolution could wait.

Bad Moon Rising

Hope you have your thing together
Hope you are quite prepared to die
Looks like we're in for nasty weather
One eye is taken for an eye...

Bad Moon Rising
    Creedence Clearwater Revival.

A new patient, flashing a sunny smile, introduced himself as Zahel. I never learned his first name, but he made an impression with his mop of blond hair that reached his shoulders.

"*The times they are a-changing,*" he said, quoting Bob Dylan. "Music is at the forefront of the culture war, Ron, even spreading Timothy Leary's message to *turn on, tune in and drop out.* Can you dig it?"

"You got that right," I told him. "My neighbors back home, especially the old European immigrants, call Rock and Roll *Nigger Music.* They hate it. My friend's dad even screams that the Beatles are Communist inspired."

"It's true, Ron." He burst out laughing like a hyena. "The oldsters are afraid we'll mix with blacks under the banner of *make love, not war*. But our generation is winning. Imagine it, our kids will study the Beatles in school along with classical music!"

"Wow, Zahel, that's heavy." His manic delirium infected me too, and we burst out laughing at the intricate working of the universe. Catching my breath, I said, "We can tell our kids and grandkids all about how *our* elders hated Rock and Roll, but we hung in and changed the world with it."

"Our parents' generation will be long gone by that time," Zahel said. "We'll be doddering old men too if we make it that far."

Laughter and Rock and Roll went together like vodka and orange juice, *shaken not stirred,* as 007 James Bond would say. We had other moods to invoke as well. Zahel was a multimedia performer with state-of-the-art stereo and speakers in his room. He selected an album from his extensive collection and put it on the turntable.

He gestured to the bed. "Sit down, Ron." Then he closed the heavy curtain and turned out the lights. "Close your eyes and just experience this."

The strains of the Beatle's *Abbey Road* ran through my nervous system. The tinny guitar began in a childlike spirit before the heavier, yet gentle, massaging lullaby voice of George Harrison took over. *Here comes the Sun...* George's comforting vocals assured us we were his *little darling*, that we'd been through our *long cold, lonely winter*, but *It would be alright*, and I believed him. Listening to the lyrics and feeling the music's vibration was a total body-mind experience.

Then followed a transition with a dreamy instrumental followed by deeper, vibrating regal lyrics. Zahel yanked opened the curtains just as *Here comes the sun king* erupted from the speakers. The effect soothed and ennobled our spirits, especially after we'd had a hit or two of pot. Like the self-empowerment of tantric meditation, it transformed us into the *Divine Pride* of that sacred deity, the Sun King.

Zahel's music became our own therapy. But I changed some of

the "defeatist" lyrics in the Beatles' *Revolution*, from *don't you know you can count me out*, to *you can count me in*. We gave Bob Dylan his airtime, too. One day, Zahel and I came back from a walk stoned on weed. Rather than enter through the front lobby, we came in through the loading dock to the service elevator that led to the cafeteria. We grabbed each other's elbows and, frisky as mountain goats, began jumping up and down to the tune of *Everybody Must Get Stoned* by Bob Dylan.

"They'll stone ya when you're trying' to go home." *Ka-blom! Ka-blom!* The slow elevator bounced and vibrated to the beat of our boots. "Then they'll stone ya when you're there all alone. *Ka-blom! Ka-blom!* "But I would not feel so all alone. *Ka-blom! Ka-blom!* Everybody must get stoned!"

The raucous song fit our mood. It was a slow ride up and by the time the door opened. We confronted the shocked face of our head nurse.

"What the hell are you boys trying to do? Your banging and shouting carried throughout the building!" It took all our apologetic flattery to keep our open ward privileges.

Marge and I loved listening to *Bad Moon Rising* by Creedence Clearwater Revival. The song spoke to me about the collapse of the old order, essential for us to bring the glorious New Age of Aquarius into fulfillment. But I changed the *whiney*, "Don't go out tonight, you're bound to lose your life" to "Let's go out tonight, we're bound to win the fight!" Everything else was spot on, as if straight from the apocalyptic prophesies of Edgar Cayce.

> I hear hurricanes a blowen
> I know the end is coming soon
> I fear rivers overflowen
> I hear the voice of rage and ruin

"What about Peace and Love?" Steph asked.

Zahel gave us both a sober look. "We could lose the fight, you know. We're up against tanks and helicopters, like the Vietnamese, and they're dying by the hundreds every day."

"Sure thing," I said. "The reality is that many of us won't make it against the repressive technology of *the man*. Like in the Doors song, *They got the guns, but we got the numbers*."

Zahel nodded, his face grim. "We may die, but our struggle is worth fighting and maybe dying for."

A pall of silence fell over us as we contemplated death. Meditation on death and impermanence gives our present life a deeper sense of meaning in Buddhism and I agreed. I'd already shared my faith in reincarnation with these friends of mine. Death could not prevent our return to resuming the struggle to create a better world. We needed to laugh at death to shore up our fearless attitude and bring the joy of spring's renewal into our experience, but some of the strait-laced nurses I chatted with took a dim view of my dark humor.

Nurses Log

11-11-69. Appears hyperactive, states has been thinking of suicide & masochistic tendencies. States is up in the air about everything & everything seems so bad that felt like ending it all. States doesn't know why changed mind. Appears to be laughing inappropriately. –B. Porter RN

Nurse Porter didn't understand that the walls were closing in on me and I had to grab all the desperate fun I could before my court date and a probable jail sentence caught up with me. Sure, I was angling for her sympathy, hoping to squeeze a little concerned affection out of her stern demeanor, but it didn't work.

Forest Home Cemetery

"Well, if it isn't my old cellmate from the County jail!" The voice sounded familiar. I turned around to see the smiling face of a curly-haired new patient.

"Pete, my man! Is it really you?" Still in his long-fringed leather jacket, Pete Fischetti looked much the same as when I first met him in the Bull Pen of Cook County Jail. His hair, like mine, was growing out after the scalping we got in jail.

I spoke in a stage whisper. "Looks like our lawyers' strategy put us both here. Don't you suppose that calling us crazy might help us avoid hard-time."

He wrapped me in a bear hug. "Wouldn't it be wild if they sent all the Weathermen to this mental hospital? It'd be just like the song." He broke into an off-tune rendition of *We all live in a Yellow Submarine*, by the Beatles, but then switched to the Weathermen version that went,

> We all live in a Weatherman machine,
> a Weatherman machine,
> a Weatherman machine.

And our friends are all in jail,
many more of us are out on bail...

"That's enough, Pete. You'll scare the nurses!" I smiled at the glowering RN sitting behind the counter. She never appreciated my rock and roll serenades. "Don't worry, Pete's only as crazy as the rest of us."

She gave me a dismissive wave. "Why don't you boys move away from the nurses' station. Go bother someone else."

I grabbed Pete's elbow. "Let me show you around and introduce you. You're gonna love it here. It's even better than jail." He burst out laughing and I joined in.

Later I met his famous dad, the political cartoonist, who seemed like a pretty-cool guy with a liberal perspective, whereas mine was a conservative Republican, who believed in the power of the unrestrained free market to fix everything. After his parents left, Pete turned serious.

"Can you sign yourself out?"

I nodded.

"Let's go for a walk and catch up." He lowered his voice to a stage whisper. "I've got some fine herb we can share."

We began a clockwise circuit of Miller's Meadow. Pete pulled a baggie out of a hidden compartment in his jacket and filled his little pipe.

"I've been saving this high-quality shit for just such an occasion," he said. "Here's to our happy reunion, Ron. Let's fire it up." We stopped and cupped our hands to protect it from the brisk wind. Exhaling smoke, Pete said, "Sympathetic friends donated this to me when I got out of jail."

We filled the bowl a second time and toked deep the magic weed while we walk at a fast clip for warmth. Before we'd finished a complete circuit of the field, the shit hit me hard. My legs kept going of their own accord as my mind listened to Pete's rambling dissertation about something I couldn't follow. His droning voice became the backdrop to my own reverie. Exclamations of "shit" and "goddamn," punctuated the tapestry of sound that washed over me like a lullaby.

I found myself back in Taos, making sweet love to Joanne, that first time. Her face kept morphing into Tike's, whose wet kisses covered my face until she vanished into a hazy white sunrise. Then Ruby, laughing at my side as she pushed and tried to trip me into the crashing breakers of lake Michigan, although it was Bonnie, not her, who'd done that. My mind settled on Karen, then Marge, until I came back with a *plunk*, into my present reality, slogging along beside Pete. He turned to me.

"It's some damn good shit, huh?"

I nodded agreement, but I couldn't get my voice to work. With an immense effort, I forced slurred words from my mouth. "Thissss isss the strongessst ever, Peeeete." My words seemed to come from somewhere far away.

"Sure, is! Damn good shit."

A buzzing sensation, like bees in my bonnet, muffled other sounds, even Pete's voice. I felt numb, airy, but at times heavy too and I'd forget what we were talking about in mid-sentence.

"Goddamn, I'm stoned, Pete." I wasn't sure if I spoke or only thought those words. My perception of time, my train of thought and full memory of what happened vanished into a haze.

Pete's face appeared in front of me, his mouth working as he seemed to ask me something. I grabbed his jacket, pulled him close, and blurted, "Huh?"

"How many times have we gone around the field, Ron?"

"Wow, I don't know, man. How long have we been out here?"

Pete started laughing. "Fuck if I know. Your face looks hilarious right now. We're totally fucked up. Better head in before we lose our privileges." Somehow, we got back across Roosevelt and onto the ward without the nurses noticing our condition.

The next day, we walked across the frozen DesPlaines river to explore the Forest Home Cemetery. Originally called Waldheim, it had been the first German cemetery in Chicago. We wound our way along meandering paths among headstones and skeleton trees that would offer leafy shade in summer. The monuments intrigued us, and we stopped to examine them.

The statue of a man in a thoughtful pose intrigued us. He rested his head on his right hand, supported by his knee atop a great pillar. Below was the year 1888, below that U. A. O. D.

"Spooky," Pete said. "I wonder what the letters stand for."

We couldn't find an inscription to clarify the mystery. Only much later did I learn that it stood for The *United Ancient Order of Druids*, a nineteenth century fraternity, whose members lay buried all around it. That put us in good company as we smoked and walked among these self-proclaimed Druids. High on pot, I felt we'd gone back in time.

"Wow, Pete, look at that one." I stopped and pointed at the black statue of a hooded woman standing like a protecting Valkyrie over the corpse of a bearded man, as if shielding him from evil. They were on top of a pyramid which stood atop a white pillar. Below it was an inscription.

"Listen to this, Pete!" Chills ran up and down my spine as I read aloud.

The day will come when our silence will be more powerful than the voices you are throttling today.

Pete whistled. "That's heavy, man. Makes the hair on the back of my neck stand up."

"Yeah, let's check out the back." There we found a bronze plaque upon which was a decree pardoning the labor leaders accused of the Haymarket bombing. The Haymarket was the very place Pete and I had marched off from to bring the Vietnam War home to America. We stood among the martyrs of the Haymarket, our ancient comrades. Giddy with stoned amazement, I clapped Pete on the shoulder.

"Dig it, man. Our getting sent to Riveredge was no mere coincidence. We have a big karmic connection to these long-dead Haymarket comrades. They may even be us, reincarnated."

We read that a following city administration had erected this memorial to acknowledge the injustice done to these martyred Labor agitators. They had been railroaded by the courts and hung despite considerable evidence of their innocence.

"Yeah," Pete whispered. "This is some heavy history, makes this sacred ground to the struggle." Pete took another hit and offered it to me. "It's spooky-wild that we both ended up right here, together, after getting busted in the modern Haymarket riot."

I laughed at the synchronicity of it all. "It's like fate put us together at Riveredge, right across the river from this memorial, and we're high enough on pot to appreciate it."

Pete nodded agreement. "Being high makes our minds more open, in tune with the spirit world. Let's commune with them."

We sat on a nearby headstone, finished the joint, and did just that. After a long moment of silence, Pete said, "Did you see me back at the Haymarket, dancing on the pedestal where the cop statue used to be?"

"Wow, yeah, now I remember. That wild fringe flapping Ghost dancer was you!" I waved my hand over the ranks of the dead all around us. "We're them, Pete, reincarnated back here to continue the struggle."

"Yeah, it blows my mind, Ron. We've got a timeless connection. I was born on the cusp of Leo, by the way."

"I figured you for a fire sign, Pete. I'm an Aries. Us fire signs make things happen in the world."

Pete looked at his watch. "Time to head back already."

In the following days, Pete and I continued roaming the cemetery, opening our minds with the sacred herb, and absorbing the vibes and perhaps the blessings of those free spirits of the Victorian era who'd gone before us. We felt comfortable among the noble dead.

Decades later, researching my genealogy, I discovered that my dad's great-grandfather, Johann Reibert, had been buried without a headstone in 1899 at Waldheim-Forest Home. Neither I, nor my father, had known that. The small rise of his unmarked grave in the northwest section was a spot Pete and I often strolled by as we smoked. Perhaps our stint at the Edge put us exactly where karma demanded, right across the river from that ancient burying ground.

Ordinary life is more extraordinary than most of us realize. If we expand our mind and pay attention, we find that it's packed with synchronic events tying our existence to a larger, more fulfilling cosmic relationship. We don't recognize our interconnection only because the daily grind of duties and terrors that crush our spiritual feelings overwhelm us.

Artistic expression

D own in the first-floor recreation studio, I molded clay into a hooded Franciscan monk praying on his knees. His eye holes stared sightlessly into the great void. Watercolors offered a challenge. The colors flowed, blending into a wavy-gravy psychedelic haze that I titled "acid trip," although it had no resemblance to any trip I ever had. Crayons and colored pencils were easier tools for my propaganda. I drew a cartoonish pig dressed in a blue cop's uniform pointing a gun at the viewer entitled "Cops are Pigs."

Christmas was coming, so I drew a turbaned figure leading a camel across a bleak desert landscape, one of the "wise men" on his way to link up with his two Hindu or Buddhist companions in Bethlehem. Theirs was an astrologically driven pilgrimage to far off Palestine where they would pay homage to the Boddhisattva Jesus. It was obvious to me that Christianity had been influenced by those more expansive religions. Jesus quoted Buddha's compassionate love for all, even enemies. Jesus broke out of the narrow mold of the intolerant faith of Moses and Joshua that required the genocide of the people whose *Promised Lands* they took, much as we, following their template, took this land from the Native Americans.

Dr. Ghattas saw my art differently. To him, this weather-worn "wise man" standing alone against an open landscape represented a pathological inner loneliness.

"Well sure," I told him. "This is the bald face of reality peering back at us from the mirror. Even when surrounded by our friends and family, we are essentially alone, responsible for our own karma on our journey from the cradle to the grave and beyond."

He shook his head. "Your outlook is far too morbid."

"Morbid? We must confront reality. Most people cling to comfortable lies hiding from the truth. We're cosmic beings, Doc. Part of an eternal ebb and flow until we break free of the cycle of birth and death." I decided the best way to explain myself was to tell Dr. Ghattas about the vision I had when I was between three and five years old.

"After being put down for an afternoon nap in my parent's bed, I awoke to an eerie humming while I levitated up toward a stern yet kind face. It felt like I was going into another dimension, but fear overwhelmed me, and I turned my head and broke the spell, to land bouncing back on the bed."

Dr. Ghattas frowned and scribbled on his pad. I waited for him to finish. I'd only shared my description of that mystical experience with a few friends and worried that I'd said too much. Marge said our Shrinks were part of the Establishment, so it's like talking to a cop. Saying too much could boomerang back against me. He looked up and blinked.

"Go on, I'm listening."

"You might call the experience I had a mere dream, but the vivid sensation stayed with me all these years, giving me hope and keeping me from obsessing over all the petty crap society demands of us. I mean, what could be more relevant to each of us than asking who we were before our birth and what is our destiny after death?"

Dr. Ghattas kept his eyes fixed on me. "Tell me about your relationship with your father."

"Both of my parents mean well. I've nothing against them.

They're just human beings from the generation that's passing away, afraid of the inevitable change that's coming, the change that we, their children, are bringing. We're here to create a new society based on racial and social equality."

I decided to make this more personal for him to understand. "You yourself, a Lebanese man with a darker shade of skin, must experience some prejudice in this society."

"This is not about me," he said with obvious irritation. "You are the patient here."

Dr. Ghattas called my parents in for a conference. Sitting across from us, he asked me to express my honest feelings about my family. When I repeated that I bore no grudge and only wanted to change our society, he rustled his pad of paper with agitation.

"Quit avoiding the subject. It's your difficulty with your family, your father especially, that you must confront to resolve your issues."

"Whatever family we're born into is only a launching pad, Doc. We need to be more than a carbon copy of the generation that's gone before, or it will hold us back from evolving and fulfilling our higher destiny." I'd resolved this issue long before, and struggled to explain my views, imperfect as they were, to the good doctor.

Dr. Ghattas' crumpled the notes in his hands. "You are so obstinate! Tell them what you told me about your childhood hallucinations. You've taken LSD, which can only compound the delusions of your dreamworld and your inability to take responsibility for your actions." He nodded with pressed lips to my parents. "There is compelling evidence of schizophrenia in your son."

He'd done the unthinkable, transgressed our doctor-patient confidentiality by blabbing about my childhood vision. Even so, I kept a dignified silence with my raging emotions in check. Let him draw whatever conclusions he wanted. I vowed to tell him nothing more about my inner life.

"If my mystic visions were mere hallucinations, then all the prophets who founded each of the competing religions underpinning or culture were nothing but raving lunatics. Our ancestors killed and died for the insubstantial dreams of long-haired hippies like Jesus Christ, Moses and the bloody-handed Elijah who murdered his Baal worshipping competitors."

Despite his frustration with me, on November 24th, Dr. Ghattas granted me three hours of open ward. I could wander farther and hang out longer with Zahel at Zayre's, the nearest department store. My friends wasted their dough on junk food, but the cafeteria food was enough for me, frugal as I was with my few dollars. I'd taken the yogic path to focus more on the spiritual landscape.

On November 26th, a nursing assistant wrote, "seemed on a good level – spending time with his peer group – went to small group meeting in the afternoon." The next shift added, "pt cooperative and pleasant. Went for walk with group, behavior good." The next day, the seven in the morning to three in the afternoon shift noted, "Pt seems on a good level this am – spent time in act. room listening to records with pt group – staff questions if pt may have been involved with the smoking of grass with the others."

I see from this that they liked me better stoned. I'd mellowed out, getting away from my political rhetoric and turning my thoughts to more timeless things.

Marge told me, "Some people have gotten caught smoking grass here. If it's serious enough amount, they may turn you over to the police." She nodded for emphasis. "Pretty fucked up. Huh?"

It was important to never get caught. We hid drugs under dressers, and taped to bottoms of drawers or behind a loose ceiling tile. Given an ounce or two to hide, I discovered a wonderful place in the bottom end cuff of the heavy curtains in my room. I tore a little of the thread to form an enclosed pocket. The package had to be flat-tened out so when the curtains opened and closed, a bulge wouldn't stand out. The random checks for contraband focused on the others and ignored me at first because I was coming out of isolation on Two North, and they knew I had less dough and less contact with the outside than the others. So far, so good, but after watching coverage of the war and political repression on TV, I still vented my rage and frustration.

Nurses Notes

11.29. Pacing up and down hallway, rambling, stating, "I would like to kill some pigs." Refused to take meds at 9 PM, finally takes them at 10 PM. Appears upset & anxious.

The Court Shrink and the Murder of a Hero

It was December second, my first court appearance. I expected to see the press corps with flashing lightbulbs and Weathermen defendants enacting wild shenanigans like the exuberant Yippees on the Conspiracy trail. Instead, I found a bunch of people in casual dress chatting with their lawyers. When I started over to greet them, my lawyer grabbed my elbow.

"Don't talk to them," he whispered. "We want to plead your case separately. You're an underage juvenile first offender. If we're lucky, I might be able to get you off with probation. Mixing with those hardened radicals could only increase your sentence."

The suit I hadn't worn in years still fit me, sort of. My parents and I sat with the lawyer in the courtroom, making small talk as we waited for the judge to come in and start the day's proceedings. Two men I didn't recognize entered the courtroom and sat behind us. The dark-haired one sneered, "That's the bastard who tried to steal my badge!"

"Yeah," his blond partner said. "He must've been high on dope, because he didn't give us much trouble." Without their helmets and bulky riot gear, the cops who arrested me looked trim and younger than I remembered.

"All rise," the Bailiff cried out. "This Court with the honorable Judge Saul Epton presiding is now in session."

My lawyer approached the bench, handed over some papers and asked for a continuance, which the Judge granted, and we walked out. The lack of dramatic fanfare in the courtroom disappointed me. I felt I'd been cheated of the ennobling catharsis I expected from standing up, shoulder to shoulder, with my comrades for our righteous anti-imperialist cause.

My lawyer stopped us in the hall and put his hand on my shoulder. "You've got an appointment with the Court psychologist." He led me to an office deep in the sprawling courthouse. The wrinkled, bent, white-haired man had to be in his eighties. After a few preliminary pleasantries, his face broke into a mischievous leer.

"Do you get a lot of sex?"

"Well, gee, I suppose. I had a regular girlfriend before I got busted."

"Did you ever have a girl go *down* on you?"

"Go down?" I wasn't sure what he meant. "You mean lay down with me?"

His leer broadened. "I mean, give you a blow job, oral sex. Did a girl do that, or did you ever eat out the pussy of a girl?" He went into details, asking whether she used her lips or let me stick it back into her throat and if her teeth or braces got in the way.

"No." I felt my face flush but decided to be truthful. "I've only had four lovers, all of them this year and, ah, I just haven't got around to any of that other stuff yet."

His primary interest was my sex life, not my association with radical or criminal groups. That led me to wonder if he was getting his jollies as much as assessing my fitness for trial. Since we were on the subject, I asked if he knew the term *balling*.

"Yes." He leaned back in his swivel chair, put his fingertips together and launched into the history of the term.

"It comes from 'high balling,' a railroad term from the early days before electricity. The railroad men hung lanterns up high on the track, as a signal that the train could leave the station at full speed." He winked at me.

"There used to be cathouses, houses of prostitution near the railroad tracks. Those railroad men hung their lanterns up on the porch when they went in to enjoy the ladies. Any other men knew what they were up to, and the red glow of the lanterns became a sort of advertisement for the house as a place for *balling,* where a tired working man could go and refresh himself with some good fucking after work."

I'd gotten him off my case and onto his favorite topic. We had a nice chat together, and I assumed it went well. The lawyer's strategy continued to be delay. Each time we came back to court, he requested a continuance. After each court date, I had lunch or dinner with the folks. It would have been pleasant enough if I could numb my mind and coexist with the whole suit wearing middle class culture that felt so alien to me. On my return from court for the first time, the nursing staff noted that I said, "I am glad to be back. Home is bad news. Mother stated pt. did not want to take his medicine while on pass."

I didn't want to carry the meds around all day to give them to Steph or Marge later. The next morning, my parents stopped by with two gifts. The zippered, red letter, King James translation of the Bible, that my grandparents had given me on Christmas 1959, and a newspaper clipping.

"We thought you might get some comfort in here from reading the Gospel," Mom said, a frown playing at her lips. "Especially after you read this." She watched my face as I read the clipping.

29 indicted, more likely in SDS war.

State's Attorney Edward V. Hanrahan said Tuesday he expected a special grand jury to indict about 30 more members of the Weatherman faction of the Students for a Democratic Society. The jury

Monday indicted 29 Weatherman members in its investigation of street disorders in Chicago in October. Hanrahan said that he expected the jury to sit for another two or three weeks before completing its investigation of the disturbances, in which 268 persons were arrested... "These indictments and our forceful prosecution of them should emphasize that Chicago will not tolerate wanton destruction of property or abuse of civilians and police officers perpetrated under the guise of protest." Only three of the 29 indicted were from Chicago. Three others were from the Chicago suburbs. The jury recommended bonds ranging from $20,000 to $50,000...

My name was fifth on the list: "Ronald Schulz, 17, of 291 Addison Rd., Wood Dale, a stock boy, aggravated battery, aiding an escape, resisting arrest and mob action, $35,000." I felt a twinge of pride at being the youngest among the twenty-nine heavies and showed the article to Marge later that day.

"Wow," Marge said after she read it. "Thirty-five Grand! It's a hefty price on your head." Her eyes sparkled with interest, exciting my hopes, but before I could reel her in for a hug, Rick turned up. "Look at this, Rick." She handed him the article while sliding her other hand into his. He nodded his head before handing it back without a word.

She flashed a crooked smile and winked at me. "Come on guys, let's go outside and light up a joint with Pete."

If I was to win over Marge, I'd have to elbow Rick out of the way, but my conscience forbade me. He was a steady, reserved guy, quite the opposite of Marge's effusive personality and as malleable as putty in her hands. We were a merry band, doing time together, which made our incarceration a holiday. I couldn't let my selfish desire ruin the goodwill between us. Marge would make her desires clear if I didn't rush things.

That evening, we got a little too rowdy in someone's room. The staff on night duty came running down from the nurse's station. "Stop making so much noise! Go to bed!" We scattered like chickens to our respective rooms, pulling the covers over our heads and pretending to be asleep like naughty children, all in good-spirited fun, but of romance I had none.

The next morning, Stephanie ran up to me in the hall. "Ron. Did you hear the news?" She didn't wait for my answer. "The pigs killed Fred Hampton. He was shot dead in his bed."

That felt like a punch to my gut. I couldn't say anything for a while. Stephanie must have thought I didn't understand.

"He's the Black Panther guy you told me about, right?"

"Where did you hear this?"

"It's on the TV. Come watch in the dayroom."

It was December fourth. After a silly commercial, I watched the happy faces of the uniformed killers laughing as they carried their dead enemy, a trophy covered by a sheet. Hampton and Party member Mark Clark were killed in a pre-dawn raid on Chicago's Panther Headquarters. The official police version claimed the Panthers fired first, but as more details emerged, that story didn't hold up. The bullet holes they claimed came from the Panthers, were in fact nail holes, but it would be years before I learned the whole truth.

An undercover FBI agent drugged Fred Hampton's lemonade before the raid, so when the police burst in shooting, his pregnant girlfriend couldn't wake him up, even with bullets flying all around them. After the one sided "battle" ended, he remained unconscious, wounded but alive. His girlfriend watched the police finish him off with a shotgun blast at close range. The guardians of law and order thus silenced the man who brought the white, brown, and black People's movements together in the Rainbow Coalition.

Although I'd only seen Fred Hampton once, at the rally in support of the Conspiracy Eight, his words still rang in my mind. "Adventuristic, opportunistic and Custeristic" was how he'd characterized the Weatherman action I joined. Fred was dead, but I, a white-skinned son of the middle-class, still lived. Thanks to Chairman Fred, I was a little wiser and less Custeristic, and feeling a little guilty about enjoying my luxurious confinement at the Edge. White skin privilege, as the Weathermen said, was all that prevented me from the harsher punishment meted out to our black and brown comrades. The pig bastards mowed down my darker skinned compatriots without remorse. This was an unequal war, but we had to smarten up and keep struggling for justice and the equality of all people.

Marianne

After showing my art and flirting with a pretty Nursing Student one quiet day, I did some stretching and meditated in my room until a woman's bloodcurdling shriek shocked me out of my reverie. Curious, I ran down the hall to the nurses' station where I saw a heavy-set platinum blond woman screaming at the staff.

"God damn you fuckers to hell!"

Pretty Ms. Huebner, and Mr. Doaty, the white orderly on duty, stood wide-eyed in shock as the fat girl slammed her fists on the counter and threw every profane invective at them, and I couldn't imagine what they'd done to deserve that. This was my chance to score some Brownie points with the pretty Ms. Huebner.

"Hey," I called to the mystery gal. "What's all the fuss?"

She turned on me like a caged tiger with bared teeth. "Who the fuck are you, asshole?"

Her extreme rage unsettled me, but I stayed calm. "I'm Ron, a patient here just like you."

"You better not be playing any fucking mind games on me like these other assholes." Her face relaxed. "I'm Marianne."

"Hi, Marianne, it looks like you'll be joining our merry band here on South."

The victims of her outburst watched with wary relief as she turned her attention from them to me. I needed to stay on this ferocious woman's good side. Maybe she was just having a rotten day, but Marianne would prove to be anything but merry.

"Give me a hand, will ya, Ron? I'm moving in." She shoved a big blue suitcase at me, put a fur coat over her arm, and picked up a couple of shopping bags. "They said my room's down at the far end of the hall, but the fuckers wouldn't help me with my stuff."

Marianne Calvi was from Melrose Park, an Aries like me, but a year older. Her bloodless complexion, too pale for my outdoorsy taste, reminded me of the thick white paste smeared on kindergarten art projects. Her silver-tinged bleached white hair, cut butch style short, wasn't to my liking, neither was her pear-shaped figure augmented by tiny breasts. Although I found her unattractive, even repellant, I reminded myself that looks aren't everything, and I needed to be compassionate. On our walk to her room, she rattled off her brief biography.

"Let me tell you, Ron. That's your name, right? I've done it all, man, lived hard on the wild side. I've been a prostitute too." She shot me a brazen wink and erupted into a throaty laugh. "Or maybe I'm just taking a break from it. That work pays much better than a straight job. You ever been with a real whore, Ron?"

I felt myself blushing. "Well, no, but it has been one of my fantasies."

After the words left my mouth, I worried that I'd said too much. If Marianne was even a little more attractive, I would have been turned on. Just hearing a woman talk like that, call herself a whore, like my dear long-lost lover Ruby had, could make my cock hard as a rock. But not this time, not with Marianne. She scared me.

Stephanie wasn't my type either, but she'd been growing on me, leading me to expand my appreciation for a wider variety of feminine charms. She gave me gifts but kept me at arm's length, so getting together with her as more than a friend hadn't worked out. Marge, who'd tried to set us up, was still with Rick, although her flirtatious attention convinced me that we'd end up together if I hung in there. Meanwhile, as the odd man out, I'd have to make the most of the cards I'd been dealt.

On the evening of December 6th, we all hung out in a magic circle on the floor in Pete's room. Marianne, in a flimsy moo-moo negligee, plopped down across from me, giving me the eye. Marge, smiling like a Cheshire cat, sat between her and Rick, with Stephanie on his left. Next to me sat Pete, and on my left sat Zaher. Pete lit up a dobie, and after it made the rounds, Marianne, reeking of too much sweet perfume, crawled over, and snuggled up to me, her hand on my thigh. Marge hung on Rick's shoulder and giggled, causing me to blush.

Even if I overcame my lack of interest in Marianne, with Marge looking on, I couldn't respond to her. If I was older and wiser, I would have. I had nothing to lose and everything to gain by making either Steph or Marge jealous. Instead, I acted like a dumb boy scout, accepting Marianne's ministrations, enjoying her caressing arm around my waist, her other hand stroking my thigh with passive compliance, surfing along with events, but all the while my overactive conscience troubled me. I tried to be *kind*, fraternal, although her eager fingers told me that she needed much more. I didn't want to be rude or selfish. Her attention relaxed me, and I tried to be grateful.

Maybe with a little sun, exercise, and a better diet, Marianne could turn into a swell-looking chick. Her warm breasts brushed up against me, fuller than I'd first thought. Maybe I should let things happen as nature intended, but I'd been reading too much about what honor and self-discipline entailed me to do.

Poor Marianne, by accepting her caresses, I suppose I was leading her on, using her for my own selfish enjoyment. Maybe I was turning into one of those selfish bastards the British called cads. Although I railed against monogamy and enthused about Free Love, I didn't feel right making love to *this* woman. It didn't help that Marge was laughing and whispering in Stephanie's ear, making me worry that I'd ruin my chance with either of them by accepting Marianne, as if they even cared what I did. Smoking Pot made me paranoid, and I already had more than the couple of hits I usually allowed myself.

The others began leaving for their rooms. Marianne took my hand, leading me across the hall into her darkened room, but I could make out her greedy eyes well enough. Wordlessly, she put both my hands inside her Mumu to touch her warm flesh. My response was so wooden that she had to place them herself right where she wanted them, where I would want them too if she was someone else. She began moving my hands over her body, masturbating with them. It felt good to me too if I'd just let myself go with the flow.

Part of my brain screamed, *"Don't be selfish. Go ahead.* We both need someone. Another part of me countered that I'd get stuck with her jealous rage when Marge, or another girl more to my liking, became available. Exclusivity was more than I was willing to give Marianne, and I'd seen her fierce anger. A break-up could get nasty. With some reluctance, I made my decision and withdrew my hands from her hot, moist body.

"Sorry, Marianne, I'd better not."

"What's wrong?" Her eyes, liquid and softer than usual, pled with me. "Why not? I'll be your little whore. You can do anything you want to me. Come on, baby..." Her hard edges softened into the guise of a loving, compliant woman. I almost gave in, but I feared I'd only hurt her more if I let this go on.

"Sorry, I just shouldn't. I'd better get back to my room." Like a wind-up toy soldier, I turned on my heel and marched out the door. In a quick glance back, I saw a lightning flash of anger transform her face from stunned amazement into the white-hot rage of a demoness.

In the sterile solitude of my room, I had second thoughts. Maybe I ought to return and discover what 'anything you want' could mean, but before I had time to return to her, Marianne barged in, shrieking.

"You fucking bastard! Think you're too goddamn good for me, huh? You're such an asshole, Ron. You know that? A fucking asshole!" She swung, slugging the middle of my chest repeatedly. I didn't block her punches, I deserved them for all my past screwups with former lovers, and to clear my bad karma from losing Karen. Marieanne could never punish me enough for that. All my present sorrow flowed from that worst mistake of my life. If Marianne pulled out a knife and stabbed me, I'd accept that as partial payment for my sin.

My passive response only intensified her rage. She reminded me of my mother's tantrums against my father and the old saying popped into mind. *Hell hath no fury like a woman scorned.* I should have grabbed her, thrown her down on the bed, and let her hateful passion arouse my thwarted lust. Fuck yeah, I should unleash my own demons, allow both of us to spend our passion in a lust more sacred and satisfying than our lonely abstinence. If I'd been older and wiser, sure I would, but young and idealistic to a fault, I steeled my heart against it.

Under her barrage of curses and blows, I walked to the nurses' station. Doors opened along the hall and an audience formed into a parade as we passed. Mr. Doaty, the orderly on duty, set his coffee cup down on the counter as we reached him.

"Whoa, settle down now and tell me what the problem is."

Marianne slugged my shoulder. "Ron is a fucking asshole, that's what!"

"Did he hurt you?"

"Fuck no, this fucking bastard could never hurt me. He's a piece of shit. I'd kick his ass."

The avalanche of Marianne's verbal abusive words gave him no reasonable explanation for the ruckus, and I just stood there, saying nothing, ignoring her insults and slugs with as much forbearance as I could. Doaty's face betrayed some sympathy for my plight. He, too, had experienced her wrath.

Marge ran up and took Marianne's arm. "Come on, sweetie," she said as Stephanie arrived to grab her other arm. "Let's go have some girl talk."

I remained leaning at the counter as they coaxed the overwrought woman back to her room. Mr. Doaty took another sip of coffee, sighed, and asked, "What the hell was that all about?"

I shrugged my shoulders, feigning innocence but not feeling it. "Gee, it doesn't take much to set her off."

"Well, I think you handled her as well as anyone could." That was a rare bit of praise from him. "The best advice I can give is to steer clear of her. She's real trouble."

As I withdrew to the silence of my room, I rewound the tape in my head and found my sin of omission less than honorable. I'd acted like a selfish prig, leaving poor Marianne without the satisfaction I could so easily give her, and me too, without losing any ground with Marge.

Nurses Notes

12-6. Saturday 3-11. Pt appears to be very talkative, had a slight argument with Marianne was trying to avoid her, was visited by parents.

Snow Angels

The next morning was December seventh, Pearl Harbor Day. The events of the night before with Marianne faded in my mind. Stephanie called me to the dayroom window. "Will you look at that, Ron!" Deep snow had fallen in the night, blanketing the sooty black roads and leafless trees into a magical white wonderland.

"Come on Ron, let's play out there!"

As we put on our coats and signed out, she asked, "Did you ever make snow angels?"

"Gee, I don't know. What are they?"

"Jeez, Ron, sounds like you never had a freaking childhood. I'll show you."

We walked through knee deep snow to the cemetery fence at the back of the building. She laid on her back on the snow and moved her arms and legs side to side, then got up.

"See?" She pointed to the image she'd made. "Doesn't it look like an angel with wings and a wide gown?"

Womp! A big fluffy snowball hit my back, showering us both in cold, damp powder.

"Got ya!" Marge ran back around the corner of the building. "Bet you can't get me!"

Yelling like kids, we began a free-for-all snowball fight. When our frolic was done, we made extra snowballs to smuggle inside. A glum faced orderly sitting at the nurses' station became the target of our volley.

"Hey." He brushed off the snow. "You kids can't bring that in here. Wipe it up."

"Aw, come on," Stephanie said. "We're just having a little fun with you. Where's your Christmas Spirit?"

"Christmas is still weeks away and I've got to drive in this shit. Winter isn't my thing."

By evening, Pete decided on one last stroll around Miller's Meadow before it got too dark, and we had to be checked in. I hung out with Marge and Rick instead. The wail of a siren didn't grab our attention until we heard it pull into the parking lot below the dayroom window. We watched the back door of an ambulance open, and white-coated men pulled out a gurney.

Rick's brow knotted in a puzzled expression. "Gee, I wonder who they're bringing to the ITU."

Pete popped into the room, wild-eyed, dripping with melting snow and huffing from exertion. "Guess what!"

"What?" Marge and I asked at the same time.

Pete caught his breath and launched into his story. "It was already dark, and the park was empty when I started out, but the white snow gave off just enough light for me to follow the trail along the woods. I saw a dark shape off to my right that appeared to be a log, and I almost passed on by, but then it moved. I figured it was a racoon or something and leaned over for a better look, when it moaned."

By that time, everyone in the dayroom had crowded around to hear. Pete raised an eyebrow as he scanned our faces to be sure he had our rapt attention.

"You'd never believe what I saw. It was a body, but not just anybody. Marianne lay moaning in the snow. I asked, 'Are you alright?' She told me to fuck off. Typical Marianne. Right? I didn't want to disturb her, but something had to be wrong. When I kneeled beside her, I saw the blood." Pete panned over his audience. "Shit, man! She'd slit both her wrists. It's damn lucky that I came by. No one else would have come around that late, and she'd probably die out there."

Pete wrapped up her wounds with her scarf before he ran back to the Edge to call for the ambulance, becoming a Riveredge hero by saving her life. Once again, as with all unsuccessful suicides, our savants debated the seriousness of Marianne's intention. Whether the wounds were deep enough or too superficial, done for pity and attention rather than to carry out the dark deed of self-annihilation. Either way, if Pete hadn't found her when he did, she could have lain all night in the snow, weakening from cold and blood loss until hypothermia took its toll.

A tidal wave of guilt overwhelmed me, and I collapsed against the wall, feeling nauseous. I'd let her down. She wouldn't have done this if I'd fucked her. My 'chivalry' was a sin of omission.

Marge slumped down beside me. "It's not your fault, you know." She took my hand and spoke in a quiet voice. "Most guys would have fucked her, whether they liked her or not."

I felt a thump in my chest. Marge was my soulmate. She read my mind as if she was a part of me.

"Oh, yeah, Marianne told me all about it, Ron. I think you acted like a real Mensch."

"Mensch? That's German for man, isn't it? You mean I acted like a typical male chauvinist guy?"

She giggled. "No, silly, that's Yiddish for a *stand-up* guy. Believe me, it's a good thing you turned her down. That chick would have been big trouble no matter what you did. I've seen some crazy chicks come through here, man. Maybe she'd cut you up as bad as she cut herself."

Marge's brash exterior covered a warm heart, tempting me to roll the dice and confess my longing for her, but before I could form the words Rick came over.

"There you are." He squatted down and pulled her to him. "Do you think they'll ship Marianne off to the state hospital?"

"Oh." Marge let go of my hand to embrace him. "Not right away. She'll be in ITU for a while."

Rick pulled Marge to her feet, and they ambled off. I'd be making a fool of myself if I chased after them. Too often, I crashed into situations too impetuous to succeed. That's how I ended up in jail, and the Edge. If I came on too rash and demanding, I might chase her away. I needed to let Marge make her choices. Her compliment, calling me a *Mensch*, comforted me. Destiny would ultimately bring us together. I had faith.

Nurses Notes:

12-7. Sunday. 9:30. Out to play in snow, brought back a ball of ice with him. In and out on open ward.

Flying Hamburgers

On the 12th of December I returned from pass to find a cheerful fellow taping colorful cartoon pictures up on the walls in my room.

"You must be Ron. I'm Fred Fagely, the artist, your new room-mate. What do you think of my work?"

"Pretty cool," I lied. Pop art, a la Andy Warhol, didn't grab me. In this case, plates of hamburgers, some with all the trimmings of fries and even a malt, were *whooshing* like strange UFO's above idealized contemporary scenes of suburban streets and drive-ins. The idea might be okay for one or two pictures, but Fred seemed to be in an artistic rut. The only thing that varied was the background.

"You must like hamburgers, huh?" I said, trying not to offend him. "Do you draw anything else?"

"Nope, this is my flying hamburger phase."

He covered our walls with these flying hamburgers, even removing my watercolor, *Acid Trip*, which he left on the desk beside my praying monk statue, to make way for another of his hamburgers. I debated whether to confront him about it. I'd been struggling to conquer my ego as part of my spiritual development, and it was difficult to know where to draw the line. Instead of *my* room, this was *our* room. Art wasn't my thing and anyway, I spent most of my time outside or in the rooms of my friends.

Later, after I returned from a walk with Pete, Fred was gone, and I noticed a peculiar musty odor emanating from the bathroom. I pulled back the curtain to find what appeared to be a fully clothed body immersed in reddish brown water in the tub. Horror! The shower murder scene from Hitchcock's Psycho had burned itself into my brain when I saw it as an eight-year-old. The camera played over the murdered woman's bloodstained body, too real for me to handle at the time. It looked like my artist roommate had killed someone or drowned himself.

After swallowing my shock, I poked the sodden mass with one of Fred's paintbrushes. Where the head should be I pulled up only a ball of sopping wet clothing, a white shirt, and below it a brown suit coat. Maybe he was washing his clothes in the tub, which didn't make sense because the dark colors were bleeding out and staining the whites. I sat on the edge of the tub to make sense of the mess. Then I recognized the clothes. They were mine.

I opened the closet. On my side hung only bare hangers, while his clothing remained neat and dry on their hangers. Fred walked in, whistling a happy tune.

"Fred, what the hell did you do to my clothes?"

"What's the problem?" He blinked at me as if wondering what I was talking about.

"Why are my clothes soaking in the tub?"

"Oh, *he-he*, that's my new sculpture. I'm a creative artist, and someday I'll be as famous as Andy Warhol. You should be grateful that I honored you in this way."

Fred was a genuine crazy. Not just an emotionally disturbed, suicidal adolescent like so many others around there. I went to the Nurse's Station to fetch Mr. Doaty.

"Look at what Fred's done to my clothes." His expression of bored indifference didn't flinch. "Why did you put your clothes in the tub, Ron?"

"I told you, Fagely did it. He said he's turning them into a sculpture." He shot me a suspicious look. Fred Fagely sat at our desk like a nice, well-mannered boy, the picture of innocence, as he churned out another hamburger picture. Mr. Doaty must have assumed that I'd done it myself to blame my new roommate.

"Clean up this mess," he said before walking away.

Dumbfounded, I began wringing out my clothes. Fred popped in and yelled, "You're destroying my art!"

"Leave my clothes the fuck alone, Fred," I said, my patience at an end.

"No, Ron, this is *my* masterpiece."

"I'll rip your stupid hamburgers to shreds if you do it again. I mean it!"

"No, no, no, you wouldn't dare."

He was right. That would boomerang back on me. He stalked out into the hallway, and I hung my wet things over the heater and shower curtain rod to dry. Eager to tell my tale of woe to my sane friends, I left, but when I returned later that day, my duds were back under water again. As much as I wanted to, I didn't punch Fred, nor did I follow up on my threat to tear apart his precious art. I complained to the RN, asking for Fred to be moved to another room, all in vain. I couldn't sit and guard my clothes all day. This is how the staff charted it.

Nurses Notes

12.20.69. 7-3:30 shift. In and out on open ward, talking to roommate, stating he is really acting "strange." Appears somewhat concerned about this. Appears somewhat depressed this afternoon. - S. Stover LN

3-11. Socializing on ward with other pts most of evening. Expressed concern about Fagely's bizarre behavior. -M. Johnson LPN

Flying Fagely

Nurses Notes

    12.21.69. 7-3:00 appears to be very upset about his roommate F. Fagely. Asked if pt. Fred could be transferred to ITU because it bothers him to see Fred like this. I asked Ron if he knew why Fred was acting like that. He stated no. He guesses he was just out of it. - J. Harris LPN

No sooner had the ink dried on that last log entry than a new crisis developed. It was Sunday, the 21st of December, and Fred's parents came to see him. They seemed a pleasant, if rather anxious, couple. He'd been telling everyone that he was going home for Christmas and had dressed up in a suit and tie. Mine were still drying out in the closet.

My folks came too, and we hung out in the dayroom to give the Fagely's space. When the visiting hours ended, I walked them down to the parking lot. When I got back, I saw Fred at the nurses' station, a large suitcase in each hand, pleading with the RN, as Mr. Doaty stood by at the ready, as if blocking Fred from leaving.

"My parents are supposed to take me home," Fred said. "They forgot and went down without me. You need to let me out of here now. I have to get to the parking lot before they leave!"

"I'm sorry, Mr. Fagely," a weary nurse said. "But they said you are *not* staying with them this Christmas. Please, take your things back to your room and settle down." She shot a stern glance at Doaty, who nodded.

Fred screamed at them. "You'll be in big trouble for this!" With his fierce face turning red, Fred spun around and marched down the hall, lugging his suitcases to his room. His grimace told me he hadn't given up but was up to something. I followed close behind to protect my belongings and Doaty, with a wrinkled brow, followed several paces behind me.

Fred barged into our room, dropped the suitcase in his left hand, raised the other one above his shoulder, and ran to the large picture window overlooking the parking lot. With a mighty heave-ho, he threw it at the window. The suitcase broke through the glass and fell into the parking lot below, leaving a good-sized hole in what I'd been told was unbreakable glass.

The next suitcase followed, widening the hole even more. The remaining glass shattered into large, spider-webbed shards. Fed grabbed the glass to either side of the hole and pulled more of it out of his way, expanding the hole before he jumped on the desk and wormed his upper body through, preparing to jump.

"Mom! Dad!" he yelled. "Wait, I'm going with you!"

Doaty was too far back. I was right behind Fred, which put me in a crisis of confused loyalties. Should I interfere, and on whose side? His parents had long gone. Jumping from that second-story window and landing on glass would injure him and he wouldn't get far. I grabbed Fred's belt and elbow and held him back. Doaty came up to take hold of Fred's other arm and together we pried his grip from the jagged glass and pulled him back inside.

"Whew!" Doaty looked at me with amazed relief. "That was sure a close one."

"Yeah, exiting! I never expected that unbreakable window to break."

Doaty searched my face. "Thanks Ron." I knew he meant it. Maybe he'd believe me about Fred soaking my clothes.

Fred, still screaming and demanding to go home, had only a couple of minor cuts to show for his effort. Other orderlies arrived to strap him down and hit him up with sedative. This would be his ticket to a stint in the ITU. The log entry gave the following report of the event, which, as always, didn't give much of the whole story away.

12.21.69. 4:00 p.m. Ron transferred to Rm. # 282 because his roommate broke the window. - E. Peterson RN

Mr. Doaty, O, wanted to praise pt. in the manner he helped him with another disturbed pt. From jumping out the window. --- E. Peterson RN

Ron was up and about unit socializing with other patients. Later was in rec. room listening to records. At times appeared depressed and then began banging his fists on nurse's desk at times. --- E. Peterson RN

Mr. Doaty became friendlier to me after this. However, I still rankled Ms. Peterson, who hated me rapping out rock and roll drumbeats on her countertop. To her, I was just one of the wild, alienated youth of America placed under her wary care to mold into useful citizens.

Mindful of the Mindless

Steve Kay said he came from a super-rich family in Flossmoor Heights, an affluent suburb on the far south side that I'd never heard of. He took a gloomy view of almost everything. Speaking of his hometown, he repeated over and over, "It's so mindless, full of spoiled rotten rich brat kids."

Mindless was his constant refrain, peppering his conversation on every topic, intoned with the same awe and bewilderment Freaks used when saying "Far out," except for his implied disdain bordering on contempt. He directed that word at the rules we lived under, our nation's leadership and foreign policy, the wars, the social and economic inequalities. They were all "mindless" to him, as if to imply that no conscious thought had gone into them. He was right, but I thought he needed to temper his disillusion with a more positive spirit of adventure.

Despite his pessimism, Steve and I hit it off. I did my best to punch through his glum attitude, and every now and then, I got a half-hearted laugh out of him.

"This universe we live in *is* insane," I said. "We've got to be crazy to survive here, so we may as well enjoy our ride to the far side."

He shook his head and rolled his eyes. "It's just so mindless."

"Come on, Steve, let's get outside." I grabbed his shoulder and yanked him along to the nurses' station, reached for the clipboard, and signed us out.

Instead of Miller's Meadow, we headed east on Roosevelt. Over the river across from the cemetery stood a big double A-frame building with two slanted rock chimneys, Sambo's pancake restaurant. The sign pictured a cartoonish little black boy running from a tiger.

"See that?" I nudged Steve. "Now, that's mindless. Do you know the story of little black Sambo?" When he didn't answer, I went on. "My grandmother read the Little Golden children's book to me as a kid. Sambo tricked a pack of hungry tigers into chasing each other around a tree until they melted into butter. His mother put the butter on her pancakes. That's a great theme, making me hungry, man. I love pancakes."

Steve didn't react, so I kept trying for a laugh. Beyond the restaurant, cemeteries stretched to the horizon on both sides of the road.

"Wow, Steve. It looks like the dead outnumber the living here."

"Yeah," he said. "There's no more forest in Forest Park as it fills up with the dying from this overpopulated world."

"Ha, ha, that's a good one. You crack me up, Steve."

From DesPlaines Avenue on stretched car dealerships and then more cemeteries before we reached the dense residential zone near the border with Chicago and turned around. We'd almost reached the river when a car pulled over in front of us.

"He must think we need a ride," I said. We looked in the passenger side window to see a midget at the steering wheel. He sat on a custom-made raised seat, the brake, clutch, and gas pedal also extended to reach his baby length legs. I bit my tongue to keep from laughing.

"You boys wanna buy some cut rate jewelry?" The fellow's elfin body contrasted with his street-tough banter to create the most surreal thing I'd seen without taking LSD. Neither of us had smoked any pot that day. This apparition had to be real.

He opened a briefcase on the seat beside him. The glitter of gold and silver bracelets, necklaces, rings, and watches sparkled as he held them up to us. "Look, I got some great stuff here. You guys oughta give some of this to your girlfriends, you'd make a real hit with 'em. How about your mamas? They'd appreciate something nice like this, all women do."

Steve glanced at me as if to be sure I saw what he did. I overcame my amazement.

"Sorry, man, but we don't have *any* money."

He held up a gold chain. "Okay, look, I could give you this for ten bucks." I shook my head. "Okay, five. It's a steal, kid!"

"I don't even have that much. How about you, Steve?"

He just shrugged and shook his head.

The midget threw down the chain and slammed the briefcase shut, shouting, *"Fuck this shit!"* He threw the long levers of his car into gear and, with squealing tires churning gravel, he sped off.

Steve watched him disappear, and said, "That is totally fucking mindless, man, *un-fucking real.*"

"Yeah, it blew my mind, too. I never saw a midget selling hot merchandise from a souped-up car before. Reality is way weirder than fiction." We both cracked up. I laughed until my sides hurt.

———

The next day, the adolescent activity workers took our group out to eat at Sambo's. The murals inside depicted scenes from the story of tigers, Sambo, and his mother amid waving palm trees for the patron's amusement.

Julie, a social worker in her mid-twenties, harrumphed. "Some people say these are racist depictions of African people, but the original story featured Sambo as an east Indian, not a negro child. I don't find that objectionable at all. Do you?"

I looked around the room packed with as many black diners as white. "They don't seem to be offended. The murals look attractive, real art. Some people are too damn sensitive."

Stephanie laughed. "I think it's mean to animals. Sambo tricks a bunch of tigers into chasing each other around a tree, melting them into butter so they eat them on their pancakes." She scrunched up her face. "How awful if you're a tiger!"

"Tigers gotta eat too," Zaher said. "It could just as well have been the kid; except he used his head. It's survival of the fittest, law of the jungle, you know."

The Sambo's chain of restaurants eventually succumbed to the growing political sensitivity in the Seventies. They changed to a tamer and more forgettable name, became too ordinary, and eventually went out of business. That's survival of the fittest in our hyper competitive modern times.

Under the Star of David

Hatha yoga and meditating in my room kept me mentally and physically fit, and life at the Edge fell into a comfortable routine. Even though my flirtations hadn't scored me their love, Marge and Stephanie's attention kept me somewhat balanced. My feast and famine life on the road had left me underweight, but the regular nutritious meals I'd been eating put an extra ten pounds on my frame. It couldn't last forever. I had to prepare myself for jail or whatever else was in store for me.

I ventured out alone to explore the acres of cemeteries that stretched well to the east of the DesPlaines River. I'd join them soon enough in the hereafter. Many of the tombstones were Jewish with ornate Hebrew lettering with metal covers, like door knockers, over pictures of the deceased, older ones were black and white and more recent ones in color. I gazed into the faces of men and women, young and old, and felt a kinship spring up, as if I was hailing friends across a wide river. We were all thrust into a mortal frame to experience this world with as much skill as we could, only to be taken back beyond the shroud into the great mystery we came from.

Although I didn't consider myself a vandal, I surrendered to an

144

impulse to bring one of these into the land of the living as a talisman and kicked off a twisted hinge with a star of David embossed on it. Stephanie had given me a long leather thong that I used to hang the talisman around my neck, star of David facing out, like a breastplate. I rejoined my live friends that evening in a circle on the floor in Mike's room. My ornament was a big hit with them.

"Wow, Ron," Marge said. "I didn't know you were Jewish. Where's your yarmulka?"

"I'm not a Jew, but I had a Jewish girlfriend in Greenwich Village."

She laughed. "I'm supposed to be a Jew, but a lot of bullshit goes with it."

"Right, I'm more into open spiritual paths that respect others."

Rick fidgeted beside her as she leaned over to lift the ornament off my chest.

"Jeez, it's heavy, Ron. Where'd you get it?"

I shot her a mysterious smile. "I was communing with the spirits of the dead when it popped up from the grave like Excalibur, King Arthur's sword of Destiny."

Mike coughed. "Jeez, man, you sure can spin a yarn. We don't even have any smoke today. Aren't you afraid of picking up negative vibes from the cemetery?"

"Negative vibes? We're surrounded by them everywhere we turn. You know the Buddhist path, Mike. We have to confront and transform the negative with positive wisdom and compassion."

Speaking the words "wisdom" and "compassion" stirred my conscience. My desire for Marge and hers for me caused suffering for Rick. He reached out and tried to put his arm around Marge's waist, but still admiring my trophy, she pushed him away.

"Give me some space, dude," she said before rolling her eyes and smiling at me, sending a hot wave of life enhancing lust through me. This could be the magic moment for me to reach out and claim this beguiling woman. She needed me as much as I needed her, but my conscience derailed my rash instinct, twisting my will in knots.

A song by Joanie Sommers from way back in nineteen-sixty-two popped into my head. *Johnny get angry, Johnny get mad. Give me the biggest lecture I ever had. I want a brave man. I want a caveman...* Yes. I wanted to be the caveman who, like the bullies I'd known in school, took the initiative and got what they wanted from girls who melted like cotton candy in their arms.

I cleared my throat. "Marge." Then my mind blanked on how to proceed. What words could I use that wouldn't make me sound like a pompous ass? Maybe it takes a pompous ass to get the girl. That was a scary thought.

Rick shot me the look of a whipped puppy and rose to his feet. "I'm going to bed, Marge."

"Wait." Marge scooted back and reached her hand out too late to stop him. She turned back to me. "We'll talk later, Ron. I gotta go now."

"Wow, man." Stephanie clapped her hands. "Things are really happening tonight. I wonder what house the moon is in. I'm still studying the stars to draw up our charts, but I'm looking into how numerology works too. Our names have deep impact on our personalities."

Mike sat up in his bed. "Do you really think our names can affect our personality? What if we change our names? Does that change who we are?"

Marge didn't come back, and as Stephanie expounded on her interest in numerology, she offered Steve and me a reading before we all trooped off to bed. My quandary, whether to be a brutish caveman or a man of honor, remained unresolved. Our nurse had a far different take on my personal adornment that day.

12-22. 9:45. Walking around with three objects hanging around neck exhibiting psycho motor activity increase.

Wise Guys Bearing Gifts

It was about one o'clock on December 29th and I'd just returned from court. I sat trying to meditate on my tantric visualizations. The effort of raising my kundalini, the coiled serpent power, from the chakra at my gonads up to the crown of my head often rewarded me with swirling waves of bliss. However, with my mind distracted by my worldly prospects, that heady sensation eluded me.

My lawyer got another continuance. He didn't seem to have any other strategy except to delay and try to keep my case separate from my fellow defendants. With the FBI cracking down on protesters, aided by Chicago Mayor Daley's anti-radical Red Squad, my conviction on the felony counts seemed inevitable. All I could do was align myself with the spiritual forces of justice and psych myself up for jail.

Knock, knock. A male orderly poked his face into my room. "Mr. Schulz? You have visitors."

"Really? Who are they?" I'd never had any visitors except my parents, and they always came without being announced.

"I don't know. The receptionist called us. You have to see them down in the lobby."

A jolt of excitement shot through me. It could be Marge playing a joke, but just maybe my beloved Karen had somehow tracked me down. I pulled my legs from their locked position and stretched, waiting a few moments for the sharp needles of tingling pain to subside before I stood up and made for the door.

In the lobby, I found a familiar bunch of guys sitting on the plastic sofa. My West End friends, the Delmonte brothers, Chris, Steve, and Patrick, along with John Borley and Bubba Fichter, their broad smiles melted my bummer feelings like snow under the sun. I'd called Chris as soon as I got my telephone privileges back in November and told him where I was. He'd promised to visit and bring me something to take the *edge* off my incarceration, but time passed, and I assumed he'd forgotten me.

"Hey, guys! Lucky that you caught me. I just got back from court."

"Yeah," John said. "I heard about you getting busted in Chicago and all. Gimme some skin, man!" He laid his hands atop mine for a horizontal swipe and then reversing them for me to slap in an elaborate handshaking ritual. Then he gushed a torrent of words.

"We walked down on the frozen DesPlaines River, one hell of an adventure. At one point, we heard a loud cracking sound. Man! It was a close one, but we all jumped clear off the ice – fast. After that, we spread out single file to redistribute our weight."

Chris beamed and clapped his hand on my shoulder. "I told you I'd come, didn't I? It's only about ten fucking miles! We started early this morning, walked to where Lake Street crosses the river." He glanced at the receptionist, lowered his voice, and gave me a conspiratorial wink. "Can you go out? We've got something to show you."

I signed myself out and followed them around the side of the building, among the trees along the frozen river. Chris reached behind a tree, brushed off some snow, and pulled up a heavy knapsack.

"Here Ron." He handed it to me. I saw about seven bottles inside.

The labels read Seagram, Johnny Walker, Smirnoff, Bacardi, and Jose Cuervo. A selection of whiskey, vodka, rum, and tequila. Serious booze!

The West Enders and I considered ourselves Robin Hoods. Chicagoland, still haunted by the legacy of Al Capone and John Dillinger, imbued a certain gangster ethos in those of us who grew up in its shadow. We saw the justice system as slanted in favor of the rich and powerful and ourselves among the disinherited, robbed of our equal share of wealth. Therefore, we didn't concern ourselves over the fine points of private ownership, so long as it wasn't purloined by a friend or deserving stranger. Among ourselves, however, we expected honor and openhanded generosity.

Steve and John counted. "One, two, three. Merry Christmas, Ron!"

"Thanks, guys! Merry Christmas back at you. This is the best present I've gotten. Where'd you get this?" None of us were old enough to buy it, and I knew they'd stolen it like we had "liberated" cheap beer and wine on past raids, but this was quality hard stuff.

Steve winked. "We broke into John's Three Pines Tavern the other night. The owner cheated Chris out of some dough for work he did, so we helped him grab a few things to get some payback."

"Yeah," John said. "Chris went straight for the cash register and got it open while the rest of us grabbed the bottles, but you know Bubba."

We glanced at Bubba, who smiled back in all innocence.

"He wasted his time struggling to bust open the gumball machine only to find about fifty cents in pennies."

We all had a laugh. Bubba was famous for uttering straight faced lines straight out of Mad Magazine, like "If we lived here, we'd be home by now." He even looked like Alfred E. Neuman, the magazine's comic mascot boy.

"Let's crack one open and toast your successful journey," I said. "Any preference?"

We settled on rum. None of us were heavy drinkers, so after passing the bottle around a few times, we only managed to gulp half of it before the merry crew needed to head back. I twisted the cap back on and lugged the sack to a snowbank at the back of the building. It was near the hallowed spot where Stephanie and I had made snow angels. After burying the bottles deep in the snow, I handed the empty boy scout rucksack back to Chris.

"Don't drink it all at once," he said, then burst out laughing. "Or I'll have to bring more!"

Chris had proven himself a loyal friend, and I pumped his hand with vigor. "Wish I could go back with you, guys!"

My tipsy companions stumbled their way back along the frozen river, keeping enough distance between them to spread their weight and not break through. I stuck the half empty bottle and a full one of whiskey into my pants and hoped that my winter coat hid the bulge.

Still tipsy, I sauntered past the Nurse's desk to Pete's room without mishap.

"Look what I got, Pete." I pulled it out of my pants with a flourish. "This is your late Christmas present, payback for all the pot I smoked with you. Plenty more stashed outside."

He chuckled in appreciation. "Man alive! I've got a great hiding place for that." He patted his belly, grinning from ear to ear. "Remember the place I showed you?" Pete kept his pot stashed in the doubled-up seam at the bottom of the curtain. If he didn't put too much in, the bulge wasn't obvious. Despite staff suspicions, we'd kept our pot smoking a secret, despite the inevitable musky odor that clung to us, and some savvy staff recognized, but they found no hard proof.

After finishing the rum and stashing the whiskey for later, Pete and I carried the empty bottle outside for disposal so we wouldn't tip them off when the janitor took out the garbage and found it.

Pete dropped his voice to a whisper. "Don't tell anyone where you stashed the rest. They might blab."

After my head cleared a little, I ran into Zahel. Despite Pete's warning, I counted him as a righteous dude I could trust. So, I took him to the snowbank to show off my booty.

"Jeez, man, that's an impressive haul!"

"Yeah, let's bring in one a piece. We've got to drink it up or find a better place to stash it before the snow melts." I chose a couple of flat flasks that wouldn't bulge our pants too much. "Here." I handed him a bottle. "Slip it down your pants like this." I stuck the other down mine under my coat. "We'll just bring in these two to share with the others."

His forehead wrinkled. "But what if we're caught? We could lose our privileges."

I *tsked* him and laughed. "No sweat, man. I already brought two in without a problem. Just go in like you always do, stash it under your clothes in your room, and we'll share one tonight and the other tomorrow. Dig?"

He relaxed, but when we reached the Nurses' Station the worried look returned to his face, arousing the suspicion of the RN. "Just a minute, you two."

With a cherry *hello* I breezed on by as if I hadn't understood her, but Zahel froze.

"What have you got there? You too, Ron. Get over here."

"I've got to pee," I shouted over my shoulder and took off running to my room. In a flash I hid my bottle in the bottom of the curtain, threw my coat on the bed, ran the water a few seconds in the bathroom, and despite the heavy throbbing of my heart, walked back as if I hadn't a care in the world.

An orderly stood next to Zahel, holding open his coat. I'd expected him to follow me, but he stood frozen to the spot like a deer in the headlights. I should never have relied on him for this.

"Pull it out!" The words of doom rang down the hall, and Zahel complied. With the bottle in her hand, the nurse turned to me. "Mr. Schulz, you'd better let me see what you have too."

One precious bottle was as good as gone, and only luck could save the rest of my stash from confiscation. I raised my hands. "I've got nothing." The orderly ran his hands over my belt and pockets, finding nothing. "He's hid it in his room. Let's go."

They ransacked my room while Zahel, blanched white as a ghost, stood beside me like a condemned man awaiting the noose. It gave me a fright when they yanked open the curtain. The bottom, weighted by the bottle, swung like a pendulum but didn't give itself away by clinking against the wall. I hid my anxiety by focusing my gaze on the dresser opposite.

The Nurse followed my gaze and motioned to the orderly. "Over there. Go through everything. It's got to be here somewhere." They moved the dresser and pulled out the drawers, fingering through all my clothing and along the underside and edges of the drawers for taped on packages. Nothing. They expanded the search to every corner of the room, behind the toilet and under the sink.

Pete, meanwhile, alerted by the ruckus in my room, responded to the crisis by chugging as much of his bottle as he could, pouring the rest down the sink, before slinking down the hall to dispose of the empty bottle into the Nurses' Station trash can where they found it later. All available staff were busy in my room and anyone who had something to hide had time to dispose of it.

Under the RN's direction, nurses and orderlies came in from other wards and, sending all patients into the hall, began a systematic search of all the rooms, including the trash cans, where they found a few empty baggies that smelled of pot. Frustrated at finding nothing else, they tried to bargain with me.

"Just tell us where it is, and we might not put you on restriction." I didn't fall for that. Having long been part of the West End gang's revolutionary-criminal underground, I kept my cool, and gave them a plausible alibi.

"Okay, you got me red-handed. I gave that bottle I'd bought at the Zayre's to Zahel and asked him to carry it in for me because I was too chicken and didn't want to get caught." I turned to Zahel, who stood there open-mouthed. "Sorry to get you in trouble, man." I winked at him, hoping he would get the message to clam up and let me do all the talking.

"The baggies you found are mine too, but I don't want to get anyone else in trouble over that." By taking the rap, I expected to allay suspicion on our real suppliers, and it worked.

Although I got restricted to the unit, my bottle remained snug in the curtain, hidden away, until things cooled down a couple of days later. It would help us welcome in the New Year.

As for Zahel, I didn't reprimand him for surrendering without a fight. This was the first time he'd been under the heat. At least he didn't tell them about the big cache buried in the snow. We remained tight, but I never asked him to carry in another bottle. The Nurse put it this way in the log.

Nurses Notes

12/29/69. 3-11. patient returned from open ward with Zahel, appeared to be hiding something under his coat. Pt would not stop ran to his room. Pt later admitted to nurse that the liquor found on Zahel was his, and he was too chicken to bring it in. pt. stated he had some pot, but he gave it away to others on ward but was not going to say who, because it would only get them in trouble.

ADOLESCENT PROGRAM
RESTRICTION REPORT
DATE: 12/29/69. TIME: 8:30 PM.
ATTENTION Ron Schulz is restricted. Pt went to Zayre's and brought back liquor to the room. Was to share it with another pt. rooms searched on unit. Full bottles of liquor found. Pt admitted empty liquor

bottles on unit he brought into hospital from Zayre's. & container found with specks (of) grass in it. Questioned pt who said he brought in the grass and liquor. Dr. Ghattas notified – restricted to unit until Dr. sees him. Restriction begins at 8:30 pm until Dr. sees him.

Restricted by: E. Peterson RN

1970: New Love in a New Year

We sat on the floor in Mike's room. Stephanie poured her paper cup half full of coke and passed it to me and slurred, "Give me another hit, Ron. I'm already feeling it."

Although I was still on restriction, I could chill out with my boon companions on the ward. My hidden bottle had remained undetected, a small victory against the establishment. By spiking our cokes with it, we got ourselves sloshed on holiday cheer.

"That's the last of it," I said, shaking out the bottle. "Good to the last drop. Huh? That'll have to do until I get off restrictions to fetch more. Anybody ready to go out on pass and smuggle out this dead soldier?"

"I'll take it," Zahel offered.

I hoped the snow didn't melt before I could go out and re-stash the rest of my supply. Instead of smuggling bottles in and taking the risk of getting caught, we'd sip it in the great outdoors, like we usually did with pot.

"Hurry back," Stephanie called after him. "You don't want to miss the meeting."

My restriction didn't prevent me from attending ward activities, which included preparations for the New Year's celebration. Joining the crowd in the rec room, I spotted an angelic apparition with long black hair, a new girl who took my breath away. Our eyes met, drawing me to her as if by magnetic force. Her shy, flirtatious smile at me sent a shivering thrill throughout my body.

"Hi, I'm Valerie," she said, scooting over to make room for me on the floor against the wall, with all our companions on either side of us.

I winked at her. "Cool name, Valerie. The Monkees wrote you a song last year. Right?" That got her laughing.

"No, my name is spelled V-a-l-e-r-i-e. They spelled it with r-i at the end in the song." She gave me her hand. "I'm pleased to meet you."

Stephanie was right. There was magic in the mantric vibration of our names and Valerie's name was already vibrating in my head like a church bell. I had to impress her.

"I got sent here from jail after a fight with a cop in Chicago. What are you in for?"

Like most of us, she was first admitted to Two North and allowed into the Adolescent Program on a trial basis. Her parents, she said, were the villains of her story.

"You see, Ron, this mind control crap runs in my family. My father is a psychiatrist, and my mother is a psychologist. Insanity is kind of like their job." She giggled at that. "It really is a crazy situation. They sent both me and my brother to different mental hospitals when I turned fifteen, and I suppose they're trying to get rid of us. Only our sister hasn't been committed, not yet anyway. They must have some gosh darn good insurance to cover this."

Valerie and I were soon holding hands and basking in each other's warmth before I dived in for our French kissing marathon. The strange flavor of her mouth was so unlike other girls I'd kissed. When she finally pulled back for a breath of air, she reached into her jean jacket and took out a pack of cigarettes, solving the mystery. She was super nicotine flavored.

Much as I'd railed against tobacco in the past, I no longer cared if this girl tasted and smelled like an ashtray. Came what may with this dark-eyed beauty, I was smitten, addicted to the whole package. The pungent taste of stale cigarettes became associated with my feelings of raw lust even if I had to die of lung cancer in her embrace.

In a trance, I watched her lite one, inhale a lungful, then with languorous satisfaction she leaned back against the wall, releasing wispy trails of smoke from her nose before offering the lit fag to me. Although I wasn't a tobacco smoker, I accepted her offering of glowing poison as a sacrament, willing to share her karma in a sacrifice of my ego. My boundless Tantric love went through and beyond her, to all the women who'd given me the love of their bodies and minds. I'd love them all through her, for true love should be as boundless as the sky.

The meeting wrapped up. She had to return to her ward, but with New Year's Eve on the morrow and I felt confident that we'd be together to ring it in, and through the long span of eternity after that. Indeed, we picked up right where we'd left off. Hand in hand, we wandered the halls, showing off our love to patients and staff without distinction. No one could stand in our way and be our adversary on that magic day when things seemed to finally begin working out for me.

"Ron," the nurse waved me over to the front desk. "You're being taken off restriction as of now." Her face blossomed with a benign smile. "Try not to screw it up." Then she turned her attention to Valerie. "Will you help keep him on the straight and narrow?"

She giggled as she shook her head, contented joy filling both our hearts with fresh confidence. I'd only been restricted to the ward a couple of days, but Valerie still couldn't sign herself out and there was nowhere I'd rather be than with her. More good news. In honor of the holiday, they let Valerie stay in the rec room on South until after we rang in the New Year.

Our friends counted down the seconds. *Three-two-one – Happy New Year!* With raucous mayhem, the bold promise of 1970 came alive. Valerie and I French kissed long and deep. Her tongue and eager lips on mine mingled the hot juice of our passion, assuring me of much more pleasure soon to come. The noise and jubilation of our companions was but a thrilling backdrop to the fireworks exploding in my brain and heart.

"This'll be our year," I said when we came up for air.

"For sure," she agreed, beaming a smile. The staff motioned that it was time for her to go and, with a last glance over her shoulder at me, she passed through the door and off the ward, if only for the night.

My chart for that day sounded more positive than usual.

12-31. 7-3:30. Pt up and about on unit. Socializing quite a bit with female pt. At nurses desk with female companion conversing with staff. Pt is now off restrictions.

11-7. Up in rec room until 12:30 A. M. to bed – quiet noc.

As an early riser, I ate most of my hearty breakfast in the cafeteria before Marge, Rick, and Stephanie stumbled in and joined me. Marge gave me a wink and smiled. "That was some night, huh?"

Rick shook his head in agreement. "Yeah. Looks like you got yourself a girlfriend, Ron." He seemed less anxious and jittery, as if assured that Marge and I had more of a buffer between us. Back on the ward, I awaited the return of my dark-eyed lady in the rec room, expecting to hear news of her transfer.

"Ron!" Stephanie ran up, wide-eyed and breathless. "I just heard that they put Valerie in restraints and took her to the ITU. Maybe she flipped out."

This had to be a joke. "You're pulling my leg, Steph. Valerie wouldn't do that. We were having such a great time last night."

"Yeah, but that's what I heard. I didn't get why, but they put her in restraints and hauled her out."

My dream world came crashing down. Marge, Zahel and I crossed the parking lot to the West building. In the elevator, they showed me where a staff had to insert a key for it to stop on ITU, which was off limits to the likes of us. Marge called up on the intercom. The answering robotic voices came mixed with static. In the background, I thought I heard a girl screaming, and wondered if it could be Valerie, but they wouldn't let us in to visit her.

I grabbed the handset from Marge. "Let me talk to her, please! Maybe I can calm her down."

"Sorry, we can't do that without her doctor's permission."

Back on the ward, I begged the RN for the name and number of Valerie's doctor, but it was New Year's Day, a holiday, and all I could do was leave a message with his answering service and retreat to my room and wait. Valerie had given me a couple of cigarettes, which, despite being a confirmed non-smoker, I took out of my bedside drawer and began sniffing the pungent tobacco to remind me of her. Then, I leaned back against the bed's headboard and with prayers to the all-embracing cosmic powers, I lit up, inhaled deeply, and watched the wispy white smoke carry my earnest prayers aloft. I needed to see if the sacraments of the Native Tribes of America had been on to something. Maybe the narcotic effect, like a shot of booze, could alter my state of mind in a beneficial way. It did bring me a little more distance, but not any more than my ordinary pranayama breathing, and I knew better than to make smoking it a habit for my lungs' sake.

Later that day, an orderly called me to the phone. A nurse on the other end relayed Dr. Nyquist's crisp reply. Permission denied.

"Why?" I asked, but she had no reason to give me and as I wasn't a blood relative, who was I to deserve one? In so short a time, Valerie had become a significant part of my emotional life and I missed her. As far as the soulless administration was concerned, I had no place in her life. It seemed to me that the system only sought to shrink us into numb cogs in their gray society.

The keen eyes of the RN were on me as I hung up the phone,

watching for any sign of ill temper, but I only shrugged with pretended indifference before retiring to my room. I took some comfort in meditation, my only sure refuge on the swirling wheel of Samsara, but instead of remaining aloof from the drama of love and loss, I allowed the tidal wave of dark despair to wash over me, in mourning, as my critical, observing mind watched. Instead of the Beatle's *Blackbird*, a song which comforted me earlier on, a new song-track, the Monkees Valleri, played in my mind.

There's a girl I know who makes me feel so good and I couldn't live without her even if I could. Vaaaaalleri, I love her...

Over and over, the half-remembered lyrics played in my head. The sweet memory of her warm, liquid presence came enhanced with the funky aroma of tobacco. Like a waterfall of hot lava, it sent wild arousal coursing through my veins. *Vaaaaalleri, I love her... Valleri – Valleri,* I'd tasted heaven in her arms, but sitting lonely in my room, my arms hung empty at my side.

Meditation again turned into a review of my vanished lovers. Valerie wasn't my first, nor would she be my last thwarted love, but they had each revitalized my life before the whims of fate tore them away – too soon – without even a farewell.

Nurses Notes

Thursday, January 1, 1970. New Year's Day.

7-3:30. Pt. up and about on unit early this AM Seemed very depressed in afternoon. When asked about it he said, "I feel raunchy because Valerie was transferred to I. T. U.," refused to talk more about it.

3-11. pt remains depressed. Dinner tray on unit. Socialized on ward very little this P. M. was seclusive most of evening. Asked to have Adolescent worker bring Valerie over for visit. Dr. Nyquist was called request denied. Pt. shrugged shoulder when informed of this decision retired to room.

Go West Young Man

Nurses Notes

1-7-70. Wednesday, 7-3. To gym with Mr. McKinney & other adolescents this p.m. watched t.v. for one program. Retired to room. I went down to his room he was sitting in chair in dark when asked why stated "I am meditating." I said ok sorry I will come back when you are done. He said "no, stay I was almost finished anyway." I sat and talked with him for a while. He is somewhat upset about his pending court date. Stated "I suppose I will get probation which is kinda bad because it means I will have to stay in this area which I don't want to do. I was planning to go back to the Rocky Mountains. But I guess things could be worse." When I asked about school stated "I would rather go to jail before going back to school."

To say I wouldn't let self-pity rule me was easier said than done, but my stash of liquor helped. In case the snow melted, I moved it to a safer location under a bush. On long walks through the graveyard with Pete, we'd pass a bottle back and forth as he listened to my tale of woe. I drank just enough each day to take the edge off and lighten my emotional load. Zahel's music also helped me universalize my experience. The Buddha taught that suffering is pervasive. We needed to nurture our wisdom and fortitude with compassion, born of our own experience with suffering.

A week went by. My efforts to keep a lid on my feelings worked for all outward appearances. The Nurses' notes mentioned my attitude as "good mood and humorous at times." I listened to music on the rec room hi-fi and socialized with patients and staff, but I got no news about Valerie. I kept hoping that if I remained calm, they'd eventually allow me to see her. Rumors abounded. One day, I heard that Valerie was transferred to another mental hospital to keep her away from me. All I could do was carry on.

Pete and Zahel transferred to the adult open ward on Two West, and I heard they were transferring me there, too. I feared that might take me out of the Adolescent Program and I'd not be able to hang out with Marge. She was the only constant female companion in my life, and my feeling for her only grew stronger.

After a nurse promised I could remain in both the Young Adult and Adolescent programs, the rhythm of my life ramped up with more activity. Both programs needed to spend the excess money in their budget, and I was the beneficiary of that. Otherwise, I'd never have seen so many movies, much less a Broadway play.

On Tuesday, January thirteen, the Adolescent Activity group took us to the movie *Gaily, Gaily*, at 12:30. When I got back that afternoon, I no sooner dropped off my clothes in my new room on Two West when I left for another movie, *Easy Rider*, with the Young Adult group.

The next day, the fourteenth, my run of luck continued as I

joined the Adolescent group on a bus ride downtown to watch my first ever Broadway show, *Hair*. All this excitement spun my head around. Before this, I rarely saw more than one movie a year. In two days, I'd absorbed more media entertainment than ever, coming full circle from my social isolation on Two North.

The movies had a profound impact on my appreciation for my place in the Sixties Zeitgeist. The songs in *Easy Rider,* starting with *The Pusher* and *Born to be Wild* by Steppenwolf, were already a big part of the soundtrack of my life. The opening scenes took me back a few months to my time in the free love commune in Taos. Dennis Hopper, the sidekick of Peter Fonda, in his flop hat and rugged buckskin dress, was a dead ringer to the extroverted guy who drove me to Taos from Santa Fe. I later learned that Dennis had remained in Taos after the filming, and I wondered if it had been him, I'd met there. Their odyssey swept me along to another familiar landscape, mythic New Orleans, where I'd first run away at fifteen. The last scene, in which a redneck murders the duo, brought home the fact that our culture war could be deadly. The last line Peter Fonda's character said before their murder rang in my mind like a prophecy.

"You know, Billy. We blew it."

It seemed Peter Fonda was talking to *me* because I'd blown it too. I assumed he meant that they should have stayed in the New Mexico Commune, as I should have. But in that case, I wouldn't have landed in jail and the Edge, and I also wouldn't have met Karen and Kay, and Ruby and Bonnie before them. I missed each of these lovers with equal affection. The problem was that all of them, extending even to Valerie, had vanished from my embrace like mist before the dawning sun in too short a time.

Did it mean I was supposed to abandon love to focus, monk-like, on my spiritual quest? In the past nine months, I'd lived through so many experiences that, for better or worse, left their mark on me. Each of my mistakes had opened me to new opportunities. Maybe the misfortune itself was part of the road I was destined to travel, and I ought to accept it with a positive attitude.

Gaily, Gaily, was a comic, nostalgic romp through turn of the century Chicago. It reawakened my sense of connection to Chicago's history, or at least my fantasy of it. The rioting scene in the movie reminded me of our Haymarket battle, and my obligation to continue the good fight for social justice. The technicolor nudity and sex, with a heartwarming look at life in a whorehouse, reassured me our more liberated era was breaking free of the prudishness that had made sexuality almost invisible by the nineteen-fifties. The critics panned *Gaily, Gaily,* which was a loose adaption of Ben Hecht's book by that name, but I loved it and had no regard for their artsy-fartsy bourgeois sensibilities.

That our staff took us to see *Hair* proved how progressive they were. The play broke much new ground with its unabashed nudity, which caused a lot of media hullabaloo. At the end, they welcomed the audience-us-up on the stage. It was as if the artificial veil separating art from *real* life lifted to bring us body and soul into that ecstatic celebration of this Age of Aquarius, the visceral drama of our times.

I could identify with *Hair.* Members of the cast and characters they portrayed reminded me of people I knew. I'd first heard of *Hair* from Mrs. Butler, who owned the John Birch Society's hyper-conservative *American Opinion* bookstore in Elmhurst, which touted books that claimed Rock & Roll, especially the Beatles, were either Satanic or Communist inspired.

Although Mrs. Butler oozed a grandmotherly charm upon us, we weren't taken in by the laughable Right-Wing propaganda, which we enjoyed while keeping the joke to ourselves. There was no sense upsetting the old lady, and we used the opportunity to explore the irrational mindset she subscribed to. She complained that her liberal minded relative, Michael Butler, produced "that dirty communist inspired play Hair." He took it from a little-known production, operating on a shoestring in Greenwich Village, all the way to a major Broadway hit. That's what serious money could do. He'd become radicalized and hoped to influence public opinion against the

Vietnam war, making him a right-thinking hero, whatever his aunt said.

On January 20th, Dr. Ghattas belatedly wrote a memo that officially placed me in both the Adolescent and Young Adult programs after some busybody submitted a complaint that I was being pampered. That evening I got back at 8:30, to be released overnight to my parents because we had to be at the Courthouse early the next day. The images of shameless nude actors standing tall and proud inspired my courage to face whatever fate awaited me, but it was only another continuance.

Peer Personalities

A new patient with a familiar face appeared in our Adolescent group and I ran over to him. "Chopper, is that you?"

There was only one guy in the world it could be. His large lower jaw jutted out a couple inches beyond his upper teeth, like a Dick Tracy comic strip character, thus earning his nickname by third grade.

"Ron? Put-er there, my man!" He extended both of his hands and I slapped them, then turned them over for his slap.

"It's been a long time no see, Ron. How's that hot sister of yours?"

"You mean Darlene? She was the Freshman Queen at Fenton High last year."

I knew Chopper from back in grade school. Bikers called their motorcycles Choppers, and he bragged that one day he'd join the Outlaws Motorcycle gang which added more depth to his nickname. I never knew how true his gang affiliations were. On the playground he hung out with the tougher guys, but I never saw him bully anyone, and we got along alright.

Chopper pulled me aside and ogled Marge across the room as he whispered to me. "Man, they got a lotta swell chicks around here on South. Don't they? I'm still under observation up on the North ward. They say I can join the Adolescent group on a trial basis and if I play my cards right, and maybe I'll move over here later this week."

The Staff took us to Sambo's for pancakes. Rick, Marge, and I sat at a table with him, stuffing our faces while listening to his hair-raising tales of bar brawls and knife fights that may have contained a kernel of truth as to how he ended up at the Edge. Then he winked at us and changed the topic.

"There's this new girl on North. She's super thin and pretty, but all she talks about is offing herself, suicide. I got damn sick of hearing about it, so I told her, 'Look, if you really want to *off* yourself don't yak about it, just do it.'"

Marge bust out laughing, "I bet that shut her up."

"No way. She asked for my help." He glanced around the table at us. "I mean, if that's what she wants, who am I to tell her different? You know what?"

We shook our heads, and he lowered his voice. "They didn't frisk me good when I came in here. I still got razor blades." He chuckled like a Hollywood villain. "I gave her a couple this morning."

Marge put her fork down. "You didn't? did you?"

"Yep, I sure did, early this morning." He winked at me, proud of his charity. "We'll see if that chick really means what she says. How many of 'em go through with it? I bet she gets scared after a little cut. It'd be a shame to waste such a pretty chick though."

That was the last time I saw Chopper. The suicidal girl sliced herself up before someone caught her and bandaged her up in time. She told them where she got the blades and that blew Chopper's transfer to South.

———

Zahel introduced me to another new patient on Two West. Angelo was a tall, bearded guy with long dark hair wearing sunglasses who looked to be in his late thirties. He put his forefinger to his lips and shushed us, then waved us into his room. "Can you guys do me a big favor?"

"I suppose," Zahel told him.

"I'm on ward restriction." That surprised me. It was the first time I'd heard of someone being restricted in West, which wasn't a locked unit. "I don't feel like going anywhere, anyway. The Doc put me on the Methadone program. I've been a junkie, and I'm detoxifying from heroin."

"Won't that conflict with drinking wine?" I asked.

"Man alive, kid." He let out a sigh of resignation. "I've got a hell of a lot of problems besides that. I'm also getting electric shock treatments. See? They leave me disoriented, my mind a jumble, which is what it's supposed to do. I got too many traumatic memories from being an enforcer for the Mob. See?"

Zahel and I looked at each other, unsure if he was bullshitting us.

He glared and shook his head at us to add sincerity to his words. "Believe me, horrible images of the guys I blew away keep come at me in my dreams and sometimes even when I'm awake. I need to cut them out of my mind. See?"

He reached into his breast pocket and pulled out his wallet. "So here. I'll give you boys some money to go buy me a bottle of *Wild Irish Rose*."

"We're both underage," I said. "But I've still got a stash of booze my friends brought me that I'll share with you."

"Naw, *Wild Irish* is the only kind I drink. I bet the department store won't even ask for your ID if you act naturally. The salesmen just want to make a sale."

It went according to plan. The Zayre department store was only a block to the west along Roosevelt, across First Avenue in the town of Maywood. At seventeen percent alcohol, Wild Irish Rose was a wino's delight, a strong but sweet fortified wine.

Angelo waved us into his room to savor a sip with him. With a conspiratorial wink, he put his finger to his lips and began his story. "I really shouldn't be telling you boys this." He unfolded his tale of Mafia heists and hits, punctuated by slugs of Irish. It made me wonder if he was breaking the Mafia rule of omerta – silence, which could make him a loose end they'd want to eliminate, but he didn't mention names and dates, so it wouldn't qualify as evidence.

He'd started out busting the kneecaps of guys who'd been too late repaying their debts to the loan sharks. Angelo was ambitious and wanted to climb up the ladder and graduate to become a *made man.* That is, an insider, a full member of the crime family. He had to *make his bones,* which meant he had to kill whatever men his capo, or boss, gave him a contract on.

"I killed a bunch of guys," he said. "I won't give you the horrible details because it brings me back there again and gives me night-mares. That's why I started using *horse,* you know, heroin. It worked, but now I'm hooked."

The next day I found Angelo slumped in the hall beside his door-way, the way I'd seen junkies in the alley crumpled after they'd shot up with heroin. I squatted down beside him.

"Hey, Angelo." I shook his shoulder. "Are you alright?"

He opened glassy eyes that rolled back in his head and grunted before rolling back on the floor. Zahel came out of his room, and I waved him over. "I think Angelo is back on heroin again."

"No," Zahel said, shaking his head. "He just got his methadone. That gives the same spaced-out reaction as heroin. That's why it reduces withdrawal symptoms."

"I suppose it's better than going cold turkey," I said. "But looks to me like the cure is as addictive as the disease."

———

A short, pudgy guy appeared at our adolescent group meeting. Although he hadn't said a word, he stared at me from across the room with an adoration that I found creepy. As the meeting broke up, he grabbed my arm and glommed onto me.

"Are you Ron? Can I please go on a walk with you?"

"Well, I don't know..."

"Please, it would mean a lot to me."

Something about him repelled me. I ran up to the counter to sign myself out and escape, but he signed out too and shadowed me. I reminded myself to practice compassion and slowed my pace to listen to what became a lengthy list of his complaints and insecurities.

"Nobody likes me, Ron. I try so hard to make friends but it's no good, they shun me. I'm unlovable and I don't know how to fit in, or even what to do with my life. Should I end it? I just want to be loved..."

This unmasculine display wasn't how straight men connected with each other, at least not after grammar school. He had to be gay with a crush on me. I didn't want to waste my time or lead him on, but with all the attempted suicides going on, I couldn't just chase him away, so I endured his rant as long as I could.

"Look, man, feeling sorry for yourself all the time, I bet that's what makes people dislike you. Don't focus on yourself so much. Think about how others must feel listening to a guy like you!" I chuckled and expected him to laugh at that, but his face scrunched up like he was going to cry.

"Oh, Ron, don't be so cruel. I need you to help me, please."

"I am helping you. You gotta face up to it, be a man."

"But I'm not, I'm a woman in a man's body. Can't you tell?" He stepped in front of me and looked up at my taller head like a desperate, swooning schoolgirl with tear-filled eyes. "Do you like me? Please say you do, be my best friend, nobody else understands me. Sometimes I just want to hurt myself. Know what I mean?"

"Why me? I'm not gay, find a guy who is."

"Because you get along great with all kinds of people. I just want to be close to you. I'm not brave enough to kill myself, but I think about it all the time. You can help me be strong."

"Life is crazy and cruel, sure, but you've got no choice but to stand up to it. See the humor in the situation and laugh at it, don't take yourself so seriously all the time."

"Don't do something stupid like that. Be a man and get it together." I'd been hoping to see Marge later that day and this guy, whose name I didn't even want to know, was blocking my way and imploring my help. I decided to give him some tough love advice.

"We're all going to die someday. Why rush it? You'll only get reincarnated to deal with the same shit all over again. Cheer up, be nice, make friends with other people, not just me."

He exploded into tears. "Don't push me away, Ron. I'll do anything you ask, let you fuck me, blow you, anything."

This sounded like a replay of my experience with Marianne. Maybe I should have taken her offer, even an ugly woman could turn me on if she tried. But a guy? Hell no, the thought nauseated me.

"Look, I'm into chicks, man, not dudes. Go find a gay guy."

He began to blubber like a crybaby. "That's easy for you to say. You're a good-looking guy. You can have anyone."

"Shit! Your face is no worse than mine. Others have real problems, like misshapen heads, eyes off kilter. Even my friend Chopper with his stuck-out jaw. You should feel sorry for them. It isn't all about you."

I realized I didn't know his name, but he knew mine, so I softened my approach. "What's your name, by the way?"

He batted his eyes. "I'm Sonya Sunshine. My family named me Mark, but that's not who I really am, because I'm a girl stuck in a boy's body." He attempted a coquettish smile and winked. "I could be at your service, any way you want me."

His flirtation backfired. I wanted to get away fast. "Maybe you were female in your past life, man. Now your karma put you in this male vehicle to teach you something. Accept who you are in this body now. Anyway, I've got to split, be cool and find other friends besides me."

I ran off to commune with the dead in the cemetery, thinking about how Samsara, the terrifying wheel of illusory life, spins us from death to rebirth. This he-she thing made me uncomfortable. The very idea of being born into the wrong sex bothered me. The opposite poles fit together best, whereas a male-to-male bond created a weird chemistry. It's a different kind of partnership than between men and women. I needed to harmonize with a woman's magic juice and charisma, not become her.

Whether he was Mark or Sonia, his whiney churlish complaints were more than I needed, but for days afterward, Sonia shadowed me on my walks, taking up my time, as if I was his shrink or only confidant. One day, another new patient pulled me aside.

"Hey, I saw you talking to Mark, who calls himself Sonia. Be careful, I knew him before he came here. He's loopy."

"How so? Because he wants to be a girl?"

He laughed. "Way more than that. When I went to make a peanut butter and jelly sandwich at our group picnic, I found him under the table trying to saw his penis off with a plastic knife. I yelled, *Stop it!* Lucky the knife was too dull to cut."

Sonia tried to stay in touch for years afterwards by calling my parents' house asking about me, even though I'd moved on and rarely came home. My mother pitied him enough to stay on the phone, chatting aimlessly about his insecurity and problems adjusting to both the gay and straight world. She began counting on his calls coming every holiday for decades. Sonia called other acquaintances at Riveredge too, talking to their mothers, or whoever answered the phone until he died around the cusp of the new century.

Bon voyage, dear fellow. May his next incarnation be more to his fancy.

Sue

Steve Kay and I filed along to a group meeting on the first floor. A young blond girl I hadn't seen before slipped up and whispered to him. "I'll meet you later, okay?"

He shrugged her off. "No. That's just mindless. Go away and leave me alone."

She was pretty, and his rejection of her piqued my curiosity.

"What's that all about, Steve?"

"Mindless, man." He shook his head and mumbled, "That chick wants me to fuck her. Says she needs to get pregnant to keep from being sent to a convent or something."

"What? She's a doll, and you don't want to help her out?"

Steve was crazy to turn her down. With her long yellow hair, sparkling blue eyes, and curves augmented with a little baby fat that I'd love to squeeze, she had everything it took to turn me on. I shook his shoulder. "Steve, introduce me to her!"

He shot me a scornful grimace and shrugged. "Her name is Sue Tinin. She's all yours if you want her."

Before the meeting got underway, I decided to seize the moment with as much delicacy as I could muster. "Hi, Sue, I'm Ron, a friend of Steve. I can help you and..."

Her blue eyes flashed angrily. "What did that asshole tell you?"

I got close to her ear. "He's not interested in you. See? There's too much going on in his head, but I think you're gorgeous. Let's get together and talk after the meeting. Okay?"

She made a face and shook her head. "Steve's an asshole."

"But I'm not," I said, glad nobody was paying attention to us. "I think you're a real hot chick. I mean it. Look at me." She turned to me with a disappointed frown. I refused to let that discourage me and whispered. "We should get together."

Her hard features relaxed into a half smile. "You think so, huh?"

"Yes, and I can take care of you better than Steve. All right?"

Her eyes fixed on Steve across the room without answering. Romance is a competitive racket of winner take all. I had to play the game or forever be lost.

"All right?" I repeated, louder. "Come on, Sue, let's hang out after the meeting and talk."

She sneered. "I don't want to yak about it. I want to fuck right now and get pregnant. Are you up for that?" Her voice got too loud. One of our keepers could intervene and blow it. I pulled her aside for more privacy.

"Yes," I hissed. "Where can we meet? Are you moving to South yet?"

"They're supposed to move me there soon, but I can already sign out for an hour's pass."

"Great. We can meet in the lobby right after the meeting. Promise?"

She nodded, and I went back to sit by Steve, so as not to arouse staff suspicion. With my piss-poor luck, I didn't want to ruin my chance with this doll of a chick. I'd had enough disappointments.

As the meeting broke up, I followed Sue out and whispered, "See you in the lobby in ten minutes."

She smiled at me, raising my hopes. I stopped at my room to get my long winter coat before going to the lobby, hoping this wasn't yet another letdown. To my relief, Sue charged into the lobby, smiling as bright as the sun. Such a surprise after her earlier attitude. Her long blond hair streamed out from under a white fur Cossack cap and over the shoulders of her knee-length red coat. She grabbed my elbow, and we flew like snowbirds out into the brisk winter air.

Her breath formed clouds as she spoke. "Where to? The cemetery?"

"It's too open there. Someone might see us, but the park across the street has woods to cover us along the river."

"Did you ever make love in the snow, Ron?"

"No, did you?"

She shook her head. "No, this'll be the first time. Isn't it exciting."

"Don't worry, we'll make our own fire to warm ourselves. Come on!"

Laughing like carefree kids at play, we ran, dodging the traffic across Roosevelt and tramped down the snowy path into the park holding her gloved hand in mine. Winter had stripped the leaves bare, leaving little cover along the edge of Miller's Meadow, but there were very few people strolling along who might see us. We'd almost reached the far end when I stopped.

"This will have to do." I led her through dead brambles to a clear, level spot almost to the frozen river, however it wasn't as invisible from the field as I'd hoped. "Maybe no one will bother to look this way."

Her white teeth sparkled like the crisp snow around us as she laughed. "Let 'em watch. I don't give a fuck who sees." Her breath, like mine, turned to wispy clouds in the chill air. Doffing her hat, Sue shook her head, flailing her yellow locks from side to side. "I just want you to fuck me, Ron. If they wanna watch, let 'em!"

Sue instantly became the wild woman of my dreams. I gazed into her clear blue eyes as I unbuttoned my long coat. "Steve said you want to get pregnant."

"Yeah, I need to get pregnant right away. Don't worry, man, you won't have any responsibility for the kid. I won't tell anyone who the father is, and you won't even have to see it." She reached into my open zipper. "I just want your dick, man." Her warm hand made my cock jump up to fill her palm. "Man, you are *ready* for me."

She glanced around our thinly screened snowy bower as she unbuttoned her coat, then back at me. "My parents want to send me to a fucking convent. Get it? They want to punish me for my sins, turn me back into their good little girl. The nuns will make me shovel pig shit all day and pray to the stupid virgin Mary all night. Can you believe that?"

I spread my coat over the snow-covered ground. "Well, Sue, maybe we ought to run away from here, head out west to a commune I know." Pulling off the rest of my clothes, I watched Sue unveil her glorious body. Her medium breasts were pert in the chill air. She undid her pants, exposing a little plump but attractive baby fat around her middle and laid down on my coat to pull them to her booted ankles, as did I, in case we had to make a fast getaway. I kneeled beside her and ran my hands over her warm, yielding flesh. She smiled, pleased with her effect on me.

"The nuns won't take me if I'm pregnant, Ron. That'll give me nine months to figure things out. I don't know if I'll keep the baby. Maybe I'll give it up to some rich people, but I'm not going to shovel pig shit. You've only got to get me pregnant, that's all. What a deal, huh?"

I pulled her naked body to me on the coat and hugged her tight against me, our hot arousal overcame the cold. She pulled back to leer up at me. "I need to tell you something else about me, Ron." She planted a kiss on my lips that opened wide for my tongue, then pulled back to emit a throaty cackle. "Did I tell you that I worship Satan?"

"Ah, no. really?" That shook me up. A chill, unconnected to the temperature, ran through me. I hadn't seen the hit Roman Polanski movie, *Rosemary's Baby,* but from all the buzz about it the year before, I knew that it was about a girl who became pregnant with the Devil's child.

"You mean I'll become the devil's stand in, like in *Rosemary's Baby?*"

"Yeah, Satan is my lord and master. I'll serve him by fucking you, in a Black Mass." She squeezed my cock, hard. "That okay with you, down there?"

I took a moment to reassure myself that as a Buddhist, I had nothing to fear from this Satan, who was only a figment of the paranoid Christian world view. My spiritual refuge would protect me – protect us, from whatever negative force she invoked. I'd visualize myself as the terrifying horned Tantric deity, Yamataka, conqueror of death. Christian missionaries equated his fearsome image with Satan, anyway. Sue, I realized, chose Satanism in rebellion against her strict Catholic upbringing. I'd enjoy my role as her master, then take my sweet time to set her straight. Our spiritual goals weren't so far apart after all, not if I got to be her master.

"Okay, Sue." I stood, assuming Yamataka's spread-legged stance before her. "I'll be your lord and master and you'll be my shakti consort."

"Yes, master." She rose to her knees and took my cock in her hands. Looking up at me with a sly grin, she intoned a liturgy. "I hereby worship thee, my Lord Satan. Do with me as thou wilt." She'd become my willing slave girl, which had the effect of a powerful aphrodisiac on me, making me lightheaded, dizzy, yet in control, as lusty blood coursed through my veins.

I'd always made love from a dimension of equality, but hearing this gorgeous girl call me master and submit herself to my command, outbid them all for the depth of arousal I felt.

Her eyes still on mine, she kissed the tip of my cock, then flicked it with her tongue as a wicked smile spread over her face. "How do you like that, Master?"

Then she opened her mouth wide and inch by inch swallowed it to the hilt. Sue thus presented me with my very first blowjob, an erotic delight which I'd fantasized about since long before high school. Yes, it felt as wonderful as my fortunate classmates claimed. Sue blew my mind and my love for her grew within me.

It had been so long since Karen, so long since any woman had so much as touched my lonely phallus. My body bucked with waves of ecstasy as Sue gave my cock her complete, loving attention, slurping up and down, impaling her head to the back of her throat like a sword swallower, all the while moaning a mouthful of inarticulate words in praise and submission to her Lord Satan. As she served me, I played with her long blond hair and reached below her chin to squeeze her taut breasts.

My dominant role as her master, her Satan, or whatever she needed me to be was a new and heady experience, but it accorded with primordial fantasies from my dimmest memories, perhaps even from an earlier life. I became her haughty lord of the underworld, empowered to do as I pleased with her, but I would not let myself degenerate into a real Satan. I had to remain a benevolent lord, compassionate, aware of my duty to her and all living beings. As I felt myself on the edge of erupting, I had to snap out of my rapture for duty's sake.

"Wait! I'm almost ready to cum." I pulled out of her mouth and took a deep breath, gazing into her liquid blue eyes. "I promised to impregnate you. Remember?"

She nodded, and let me push her down on her back. Playfully, I rubbed our noses together, Eskimo style for warmth. Then I toyed with her clit, as she moaned a sweet erotic melody and mumbled, "Yes master, oh yes," reminding me of the harem girl from I Dream of Jeannie.

Pacing myself to last longer, I eased my steed into her corral and bucked her with a slow and gentle rythem while I continued to rub her clitoris, the *man in the boat,* with my finger. Sue erupted, trembling, and groaned her pleasure as I galloped, faster, harsher, to erupt like a volcano with my store of too long held back lava rushing deep into her cavern, the womb of our future offspring.

Whew, we both exhaled in satisfaction. I rolled over, panting, and pulled her sweaty body on top of me, like a fleshy blanket.

"We need to do that again, real soon," I said, daring to hope for more. "How about you? After you move to South, and we'll try this inside?"

"Okay, I mean, yes, master!" She giggled, and I hugged her, feeling that this was only the beginning of a long and satisfying relationship. If my seed did indeed germinate inside her to begin a new generation of rebels, our bond would grow even stronger.

Cooling sweat chilled our naked bodies, convincing us of the need to move. We shivered as we threw on our clothes in record time and ran back to the road, reaching it warmer and out of breath, we stopped.

"We've still got a few minutes," I said. "We could hang out in the lobby for a while."

She put her gloved hand to my lips. "We'd better not be seen together. If my bastard father suspects anything, he'll ship me straight to the pig farm." With a furrowed brow, she looked up and down at me. "And you? Skinny guy that you are, he'd fucking kill you for sure."

"Come on, Sue, we can figure out a way around him. Let's talk it over some more."

"You don't know my old man. He doesn't cut me any slack. Give me a couple minutes before you follow me in."

I watched her cross the road and disappear inside before I followed, whistling a happy tune. My heart skipped along, happy as a child at recess. The mad episode of our lovemaking, the sweet pungent scent of her, her pornographic endearments, and moans of passion reverberated over and over in my mind. Sue made such a beautiful, willing love slave, fulfilling all my fantasies, and even banishing thoughts of other women from my mind. My world was spinning back on its proper orbit. But could it last?

The Day After

S ue was an extraordinary girl full of surprises, and I couldn't
get her out of my mind. It seemed a match made in heaven,
or if she preferred, hell, and I looked forward to more than
the hasty encounter we'd enjoyed, if only to be certain she got
pregnant. She told me I didn't need to be involved, but I wanted
her. As she sought freedom in orgiastic slavery to Satan, I would be
her dark master and keep her from going over the edge. After
filling her womb with new life, I'd love and protect her and raise
our future child in the hip new culture we'd build together. It
would be far removed from crazy Catholics and their pig farming
nuns. As for her maniac father, Mr. Tinin would have to catch us
first.

The next day, I filed along with a new guy, Chin, and the others
from Two South to a meeting downstairs in the Adolescent group
office. Chin was a tall Chinese boy, shy and slow to talk, the first and
only non-white patient I met at the Edge. I'd taken him under my
wing, doing most of the talking on long walks around Miller's
Meadow. The little he said led me to understand that he'd been
bullied in school, causing his social anxiety, and problems speaking

up. I lectured him on the need for revolution to create a more caring society.

Chin and I sat on the floor with Zaher, joking around while I waited with restrained impatience for Sue to show up. Ruth, a redheaded twenty-something social worker, looked up from the paperwork on her desk. She spun around on her swivel chair to face us and shot me a smile that became a smirk.

"Congratulations Ron, you lucky dog. I heard you scored and got a piece of ass from Sue yesterday. Right?"

Shocked, I didn't reply. Her approval of my *scoring* at the expense of Sue's sexual reputation, which still held weight even in that more liberated time, confused me. I sure didn't expect that kind of cavalier, sexist remark from a woman, especially Ruth, who seemed to be a savvy, liberated woman. How did our secret get out? Could it be a trap? Was she just fishing?

"Don't worry, Ron. *You're* not in any trouble. That silly thing made her own grief. Man, at least you got some action before she went nuts and blew her transfer. Now she's out of the Adolescent Program and won't be joining us on South."

I took a deep breath. "What do you mean? She freaked out or something?"

"Her father wanted her to remain restricted on a locked ward, and her shrink wanted assurance from her that she'd settle down and behave herself before her transfer to South went through. She got into an argument that turned into a screaming physical altercation."

Ruth's male co-worker stepped over our stretched-out legs and walked into the small office. "Are you talking about Sue? Yeah, she got out of hand, kicking and swinging at her doctor. They called for backup. It took a few of us to hold her down and put restraint cuffs on her."

Ruth broke in. "She spilled the beans about your little rendezvous, Ron, bragging about screwing you in the snow! I bet that was cold. But her outburst ended her open ward privileges. They shot her up with Thorazine and sent her to the ITU."

It had to be more than a coincidence that all my would-be girl-friends ended up in the ITU. Sue was wild, all right. I could imagine her exploding out of control, like they said, Marianne too, but not Valerie. She didn't seem capable of such a manic blow-up unless she had a damn good reason. The administration seemed to be screwing with me.

Poor Sue, her parents' rigid control only turned her into a raging Satanist against them. She must have gotten some satisfaction from throwing the *sin* of her wanton sex into her dad's Catholic face. I admired her rebellious spirit, even to the point of worshipping Satan, but she needed to learn to cool it and not blow her chances. Too bad Sue couldn't keep her cool long enough for a few more sessions to be certain that she got pregnant.

A week later, Stephanie stopped me in the hall. "I got a message from Sue for you. She says she's pregnant."

Exit the Edge

D r. Ghattas threw up his hands in exasperation. "I'm unimpressed with your progress, Ronald. You are incorrigible, not cooperating with the program very well and if you are ever to return home, you need more treatment to learn how to conform to society. On the other hand, your father's insurance is running out. What are we to do with you?"

My parents agreed that living under their roof wouldn't be good for any of us. They needed a cheap place to stash me, so I suggested moving in with my West End friends, the Delmontes. A phone call set up a meeting with their mother. Mrs. D met us in front of her house in the chilly winter sunshine. I supposed she didn't bring us inside, because like most women, including my mother, she felt embarrassed by her unkempt house.

"Sure." She nodded in ready agreement with our proposal. "What's one more mouth to feed? My oldest boy, Ricky, is away in the Army. Ron can take his bunk in the shared room with Mike, Chris, and Steve."

Mom arched her eyebrows, veering between concern and relief.

"So, he won't be a problem then? I expect he'll move out as soon as he finds a job."

"No problem." Mrs. D seemed glad to have me. "Ron can help around the house. He's been almost part of the family these past couple of years, anyway."

She didn't need to discuss her decision with her husband. Bruno worked for the Railroad in downtown Chicago. They're more relaxed, or maybe burned-out attitude, contrasted with my argumentative, blame slinging parents. My dad threw himself into unending projects when he came home from work, no matter how tired he already was. He wasted much of his effort due to the law of diminishing returns. Projects he rushed into had to be redone, and I felt that his relationship with Mom suffered.

On the morning of January 27, Mrs. D picked me up and took me out on a pass to look for a job in the growing business district that had sprung up on what had so recently been lush farmland along the border of Bensenville and Elmhurst.

"Look, Ron. There's a help wanted sign." She parked in the fenced-in lot. "It looks promising. Huh? I'll wait in the car."

The fortyish man standing behind the counter looked me up and down with evident distaste, a prejudicial reaction I'd come to expect from the so-called *Silent Majority,* and I knew I wasn't welcome among their ilk. My hair had grown out over my ears in the three months since the buzz-cut I got in jail. It wasn't as long as I wanted, but it was too long to suit the anti-hippie bias of main-stream conservatives.

"All right," he sneered. "What the hell do *you* want?"

Ignoring his palpable disgust, I put on a brave face and soldiered on. "I saw the help wanted sign out front. I'm looking for a job."

He cleared his throat. "I don't think we need anybody, but I'll call the boss." He sat and leaned back in his swivel chair, staring at me as he talked into the receiver. "Hello, Mike?" His loud voice made sure to broadcast his end of the conversation to me.

"Say, we got one of those longhairs in here... Yeah, looks like a real weirdo, says he's looking for a job... Uh-huh... What'll I tell him... Yeah, that's what I thought... Give him the bum's rush? *He-he*, yeah, I get it... No, we don't need any of them punks in here... *He-he*, okay, I'll get rid of him."

With a big, toothy grin, he hung up. "Sorry, we don't need you."

With my anger held in check, I turned on my heel and stalked out, telling Mrs. D, "They forgot to take the sign down."

Although that fellow was the most hostile, I found no takers for my labor. Only two of them had me fill out a job application, most gave me a curt, "Sorry, kid. We don't need anyone." A couple times I heard, "We're looking for someone older, with more experience," but the overall message was clear to me. If I wanted a job, I'd have to cut my hair. To do that would imply my total surrender to social conformity. If I gave in now, my hair would never be long enough to convey my true identity as a hippie, a proud freak.

As I walked out of the last place, I overheard one of the two men standing at the counter snicker and comment, "We don't hire no niggers either." That settled it. Fuck these conservative assholes. I had to be who I was, a revolutionary, and stand with my fellow freaks, my people, including all people of color. By refusing to cut my hair, I was effectively making myself a nigger. Society had to change, not me, and society never would change if we, the children of the white ruling class, didn't stand up to force it.

"I didn't get the job," I told Mrs. D over and over. Her face creased with maternal concern. She prodded me for reasons, and my evasive answers didn't prevent her from zeroing in on the reason.

"Oh, for gosh sakes. Cut your hair! It's not that big a deal. Is it? Make your life easier."

I couldn't back down, but I couldn't explain my obstinance in words that this kind and generous woman would understand, but I wouldn't impose on her generosity for long. After winter's freeze melted under the warm spring sun, I expected to hit the road again.

Mrs. D drove me back to the Edge. That afternoon, I attended a team meeting, and the nurses noted that I appeared "very bored, quiet, depressed." It was hard to keep my sang-froid under the hammer blows of fate.

Judgement Day

Nurses Log

1/29/70. 7-3 pm. Returned from pass with parents. Says he thinks he will have to stay in the hospital longer than he'd thought in order to avoid going to jail.

Monday, 2/2/70. 7-3. Sitting in rec room early this a.m. – lotus position – eyes closed – meditating – continued meditation in this and other positions for about ½ hr. to 45 min…

"All rise…" Judge Epton banged his gavel, and my lawyer approached the bench, asking for yet another continuance. Then we left. That scene on December ninth repeated itself on the twenty-ninth. Continuance after continuance made me wonder whether my case would drag on for years as I wasted away in Riveredge.

"I'm sick and tired of these continuances," I told the lawyer. "Can't we just get it over with?"

He blinked at me, turned to my folks, who nodded, so he turned back to me. "I'm trying to have your charges reduced from felonies to misdemeanors. Maybe the court will take your age into consideration. You're a first-time offender and an inmate in a mental hospital, so you might get off with probation rather than jail."

"Great. So, when will this be over?"

"We have a little snag." He glanced at my father, who nodded approval to go ahead. "The court psychiatrist found you mentally incompetent to stand trial."

"Really? We had such a nice chat." I turned to Dad. "My legal fees must be costing you a lot, hiring a lawyer and all." He shuffled in his seat, so I knew I was right. I turned to the lawyer. "Set up another appointment with that psychiatrist. I'll convince him that I'm sane enough for trial."

Last time I'd let him run the show. This time I'd be more decisive. After knocking, I approached his desk with firm steps.

"Thanks for your help. I appreciate how you got me declared incompetent so my charges could be reduced, but now I'm ready to get this over with." He coughed but said nothing, so I went on. "I'd appreciate you changing my diagnosis. Tell them I'm no longer crazy and okay to stand trial."

He blinked in surprise, then gazed at me as if peering below the surface of a lake, taking a long moment to reply. "Alright Mr. Schulz, I'll make my new recommendation to the court." With a flip of his hand, he dismissed me. That was fast. After a few days I got confirmation, the continuations were over.

Dream yoga, one of Lama Naropa's six spiritual disciplines, helped me to confront my situation. The mastery of dreams helps build the heart of a warrior, and in conjunction with other practices, to open psychic abilities, like projecting out of your body and into the astral plane. One should learn from a master, but lacking that, I relied on books and prayers for guidance. The more I focused on it the more I was able to control the dream.

My dreams involved confrontation with armed enemies, police, or FBI, even finding myself mounted on a horse with the blue-coated cavalry of Mackenzie's Raider's, the TV show I identified with as a kid. After first assuring myself that the situation was a dream and not a real situation, I'd charge into my phantom enemies, heedless of bullets or arrows, laughing as they landed harmlessly at my feet. Other times I would find myself in an unknown house filled with mysterious passageways that led to rooms hung with ancient portraits, one of which changed into a mirror. The face I beheld wasn't my familiar, current visage, and I saw scenes that I supposed came from my past lives, others prepared me for future events.

Encouraged by this, I felt ready to face the flesh and blood judge to resolve my case. The next time I appeared in court, it was for keeps. By wild coincidence, our car had followed behind Judge Epton's on our drive to the Criminal Court Building early that morning. Watching his shiny bald spot as he drove alone in civilian clothes, commuting to his nine-to-five job as a judge humanized him to me. He'd soon don his black robe and step into the courtroom with an august judicial ceremony, but I saw him as an individual, not my enemy, not necessarily an upholder of the status quo, or an *enemy of the people*, but just a regular guy trying to do his job.

In the courtroom, I stood before the bench. Judge Epton peered over the top of his horn-rimmed glasses at me. His coal black hairline receded so far to the back of his head that he reminded me of a tonsured monk. My fate rested in his hands, and I'd take whatever sentence he imposed with calm equanimity.

He watched me intently as the bailiff read my charges, which were already reduced from felonies to misdemeanors. He took note that I was still a minor and had no prior charges against me. I contested none of the charges. Yes, I'd helped a guy escape the clutches of the police, and yes, I defended myself from the club wielding cops and tried to get away, thus resisting arrest, and yes, I'd 'accidentally' grabbed one of their badges as they beat me down to the street. I pled guilty to all charges.

The judge, gazing at me with a firm, almost fatherly gaze, pronounced his sentence. "I sentence you to three years' probation. I hope you've learned your lesson, young man, and won't appear before my court again." I nodded in the affirmative. "Do you have anything to say to the court?"

"Yes." I swallowed hard, hoping I wouldn't screw up the leniency of my sentence. "I'd like your permission to leave the state of Illinois."

My mother gasped beside me. She'd warned me not to ask this, but three years was still a long time for me to be stuck in Illinois when the world pulled me in so many directions.

"Leave the state?" Judge Epton reared back on his high throne.

"Yes. I need to look for my missing girlfriend out west."

"How do you expect to make a living?"

"Oh, I could pick fruit or herd goats. I lived on apples while hitching across New York."

His eyes grew big. "Leave the State? Pick apples? No, son, your probation must be served in the state of Illinois. If you leave, you will abrogate it and you could serve the rest of your time in jail. My advice to you, young man, is get a job and settle down."

Home at West End

It was Friday the 13th, an unlucky day for the superstitious, but ever a lucky one for me. Stephanie tried but couldn't convince me that mere numbers held such hocus-pocus power over us, as her numerology claimed. I signed out from the Edge at one thirty to spend a trial weekend at the Delmonte home before my upcoming release from Riveredge. The West End neighborhood and the adjacent Fischer's Woods had already been like my second home since the eighth grade.

The stub of West Avenue only ran a thousand feet north of Grand Avenue before dead ending at a thick wall of trees known as Fischer's Woods. The last house on the left was the home of the Delmonte family and midway back on the right stood the home of the Fichters. The boys of these two families, together with a few others who joined in occasional exploits, referred to themselves as the West End Nation. Suburban homes with tidy lawns lined Oak Lane, which meandered west off West Avenue to Highway 83, to comprise the rest of the neighborhood.

The tall oaks beyond the Delmontes house were our sanctuary. Wrapped in silent gloom, often pierced by the cry of birds or the occasional squeak of racoons and possums, the forest could either threaten or entice you to venture within, depending on your spirit of adventure.

Between the house and the woods was a muddy parking lot with several rusting vehicles, one without wheels, sat up on blocks. The litter of toys, piles of clothes, and refuse scattered about the backyard made it obvious that children lived there. Ten kids ranging in age from Ricky, the oldest who was away in the Army, to Teddy at six, made it impossible for two working parents to keep up the standards of *Good Housekeeping* magazine.

"Welcome back, Ron!" Lee Swanson, a redhead with angry red acne scaring his face, walked up the drive and grabbed my hand with a firm grip. "We can sure make use of you around here. Remember the underground coffee shop we started just before you left town?"

"Sure, Lee. I think we settled on naming it *The Place*."

"Right." He laughed. "You suggested *Nirvana*, but that hippie shit wouldn't go over with these conservative parishioners, so we opted for a bland, non-threatening name."

Zipping up his heavy coat, Lee said, "Let's take a stroll over there."

Lee and his younger brother Dave had only lived in the neighborhood about a year and remained a bit aloof from the West Enders more criminal ventures, like stealing alcohol or copper for re-sale, but he was a mover and a shaker who planned to create venues for Rock and Roll bands to come and play. *The Place* was his first successful project.

Lee negotiated long and hard to convince the pastor and the ultra-conservative parishioners of the Sunnyside Church of God to set up a folksy coffee house in their basement.

"It'll give the local youth a hangout to keep them out of mischief," he insisted. Another such establishment had opened a couple of years before in my old Wood Dale neighborhood. *The Down Under* was set in the very church basement where I attended Sunday school from age three, and confirmed a Christian at twelve, although I'd already become a secret Buddhist at heart. We copied their iconic Beatnik motif with rustic wooden spools for telephone cables serving as tables.

Lee marshaled the local kids to paint the walls of *The Place* black with dayglo art and hip inscriptions, like Tim Leary's "Turn on, tune in, drop out" that a series of black lights brought to life. Like my old Methodist church, *The Place* transformed from a dowdy empty church basement into a vibrant youth hangout. It had only just opened the summer before. The somber church folk weren't thrilled, calling it Satanic, which only increased its allure with their children.

"Come on!" Lee pulled my sleeve. "I'll show you what we've done since you split."

The Sunny Place Church of God was a short walk from the West End neighborhood, on Oak Street, directly across Route 83 from Oakdale Road. Most of the roads on both sides of 83 paid homage by their names to the remaining Oak trees that still surrounded the expanding invasion of human habitation.

The older youth with cars drove back and forth between the coffeehouses, on the lookout for the *action*. It was not unheard of for them to carry in a flask of illicit alcohol, bootleg style, to spike the non-alcoholic fare. The pungent scent of marijuana or hashish could waft in from the parking lot, where stoners toked it up while keeping a wary eye out for the police.

"Check it out, man." Lee opened the door of a small closet under the stairwell. The cramped space had become a mini head shop, stocked with psychedelic posters, hash pipes, roach clips, rolling papers and other hippie paraphernalia, with just enough room to squat at the door beside a cashbox.

Lee turned to me as a sly smile crept across his face. "You need a job, right? Do you want to run the store? You can start tonight."

"Sure thing, Lee. Quite a venture you've got here. Where will the profits go?"

"Not to the church, if that's what you're asking. I've got all I can do to keep them from shutting the coffee shop down. I'll give you a percentage and the rest will go toward my upcoming ideas, like opening a dance club in Elmhurst that can attract big name bands."

Lee handed me a recommended price list for his stock, which I inflated by a few cents or half a dollar. I'd never run a shop and wasn't sure how, so I slipped a few bills in my pocket occasionally, not too much. I wasn't greedy and didn't want to impose on his bottom line. He was too busy to keep track of sales and inventory, which I didn't record, anyway.

My first customer that very evening was a short, beefy, blond fellow with a brown-haired girl wearing granny glasses in tow. He sucked in his breath as he checked out our hash pipes.

"Jeez, man, is it legal to sell these here?"

"I guess, as long as there's no residue in it."

He gave me a broad smile, put out his hand and said, "I'm Bob." His voice dropped to a whisper. "Got any hash for sale so we can test it?"

I snickered. "No way, man. Maybe someone in the parking lot has some."

Bob laughed. "Just kidding, man, be cool."

Sales picked up from there. He and his girlfriend Madeline became regulars and were absorbed into our West End gang. I didn't have to sit in the doorway all the time, but locked up and joined people at the spool tables, ready to open and show off the wares when newbies came in. Working there gave me a mystique that attracted the ladies. Most of them, strangers to me, went to Addison Trail High School rather than Fenton in Bensenville, where I'd gone before dropping out.

Later that night, Chris motioned me over, clapped his hand on my shoulder and looked into my eyes. "What do you say we celebrate your return with an adventure tonight?"

"Sounds good."

"Great! It's been over a month since we raided John's Tavern. He still owes me back pay. Let's hit it tonight after the bar closes, so you can bring some booze back with you."

Despite being a bit cramped at ten by fifteen feet, the oldest boys' bedroom at the southeast corner of the house was a warm winter gathering place for our West End Nation. A knock at the bedroom's east–facing window, rather than the front or back door, prevented us from alarming their parents of our late-night comings and goings. That night the two Fichter brothers, George and Bubba, John Borley and Toney Joseph crowded in with the Delmontes and I to stand or sit on the lower bunks. We made up a larger than usual crew.

Like me, the West Enders considered themselves part of an outlaw culture, not bound by the unfair rules that favored the rich. We knew our place in history. We became steeped in Marx, Malcomb X and Upton Sinclair's *The Jungle*. Chicagoland was, after all, imbued with a combination of tough working class and gangster ethos. If labor unions hadn't allied themselves with the mob to fight back against the boss's repressive violence, workers would never have gotten the rights and income to raise their standard of living enough to join the middle class.

The Revolution was neigh, and we had to hone our skills for the inevitable guerilla war. Even so, stealing did not come easy to me. I worried about how the collateral damage affected unintended victims. My conscience bubbled up to accuse me. I had nothing against John, the owner of the tavern. We'd never even met. Then there was my probation to consider. If caught, I'd be back in jail with years added to my sentence, but I had to prove myself and couldn't wimp out.

February's latest snowfall blanketed the landscape in white, which reflected enough to help us see on a pitch-black night raid. It felt more like a lark than a serious mission that put our freedom at stake. We slipped out the bedroom window. Brother Mike, the committed artist busy at his desk on a poster sized Spiderman painting, remained behind. We depended on him to open the window for us upon our return.

John's Three Pines sat at the southeast corner of York and George across from the White Pines Golf Course. It was a little over a mile away on foot, if we cut through the woods and golf course, but we looped in a wide arc to approach the tavern from the rear through snowy back yards to confuse witnesses. It was my first time there and surprised me how open to view it was. A broad gravel parking lot at the back lay bare of cover under an Arclight and lighted windows from neighbors on either side. The one on the south side had the best unobstructed view of the door Chris intended to enter. Chris still had a key he'd swiped, so getting in and out should be as swift and silent as he promised.

After a quick examination from the cover of trees behind the parking lot, we retreated to huddle at the corner of a fence line in the shadow of tall pine trees, where Chris, with a military clip to his voice, gave us our orders.

"This is our rally point. If anything goes wrong, we'll assess the situation here before we *scat* back to the End. Got it?" We nodded. Chris handed his boy scout rucksack to John. "Take this and don't lose it. Okay? It's got my name and address on it." He then addressed all of us. "You guys wait here until I unlock the door, then run up silently. We'll be in and out of here in a few minutes with some booty and celebrate tomorrow."

We followed him to the edge of the bright parking lot and watched as he ran up to the white painted metal door, but minutes ticked by as he struggled to open it. Frustrated, he banged his shoulder against the unyielding door with a loud thud, then another, with no result. Finally, he ran back to us.

"He changed the lock. Bubba, I need the crowbar you brought." Like any good boy scout, we were prepared for contingencies.

Back at the door, Chris pried as silently as he could, but stymied, his efforts became louder. Precious time passed as we watched, breathless and wary. I cringed when Chris gave up prying and began hammering at the door with the bar. Dogs started barking throughout the neighborhood and a couple more lights turned on in the houses.

"Shit," John said. "I can't fucking believe that no one hears this. We should get out of here."

"Shush," Toney told him. "Chris knows what he's doing. Those guys are probably watching TV or screwing."

I agreed with John. We needed to go and fast, but I didn't say anything.

Suddenly, a cop car churned gravel, speeding through the parking lot behind Chris. Whether he'd noticed him under the floodlight or not, the cop circled around to the far side of the lot before stopping, giving Chris time to run back to us in the shadows, and we all hightailed it back to the fence line.

Chris heaved a loud sigh of relief. "Man! That was a close one."

John, wide-eyed, said, "We better get the fuck out of here now."

Chris grabbed his arm. "Hold on. Don't panic, man. Give me the knapsack."

John's mouth and eyes popped open. "Oh, man, I must have left it back there." He pointed into the darkness of the tree line. At that moment, another patrol car, its lights flashing, sped into the lot and parked beside the first.

Chris screwed up his face. "Shit, John! You gotta go back for it. It's got my name and address on it."

"Not me, man. Let's go before we're spotted."

Chris handed him the crowbar and ran back, dropping to a low crawl beside the trees. As we watched his dim image crawl closer, the cops got out of their cars and began patrolling the lot, scanning its darker edges with their flashlights. One cop shouted, "Hold it right there! You. Come out with your hands up. Now!"

"Oh, man," Bubba said. "They've got him for sure. Thanks John."

John climbed the fence until Steve grabbed him. "Just wait a sec, man. We can't just leave until we know for sure about Chris."

The cops kept probing the edge of the lot without venturing in. I watched the last place I'd seen Chris but couldn't make him out in the shadowy lumps played over by the lights. At least they didn't seem to have a prisoner yet. Their radio cackled, maybe sending backup to surround the area, and cut us off. The beams of light converged steadily on the spot I'd last seen Chris and I heard more shouting. *We see you, come out with your hands high!*

"Shit," I whispered. "Chris is a goner. I'm on probation and there's nothing we can do for him. We're all on our own."

We scrambled over the fence and fanned out in every direction except straight back to the west, which could lead the cops to our neighborhood. Steve took off southeast in the direction of the old gristmill and cemetery on Grand Avenue. I headed northeast, crossing George Street to cut through small suburban properties, having to clamber over several shoulder-high fences that stood behind each house. Barking erupted and light flooded in from neighboring yards, but I evaded the men who came out yelling, "*Who the hell is out there?*"

After a few blocks, I thought I was far enough out to avoid the police dragnet and slowed to a walk along an empty street. I no sooner caught my breath than a squad car with lights flashing, but without a siren, came barreling out of nowhere to screech to a halt beside me. The cop jumped out, and I tore off up the paved driveway of the house on my right. Fueled by adrenaline, I hurled myself over a six-foot wooden fence and kept going, cutting through yards and hopping obstacles in a southeast direction. Then I veered northwest, hoping to confuse pursuit, all the while wondering how the others were doing and if, by some miracle, Chris got away.

At York Road, I hid in a ditch until the coast looked clear and charged across to the cover of trees on the far side. I then went south, climbed over the chain-link fence topped with barbed wire to enter the huge White Pines Golf Course, which offered me safe passage to Church Road and the woods.

So far, so good. I congratulated myself as I followed the dark woodland paths, relying on my peripheral vision that works best at night. I remained in the shadows at West Avenue, watching for a sign of any police presence. If someone got caught, they might have told them where to find the rest of us. In front of the Fichter residence, I saw the silhouette of a parked car with bubble lights on top. It could be a cop, watching and waiting for us to return. I slinked through the trees and discovered that it was only a civilian car with a luggage rack on top. What a relief. Confident no one observed me, I crept to the bedroom window and looked in before I knocked. Mike still sat at his desk.

"Did anyone else get back yet?" I asked when he opened the window to let me in.

"Not yet. You're the first. How'd it go?"

"It was a total fuck-up, man." After running through the whole adventure, I flopped onto the bed.

"Mike, if the cops come, tell them I've been asleep the whole time. Got it?"

"Sure thing, Ron. That's why I don't get involved in this crazy stuff." He held up his latest masterpiece of the webbed warrior. "What do you think about this?"

"Groovy, man. Maybe you should have an art show or something." Mike was on his way to the big time and didn't need a police record to bring him down.

I lay there wondering how my luck would go. Chris was a goner, for sure, but he wouldn't squeal. John might shoot off his mouth. If he implicated me, the court could revoke my probation.

A knock at the window brought in Steve and Bubba, then John, chattering with excitement. Mike drew his hand across his throat. "Shush! Keep it down, guys, you'll wake up the oldsters." In lower tones, we dissected the night's events. Everyone except Chris had made it back from the fiasco of a robbery.

"Chris won't break," Steve said. "He'll take the rap without implicating us. The only thing we can do is play dumb and say nothing."

"Nothing more we can do," John said. "We may as well go home and get some shuteye."

He and Bubba were just about to slip back into the night when an unexpected knock came at the window. We all jumped up.

"Shit," hissed John. "It could be the cops!"

Mike peeked through the curtain, let out a sigh, and opened the window. A wheezing, haggard looking Chris climbed in, hugging his telltale knapsack like a hard-won trophy. He collapsed onto a bunk, shaking with exhaustion and emotion. As he caught his breath, he scanned the crowded room, finding us all present and accounted for.

"Fuck, man. I thought for sure all you guys got caught."

The first tears I'd ever seen him shed streamed down his cheeks as our questions peppered him from all sides.

We thought you were a goner, Chris. The cops shone their flashlights right on top of you. How the hell did you get away?

Chris took a moment to settle his nerves, then gave us the scoop. "All I could do was lay there motionless and wait them out. They must have hoped I'd give myself up if they kept shouting, but they couldn't be sure who or what they saw in the shadows and were cautious. They wouldn't want to run into something unexpected."

He gave John a severe glance. "I found my backpack in the nick of time as more cops arrived, making them bolder. Then I skedaddled. Man, it was a close shave!"

I thought the disastrous outcome of that mission would dissuade Chris from these shenanigans. It sure cautioned me, but he kept at his trade of burglary, preferring to work alone and not to trust himself with the inexperience and unprofessionalism of others.

Mescaline and Fond Farewells

Before I started back to the Edge on Sunday, Steve handed me a couple of capsules filled with brown powder. "It's Mescaline, gives you a different kind of trip than LSD."

He was right about the sensory difference. I waited until the next afternoon and popped it in my mouth as I filed along with the group to a ward meeting. As I sat against the wall on the floor, people chatted all around me as it took effect, coming on slowly, with subtle changes to my senses of sight, sound, and smell, giving me the sensation that each sense merged to enter through all the apertures of my body. Smells came in through the pores of my feet and hands, mixed with sensations of light and sounds that churned together into a multi-layered experience to all parts of my body. Hot and cold flashes ran through my body, but it wasn't my body alone as I seemed to be integrated with the perceptions of those around me, as if we were incorporated into a single entity with waves of intermingled perceptions that ebbed and flowed through us all.

My mind floated in mystic communion with all those around me, whose thoughts and tactile experiences vibrated to become mine also, but I hadn't bothered to follow the actual topic of discussion, so when it came my turn to speak about an upcoming play they were planning, I only grinned my altruistic love back at them, mere words seemed redundant. A cheerful adolescent worker leaned over me, all smiles, as she peered into my eyes. "Are you high, Ron?"

"Oh, baby." I smiled back at her, in a mystic harmony with my surroundings. "If only you felt as high as I do."

At our next meeting, Dr. Ghattas stared across his desk at me, his face scrunched in a tight frown. "I'm afraid you have made very little progress here, Ron. You are stubborn and incorrigible."

"Thanks, doc. I'll take that as a compliment. It proves that I'm not crazy. What's your diagnosis, anyway?"

He shifted in his chair and shook his head. I almost felt sorry that I'd put him on the spot, but he'd danced around this issue too long, and I deserved to know how he'd labeled me.

"Alright." He fumbled for his smoking pouch, lit up, and puffed, filling the room with the comforting aroma of his cherry tobacco before he answered. "My diagnosis is unspecified schizophrenia."

"Unspecified? That sounds like a catch-all term that could probably fit anyone." I thought it was a bullshit diagnosis.

He leaned back and looked up at the ceiling, to exhale a lungful of sweet smoke like a prayer of resignation to the heavens.

"Tomorrow, I'm releasing you from the hospital." The abrupt news sent a thrill down my spine. He took a few more puffs on his pipe before he finished. "I want to continue seeing you as an outpatient."

I nodded in happy agreement. I'd beaten the system to be free at last, but then a wave of sadness passed through me. Riveredge had become more than a mere waystation. I'd bonded with dear friends, and I feared that we'd drift apart, like all the others who'd passed through my life, and I didn't want to let them go, especially Marge.

As if sensing my thoughts, Ghattas said, "We can continue to meet here at the hospital, if you like, rather than my office in Bensenville." I nodded and breathed a secret sigh of relief.

Since my arrest on October eleventh, I'd spent ten days in jail, followed by four months in Riveredge. A new, uncertain future loomed before me. I had to decide whether to go straight, get a job, and keep my nose clean, or escape to the road again. The Weathermen cadre had jumped bail and gone underground to wage guerilla war against the system. Although I'd toyed with the romantic image of a life on the run, I decided not to follow that path. My probation, if I played it right, shouldn't constrain me too much from finding my way back into a meaningful life.

They gathered in my room, these strangers who'd become dear friends, to wish me bon voyage. Marge broke away from Rick and hugged me tightly. I took a chance to kiss her, but she turned, and I landed on her cheek. Rick cleared his throat, and she leaned back away from me. Teary-eyed, she searched my face, as if looking for a clue. I wondered whether she was trying to see if she belonged in my life. I wanted to scream YES, but the word stuck in my throat.

Stephanie came up to give me a less intense embrace. "Come visit us when you can, Ron."

"I will." I promised, holding back my own tears. "I'll catch you guys when I see Dr. Ghattas as an outpatient." This could be our last hurrah, but I still clung to a desperate hope for a sign of Marge's love.

Nurses Notes

Thursday, 2-19-70, 11-7. Awake until quite late, visiting with peers & saying goodbyes. Group gathered in his room. Up, dressed, showered, preparing to leave. 9 AM. Discharged...

Life at the End

Domestic Tranquility

In the predawn darkness of a frosty Sunday morning, Chris, Steve, Mike, and I slipped out the window. Our boots crunched through the crisp, icy snow and our breath rose in billowing clouds as we trotted for warmth. Two miles to the west, we ran across Route 83 and along Lake Street, to where it intersected with Addison Road. Our footsteps, muffled in the snow, were the only sounds echoing in the darkness. The streets were devoid of traffic. Nothing was open at that hour.

Our mission wasn't criminal, nor dangerous in the least. Our destination was the Addison House restaurant, where we'd celebrate the simple joys of life, and, as an afterthought, toast my newfound freedom with a pancake feast. This was my first visit to their favored haunt, and Chris filled me in.

"You can select music for the jukebox on the coin-operated console right at your table and they've got most of the latest Rock and Roll. It's a nickel a play."

"I see the pink elephant up ahead," Steve said. The neon sign depicted the smiling elephant curling its trunk around a tree, was a familiar landmark for as long as I could remember, and the Addison House was right next door.

"Well, I'm looking forward to some hot coffee right now," I said, clapping my gloved hand together. "Starting to feel a tingling in my fingers and toes."

"Yeah," Chris nodded agreement. "After that hike, we'll all appreciate taking the chill out of our bones." He reached for the door handle and pushed. "Oh shit, it's still locked."

"I guess he's late today," Mike said. Peering in the window, we saw no activity.

Chris chuckled. "Well, at least we can watch the sunrise."

There wasn't yet a glimmer of light on the eastern horizon and the rest of us were too busy jumping up and down and shivering to answer. Ten to twenty minutes felt like an hour before a car pulled up and a middle-aged man stepped out.

"Have you been waiting long? I had trouble starting my car. You guys are the earliest customers I've had since the last big snow."

We followed him in and sat at a booth while he turned on the lights and the stove. "Coffee will be ready soon, boys."

I stripped off my gloves and blew on my fingers before making my request. "I hate to be a moocher, Chris, but I'm flat busted."

"Don't sweat it, Ron." Chris waved his hand as if chasing away a fly. "I know you're still jobless. You'll get us next time."

We flipped through the turnstile of song selections and pumped in a few nickels and dimes. *Born to be Wild*, still a long-time favorite, was the first to blast from the jukebox. Anything Steppenwolf or the Beatles followed. By the time other customers came in, fresh hot coffee had already warmed our innards and I felt alive among loyal friends. I shouted over the music.

"This is what the Germans call Gemütlicheit, an expansive feeling of warmth, camaraderie, and tasty food."

"But there's no beer here," Steve said.

Chris laughed. "Let's make a toast, anyway." He raised his coffee mug. "To Ron getting a job so he can pay the tab next time!"

Long after we gobbled our food, we lingered over our bottomless cups of coffee. Wired up, our conversation rambled from the prophesies of Edgar Cayce to Stalinism vs. Trotskyism, from the merits of non-violence vs. proactive self-defense. The rising Black Panther movement had already discredited the passive nonviolence of Gandhi and Martin Luther King in the Black community and gained traction with other progressive movements. My friends and I agreed, supporting the People's Power Revolution was as natural as breathing fresh air, but I had to be careful not to get myself thrown back in jail. Rather than follow my headstrong Aries instincts that had robbed me of my truest lover.

The Delmonte family welcomed me. I'd settle down and find a job while deciding how best to further the Revolution in this corner of the world before running off. Mrs. D worked the late shift at the White Pantry convenience store, so keeping her household in reasonable shape needed to be a team effort. She could shout herself hoarse trying to get her kids to pitch in on household chores. Without a paying job, I needed to show my gratitude for Momma D's hospitality. Whether it was my turn or not, I tried to make myself useful, sweeping and washing dishes, to put some order in the chaos.

Her husband, Bruno, made good money working at the railroad in downtown Chicago, but their ten kids put more of an economic strain on their budget than the family of five sisters and no brothers that I'd grown up in. Dinner was often a big pot of spaghetti. While Mom brought out the main course, reliable brother Patrick would be busy slicing up a long loaf of French bread, or buttering slices of wonder bread, piling them high on a plate next to the mountain of pasta covered with tomato sauce in easy reach for all. The dining room was at the far end of the living room beside the back door. We sat around a large wooden picnic style table, bolted to the floor, with benches on either side.

As soon as he got home from work, Bruno plopped on his sofa chair by the kitchen door like a king on his throne. With an aura of benign neglect, he slouched with his reading glasses perched precariously on the tip of his nose, half watching the TV news over the top of the newspaper while shouting occasional comments to his wife and kids until he dozed off.

Although I admired his laissez-faire attitude, a multitude of unfinished jobs, such as the worn or missing linoleum in the kitchen and the toilet that remained clogged and unflushed for years, didn't faze him. "I'll get to that one of these days," he mumbled with more resignation than determination. Even with the door closed, the smell of the ancient load hung over that corner of the house, but over time, like my companions, I got used to the less than pristine living conditions and much else.

The normal locker-room odor of a room inhabited by four boys mixed with the smell of mildew coming in from the laundry room, where a damp pile of clothing lay in the middle of the floor. Catholic charity had donated it, to be picked over by the family members, however much of it rotted away as new donations piled on top of them.

An occasional shiny new bicycle and then a motorcycle or two appeared in the backyard from time to time. These were rather expensive for the family's modest means, and Father Bruno wasn't blind to the implications of their unexplained origins. One day, he gave Steve a stern look over his bifocals before issuing a warning. "Just don't get caught!"

Bruno's tacit agreement with his son's moral ambiguity seemed to arise from the recognition that the meek do not inherit more of the earth than it takes to bury them in, and nice guys almost always finish last in life's race. I later saw it demonstrated at a family funeral. The men who sat on opposite sides of the long table appeared unwilling to speak to the men across from them. Chris explained it to me. "On one side are the cops, on the other are the guys with mob connections." He shot me a twisted smile. "Hey, we're Italian. What did you expect?"

Mike, the consummate artist, did a thorough job when it was his turn. Chris, a dropout like me, was excused from housework because he worked nights and Steve was too busy with his extracurricular reading. Bruno nicknamed him the *Mad Russian* for his intense focus on the Russian Revolution.

Just sweeping the bedroom inhabited by us four boys was a challenge. I slept in Ricky's bunk, who was serving in Vietnam. Before he'd shipped out, he brought home a great quantity of ammunition that he'd *ripped off* from the Army and left stacked under the beds. In a room crowded with four boys, it didn't stay that way long. Live bullets and empty shells lay scattered all over the floor, mingled with old leaflets and underwear that hadn't made it to the wash. Even Mike, the most fastidious, grew weary of marshaling that ordinance back into the cardboard ammo boxes and kicked the bullets under the bed with the dust.

One fine sunny day I swept up everything, bullets, and all, filling two paper trash bags that I carried to the burn area out back next to the woods. I expected some fireworks as I lit the paper and stood back, watching from what I thought was a safe distance as the bags became consumed in flames and black smoke. There was a shrill *ping* and then another, then a whole series–*ping–ping–pew,* clipping a tree branch nearby, but it seemed harmless fun until the racket aroused the curiosity of Mrs. D.

"What's making all that racket?"

"What racket?" I answered, feigning innocence. "I'm just burning the garbage and it went off."

"Well, get away from there. You could get hit." She stepped back, ready to retreat inside to safety.

Cocky as I was after facing down guns in Chicago, I laughed. "Don't worry Mrs. D. These wild shots don't have the velocity to do much damage."

As I was about to turn away from the bonfire when I heard *ping–whack*, something hit the left side of my jaw and my hand came back red.

"What happened?" Mrs. D yelled and insisted on looking at it. "Lucky it didn't hit your eye. There's only a trickle of blood from a small wound that's beginning to swell." She put ice on it and admonished me. "Be careful burning the trash from now on."

A small scar over a hard lump remained on my jaw for years until a doctor decided to dig in and yank it out, a trophy to my misguided bravado.

Bob Grady's Entry

When Chris got home from his night shift, he stripped down to his skivvies in the comfortable heat of the house, moseyed out to the kitchen, and made himself a Dogwood sandwich, which he brought back up to his lair on the top bunk. There he relaxed from his nocturnal regimen of work and burglary, ate, read from his extensive collection of science fiction books, and napped. He relished his peaceful solitude until mid to late afternoon, when he might rouse himself for a degree of sociable inter-action before disappearing into the night. His quiet time was, however, often interrupted by the pedestrian traffic through our bedroom by his brothers and other members of our extensive tribe. They jabbered away and bothered him with trivial questions.

Lee Swanson was the most regular and dogged interrupter of his peace. He'd pop over in the late morning or afternoon and hound him to get up and join in one of his schemes. Unless he was in a rare, expansive mood, Chris would yell, "Get the hell out of here and leave me alone!" Sometimes he'd raise his machete, which he kept beside him under his mattress. "I need my slice of death, goddamn it!" That's how he referred to sleep.

"Come on, Chris," Lee countered. "The sun's up and the day is wasting. You'll have plenty of peace and quiet when you're dead."

"Go fuck yourself, Lee!"

Despite his ill-tempered outbursts, a thin smile might cross his face as Lee's buoyant cheer wore him down. Chris tried to hide his generous nature behind a gruff exterior, but we who knew him trusted his generous spirit.

One day at noon, I came in and was surprised to find him laughing in bed with a burly, blond fellow in a brown jean jacket that didn't reach his belt line and was too light for the fierce winter. He paced around the room, waving his hands as he raved historical bombast about Nazi Generals.

"The British called Rommel the Desert Fox because he was better than any general that they put against him. Always outnumbered, he outflanked and drove them back to Egypt again and again."

He looked up at me and dropped his hands. "Herr Schulz, *was ist los?*"

I didn't recognize him at first, and he chuckled at my confusion.

"I'm Bob Brady." He stuck out his hand. "Still don't remember me, huh? You sold me a hash pipe a few weeks ago. Chris told me you speak German and know your World War history."

Bob was a big talker, over enthusiastic about the history of the Third Reich, which he expounded upon with fervent grandiosity, who also hailed from Wood Dale, although as a year younger than me, our paths hadn't crossed.

"I'm driving up to Wood Dale," he said. "Wanna come along?"

Chris yawned and scratched his crotch. "It's about damn time! Get outta here, both of you." He leaned back and pulled the blanket over his head. "I need my slice of death."

Bob's big rusty, dented, white Ford Falcon station wagon still had intact paint in a few places. He puffed up his chest. "This is my *beast, man!* She ain't a beauty but gets me to where I'm going. Be careful opening and closing the door." He suppressed a chuckle. "It might fall off."

He turned the key, and the engine sputtered, coughed, and died. After two more tries, it roared to life, backfiring as if ready to explode. Bob shouted over the racket. "A muffler is the very least of its problems. My philosophy is to buy the cheapest pile of junk that still runs. I never pay more than fifty bucks."

"Gee, Bob, is it worth it?"

He shot me a broad smile. "Oh, I get my money's worth. When it dies, I go buy another fifty-dollar bargain. That's still more cost-effective than pouring money into fixing up the first one."

He shifted into gear, and we rattled up Route 83 and across Irving Park to a house in northeast Wood Dale. We passed the hulks of two cars along the driveway shrouded in snow. Bob jabbed his thumb at them. "They're still waiting to get picked up by the junkyard after the weather warms up." I followed Bob through the backdoor into the kitchen.

"Hi Ma, I'm home!" His voice boomed in the silent house as he looked over the contents of the refrigerator. A meek feminine voice called from another room. "Could you please do your dishes before you go, Bobbie?"

"Goddamn it, Ma, I don't have time for that now! I just came to grab a bite and we'll be leaving soon."

I recoiled at Bob's sharp retort to such a mild request – from his mother, for god's sake. "Take it easy," I whispered. "It won't take long to wash a couple plates."

Bob glared at me. "You don't understand what I've have to go through around here, Ron." He tossed a packet of lunchmeat and a loaf of bread on the counter and pointed at the cupboard. "There's peanut butter if you prefer."

After we filled our bellies up on his dear mother's food and chugged down the last of the milk, Bob tossed the plates in the sink.

"Let's roll," he said to me, then shouted. "Goodbye Ma!"

"What time will you be home, Bobby?" Her voice sounded frail and pleading.

"Gee, I don't know, Ma. When I get here, I guess."

Bob revved the engine. "Where to, Ron?"

"We may as well swing by my folks, since we're in town."

My parents were a different matter. I could never be part of their conservative, button-down world, but I bore them no grudge. Unless, as he sometimes did, Dad picked at sore points, reminding me of mistakes I'd made, even toys I'd broken as a toddler, to arouse my irritation. Bob offered to wait in the car for me, which gave me an excuse to leave early. After that we went back out into the dark winter late afternoon, our destination Zaher's department store in Addison, while a fierce wind picked up with occasional snow flurries. My flimsy corduroy coat couldn't protect me from the chill drafts leaking through cracks in the warped door. Bob, in lighter garb than me, seemed unaffected.

"You just never know," he said as we forged against the wind through the parking lot. "Sometimes this place is crawling with cool chicks."

Through chattering teeth, I yelled. "Do you really think they'll be out in this weather?" The wind carried my words away.

There were no chicks to be found, and I regretted tagging along on the fruitless search. Bob finally gave up, but back in the car, my relief was premature. The cold engine turned over but refused to start. Frantic, Bob kept pumping the gas until it flooded.

"Son of a bitch!" He slammed the dash. "We'll have to give it time to clear." After a tedious wait, he began again until the battery drained of juice. He got under the hood, played with the cables, and tried again with no result.

"Shit! I don't have any jumper cables. We gotta ask somebody." With increasing desperation, we ran up to everyone in the almost empty lot, to no avail. Bob was running out of options.

"Jesus, Bob, I'm freezing my nuts off. Let's leave the car in the lot, hoof it back to the West End and try it tomorrow."

"It's a two-mile walk, too damn far."

"The jog will warm us up. I was in cross-country..."

"The fuck you say, Ron! I'm not running or walking that far. I'll call my dad."

It was too tight to close the glass door when I squeezed into the phone booth with him, but I caught Bob's side of the conversation.

"Dad, I'm at Zayre's in Addison. My stupid car won't start. You gotta get over here... No, I mean it, you gotta give me a jump... An hour?" Bob exploded, "I can't wait that long. You gotta get over here right now, I mean it!" He slammed down the receiver.

"Christ, Bob, I'd never use that tone with anyone, much less my parents, especially if I needed help."

Bob waved his hand as if to brush aside my criticism. "You don't know the whole story, Ron. Anyway, he's not my real dad. He and Mom won't even tell me who my real dad is. Let me tell you, I've had to put up with so much crap from them it's unbelievable."

At last, a big green pickup truck pulled up beside the car and an older man stepped out. Without a word, he popped his hood and set up his jumper cables. Bob took the other end and attached it to his battery, then got into the driver's seat and turned the key. With a low rumble, the engine cranked over once but didn't catch.

Bob's stepdad seemed okay to me, a kind and patient fellow who didn't blow up at his demands like mine would. From his well-stocked toolbox, he pulled out a wire brush, scraped the battery posts, and tried again. It caught, sputtered and died.

This ill-fated adventure smacked of a Twilight Zone experience, a nightmare that went on forever. After more than twenty anxious minutes, they finally got the beast to roar. He grabbed his cables and got back in his service truck, waiting to be sure it kept running before he drove off with a good-natured wave. I wanted to hug the old man for his kindness, but Bob pulled me aboard and we were on our way.

"Dad's a television repairman," Bob said. "He's a very technical guy. His office is next to Helen's Delicatessen on Irving Park."

"Oh yeah? I used to sit on the steps outside it on a sweltering day to drink the pop I bought at Helen's. let's go back to the End, Bob. At least it's warm there."

Despite my less than blissful experience that day, Bob became our wheelman to places beyond where our feet could carry us, even though his beast had no working heater. On our next adventure that freezing February, Bubba Fichter, and I huddled in the back seat, lighting small sections of newspaper on fire, holding the flames carefully to warm our freezing hands in the few moments before we dropped them smoking to ash onto the bare metal floor.

"Just don't set my car on fire," Bob shouted over the roaring engine. "You've read about the Battle of Stalingrad, right Ron? It was so fucking cold, the Nazis had to start fires under their tank engines to get them to start."

Dating Debbie

Bob Brady took me on another aimless drive to nowhere when a destination popped in his head. "Ron, I should introduce you to the lovely Debbie Sloan. She's this pretty Jewish chick I know in Elmhurst."

That piqued my interest. "Jewish, huh?" Fond memories of Bonnie back in New York and my still smoldering love for Marge had imbued Jewish women with a sexy aura.

Bob pulled up to a large, white suburban home in a stately neighborhood with sidewalks shaded by trees. When he rang the doorbell, an ornate mezuzah fixed to the doorpost.

I reached out to touch it just as the door opened. A ravishing brunette stood there, and I watched a slow smile creep across her face as she gave me the once over.

"Hi Bob. Who's this guy?

Bob put his hand on my shoulder. "Debbie, this is rabble rousing Ron, the wild radical I've been telling you about."

Her dark eyes twinkled. "Really? Is he Jewish? He knew about touching the mezuzah before entering the house."

I smiled "No, I was raised Christian, but I'm a Buddhist now."

She wrinkled her nose. "Too bad. I don't know if my parents would approve of an idolater." Her face relaxed, and she giggled. "Lucky for you, they're not home. Come on in."

My feet sank into the plush shag carpet as she led us into the immaculate beige living room. Several framed plaques lettered in golden, sharp, pointy Hebrew calligraphy caught my eye. I assumed they were verses from the Torah. A menorah, the ritual candelabra of Hanukkah, sat with pride of place on a central table. We flopped on couches around the coffee table, sipping cokes Debby brought out.

"What's this, Debby?" I asked, pointing to a giant curved animal's horn hanging on the wall above the staircase.

"Oh, that's a shofar, a ram's horn that my dad blows on high holy days."

"Oh, yeah? I've read about it in the Old Testament."

"Wanna try it?" My best effort produced only discordant squeaks that elicited their laughter. "Don't feel bad, Ron. It takes practice. Believe me, it produces a nice tone when you know how. Have you ever heard about the Kabala?"

Bob perked up. "Sure, we have. We were yakking about it yesterday with Steven, remember, Ron? He said you guys bought some books about it at the Occult Bookstore in the Loop. Right?"

"Yeah," I said. "It's a Jewish mystical tradition. Last year I tried to make sense of the Zohar, the Book of Splendor."

Debbie laughed. "I bet you guys know more about it than me. Girls aren't allowed to study that stuff. We're just supposed to be homemakers and take care of our husbands and kids!" She shrugged her shoulders. "Anyway, I love movies. Have you seen *Hello, Dolly* yet? It's playing here, at the Elmhurst theater. Barbra Streisand stars in it. She's my favorite actress, and she's Jewish, you know."

"No, I don't know much about Hollywood stuff."

"Well, I loved her in *Funny Girl*. Did you see that?"

I shook my head. "No, I haven't seen many movies until I got locked up. Just saw *Gaily, Gaily* and *Easy Rider* a couple of months ago. Oh, and I saw the live play *Hair* too. Now that was an experience."

"Yeah." She giggled and covered her face. "I heard there's a lot of nudity. My parents would never let me see *that*. Well, I simply must watch *Hello, Dolly!* Would you mind taking me out to watch it?"

"Me? Uh, sure, it'll be my pleasure." She surprised me, but I rolled with it.

I expected a boring Bourgeois flick, but for her sake I'd give it a shot. No *power to the People* rhetoric from me tonight. I'd just be some schmuck out with his girl. But could this pampered girl, used to posh creature comforts, be happy with a rabble-rousing guy use to living rough?

Bob took off, and Debbie and I, bundled against the chill, walked arm in arm the few blocks along the leafless tree lined sidewalks to York Street. Compared to my neighborhood in Wood Dale, Elmhurst was upscale, straight out of television's *Leave it to Beaver*.

Debbie pulled me to an upfront seat, chattering about actors until the lights dimmed. It was an 1890 period piece about Jewish match-makers with contradicting love interests, and to my surprise, I became as engrossed as her. Debbie's warm presence, gorgeous looks, and even her perfumed scent, which I wasn't used to with the women I been involved with, enchanted me. I dared to put my left arm around her shoulder and thought about snuggling and kissing her but held back. Not that I didn't want to. In my relaxed state, I decided to let her take charge if she wanted to.

With her eyes still glued to the screen, she took my right hand and gave it a reassuring squeeze, but I feared offending her if I slipped my hand under her clothes to caress her warm flesh as I would if I knew her better. I felt outclassed by this *rich girl* from a pampered life. The high-end furniture, the shag carpet, the very walls of her home shrieked upper-class snob to me. I was flat broke and jobless and felt sure her parents wouldn't like me. I was a *goy*, after all, with no economic prospects, and she sounded like she was too close to her parents to run off and be a hippie like me. She appeared too sleek, dressed in too fine a wardrobe, too upper middle class comfortable and less the wild rebel I looked for in a mate. What political consciousness could I expect from her?

Marge, my rebel Jewish gal, still weighed on my mind and heart. She'd be more my type than some frilly, spoiled rich girl, but Marge wasn't available and maybe I was selling Debbie short. I decided to keep an open mind, take it slow, and let her make the moves. The movie ended, and we walked out into the bracing cold.

"Wasn't it wonderful, Ron!"

"Sure! I liked it way more than I expected."

"Really?"

"Yes, I dig history and got off on the period scenery as much as the story."

We strolled in silence along the dark streets while I considered my move. It wasn't like in the movies, an unguarded moment when I was supposed to kiss her. Would she think it too soon, too impetuous, unwanted? Should I wait for her cue or get all the way to her front door first? And what if her parents were home? I dreaded rapping with them as I would with my own folks.

When we'd gone about halfway to her place, under the illumination of a streetlamp, she stepped in front of me and drew herself up on her tiptoes and inhaled a deep breath as if she had something important to say. Her black eyes probed mine, reaching deep into my soul and in that moment, I saw all my missing lovers down to her in a rapid slide show, as if she was the missing link that would connect me to the great cosmic Yin, the compliment to my Yang. Her earnest disposition made her so alluring that a sudden tidal wave of love rose in my heart. As I started to reel her in my embrace, she turned and broke eye contact. I stopped, waiting for encouragement or instructions.

"Here Ron." She faced me again, with tears in her eyes.

"Yes?" I gulped, expecting the very cosmos to open above us with her words.

She pressed something hard into my hand and squeezed my fingers over it. "When you find her, give her this." And she ran off.

Stunned, I opened my hand to stare at the small wire ring she'd pressed into it. Whether it was a cheap trinket or an heirloom of immense value, I couldn't say. What did she mean 'when you find *her?*' Did she want to get rid of me, or did she expect me to run after her? Was she hinting that she, herself, might be the one I was looking for?

She stopped at the far corner and glanced back. I called out, "Wait, Debbie, what do you mean?" She ran on ahead. What was my role, and my lines in this tragic comedy of a romance movie we were living. Was this my cue to shout out, "Debbie, it's you I want!" But did I, or should I?

Maybe she'd taken my lack of aggressive zeal in the theater as disinterest. I'd been trying to act with more deliberation, less mad impulse, and remained rooted to the spot, my mind going over the situation for a rational response. But of course, rationality had no place in the complex puzzle of sexual relationships. We are all winging it.

I expected that we'd straighten this out the next time I saw her, however, the next day we didn't connect. Something always seemed to come up. My life and hers began moving in contrary directions and I never saw her again, but at least we always had the memory of *Hello, Dolly!*

At *The Place* one evening, I showed Debbie's mysterious ring to a friend's girlfriend. She claimed to know something about jewelry and held it up to the light, turning it over with her eyes knitted into a serious frown.

"Sorry, Ron. It's just cheap trash, like what kids get in a bubble gum machine."

I held onto it for years, half-forgotten in the pocket of my back-pack, until a girl who'd already broken up with me rummaged through my stuff and found it.

"Oh, Ron. Can I keep this?"

"Sure, maybe you were the one it was meant for."

She put it on, *ohing* over it, as if it was a gem beyond price, which it was. Like all material things, the value lies in the feeling we connect to it. It didn't improve our relationship, however. She slept with me a few more times – for old times' sake, she said, but she dumped me for a guy in Law School. The morning after our last tryst, I discovered that she'd also taken all my yoga books.

In retrospect, I should have chased after Debbie Sloan on that cold winter night in 1970. Everything in our lives might have turned out better. I'd like to think so.

A Con Job

"**R**on!" Chris squatted down where I sat on the floor in the doorway of my mini emporium at The Place. "Come, there's someone we gotta talk to."

Business was slow anyway, so I closed and followed him to a table in the half empty establishment, where a rail thin guy sat, his frizzy blond hair ratted out into an Afro around his pale head.

He held out his hand. "So, you're Ron, huh? I'm Bill. Chris tells me you might be interested in pulling a job with us."

"Well, I'm on probation and can't afford to get busted again."

"I dig that, man, but don't worry, we'll hit a location that's safe. The Churchville School isn't patrolled too carefully at night. You're in the Revolution, right? The schools are where they indoctrinate us in racist capitalism. We're going to strike back at the establishment, man!" He appealed to my need to strike back against the system, and that won out over my caution.

"Don't sweat it, Ron," Chris said. "I worked there last year. The cops only drove through the parking lot and flashed their lights over the football field. Once or twice a night they might rattle the doors outside, but we'd keep them locked behind us."

Bill bragged about his experience as a burglar. Under his direction, we borrowed a neighbor's license plate to replace the one on his car. As he put it, "This will cover our ass if someone calls the license plate in." We'd have to return it to the other car before dawn to avoid suspicion.

We parked at the far end of the football field obscured from the road and parking lot by bushes and followed Chris in a silent dash across the football field, trying to avoid leaving footprints on the hard packed snow. He led us to a side entrance where he used a screwdriver to remove a tiny window from its hinges and then he, the smallest of us, wriggled in to open the door from the inside for Bill and me.

"We'll just take merchandise we can sell quick," Bill said, looking around the school offices. We unplugged a couple of electric typewriters, radios, and a television, which we stacked at the door.

"Okay, guys," I whispered. "Let's get out of here."

"What's your hurry?" Chris said, as he ambled over to the refrigerator in the teachers' lounge. "Look, they have Coke and Seven Up. Relax and catch your breath before we haul this stuff out." He popped himself a cold one and leaned back on the couch.

Bill blinked and shook his head. "Man, you've got some nerves. Any Orange Crush in there?"

My nerves weren't so steady. I remembered the fiasco at the tavern too well, but I sat down with pretended calm, praying that we'd pull this off without a hitch.

With a loud belch, Chris got up and stretched. "Well, I suppose I'm ready. Let's load up."

We each carried as much as we could and made two trips back across the field to fill up the trunk and half of the back seat of the none too large car, leaving just enough room for Chris to squeeze in while I sat up front with Bill.

We drove up York, across Lake and Grand Avenue, and turned into the White Pine neighborhood on the other side of Fischer's woods. It was bitter cold, and a sheet of ice covered the roads that gave us a slipping, sliding, fishtailing ride on the side street to within a block of Bill's house. The car's engine coughed, sputtered, then conked out. Bill turned the key. Nothing happened.

"Goddamn it!" He slapped the dashboard. "We're so damn close and yet so far."

Chris leaned up from the back. "We better check the battery." We all got out, opened the hood, and played with the cable connections.

"It's lucky there isn't any traffic at this hour," I said, to put a positive spin on things. Then, with amazing synchronicity, a car pulled up from behind, its bright headlights blinding us, but illuminated our haul of stolen goods in the back window.

A voice called out of the darkness, "Do you boys need any help?"

I watched Chris walk to the driver's side said, "Our car gave out on us on our way home."

"Do you need a jump?"

"Nah, but we'd appreciate a push a few feet up to our driveway."

Chris came back, whispering, "It's a cop, don't freak out. Play it cool."

The cop shone his spotlight on the back of our car. If he noticed the office equipment, we'd never be able to explain it. Bill jumped behind the steering wheel and officer friendly inched forward and pushed the car about fifty feet until Bill turned into his driveway. A dense hedge of bushes encircled the yard, offering seclusion from neighbors.

The cop shouted, "Are you boys going to be okay now?"

Chris waved and cried out, "Thanks, man. We can take it from here." With tremendous relief, we watched him wave and drive off.

Bill exhaled a mighty sigh. "Jesus, that was close!"

If I hadn't been there, I'd never believe that the Bensenville police assisted us in pushing our loot laden car to a hideout. The downhill grade helped us push it farther through the snow into a dilapidated shed. We locked it in there after removing the license plates and returned them before dawn. Then we scuffed away the tire tracks to disguise where the car ended up.

"We'll let it set there a few days to cool off," Bill said. "I'll check with some buyers I know, then we'll split the proceeds and plan the next raid."

Chris and I retreated to our West End lair, congratulating our success before hitting our racks and drifting to sleep. Visions of sugar plums danced in my head in expectation of the payoff we'd earn.

The next day I saw Bill at The Place and he had a new proposition for me.

"Did you ever rob a store? I mean, use a gun, armed robbery?"

"No," I admitted.

"Well, I have! It's ready cash, more lucrative than trying to sell hot merchandise. We'd be in and out in no time." He motioned me closer and opened the flap on his heavy coat to show me the butt of a handgun. "It's a Saturday Night Special, and I bet we won't even have to use it. They'll hand over the dough when they see it. We'd be in and out of there in no time." He stared at me for a minute. "Are you in or not?"

"I'll have to think about it."

"Okay, we'll talk about it tomorrow."

My knees felt weak, and I collapsed into a chair to consider. Although my first reaction was to say no, it could bring me the vocational skills I needed to serve the Revolution.

A day later, Chris and I met a more subdued Bill at The Place.

"Sit down, guys." He cleared his throat. "I've got some good and some bad news."

Chris raised his eyebrows. "Did the cops find the car?"

"No, that's the good news. I got it running and drove out to a dealer I know, when I noticed a suspicious car following me. I managed to lose him and dumped the goods in a vacant lot. After a couple of hours, I drove back. The cops must have found it, because all the stuff was gone. Would you believe our luck?"

Chris and I shared looks of disbelief. "You're feeding us a load of crap," I said.

Chris added, "You just want to cheat us out of our share."

"No, man, it's all true! I didn't sell anything. We can count ourselves lucky we didn't get busted. Right? Better luck next time."

Bill jabbered on about pulling a stick-up at a convenience store, but I was done with him. He was no Robin Hood, and the saying about honor amongst thieves proved to be a lie. Stealing from the rich to give to the poor was great in theory, but I didn't have a clear conscience about some of the victims. We never got a penny from that Churchville raid, and I'd taken enough reckless risks. My life of crime was over.

Jenny and a Job

I began making day trips into Chicago, taking the bus from Elmhurst to Oak Park where I caught the El, the elevated train into Chicago. At the psychedelic *Seed* underground newspaper office, I'd pick up a bundle of papers to sell on the street. It stood right under the El tracks beside Alice's Restaurant Revisited, where I'd met Ruby and cavorted with Bonnie and then Karen before my arrest the year before. No one I asked recognized the names of my lost loves, and I'd resigned myself to having to build my love life anew.

There were plenty of other freaks hawking the Seed in Lincoln Park and Old Town, so I continued all the way to Randolph Street in the Loop, hollering, "Buy the Seed, buy the Seed, buy the beautiful Seed!" If I managed to sell all the copies on the way, that was unusual, a few always remained that I took back to the End. Perched in the door of Lee's closet Headshop at the Place, I might sell a few more, but I never sold enough to do more than just get by. Even though I refused to cut my hair, an abject surrender to the culture of conformity I struggled against, I kept looking for a job that paid real money.

Sometimes I found myself drawn into one of the marches

protesting Nixon's escalation of the ever less popular war in Viet Nam. The energy of my peers electrified me, although I hadn't found a place to crash and stay on a more permanent basis.

A skinny girl boarded the bus one day in Oak Park, long strings of unkempt auburn hair fell over her face. She gave me the eye as she sat across from me and smiled.

"Hi, I'm Jenny. Are you going to Elmhurst?" Without waiting for my answer, she rattled on. "I'm on my way to my capitalist sales job. She rolled her eyes as if she dreaded it. It's easy money though. Getting people to subscribe to newspapers is something they need anyway, so I don't feel like too much like a sellout." She broke into a nervous giggle, giving me time to introduce myself and say, "Think they'd hire me? I need a job."

"Oh, God, yes. They don't care about your hair either. Some of the college guys I work with have hair longer than yours."

Our conversation got loud and giddy as we exulted in our identification with the counterculture and protest scene, which irritated the driver, who kept scowling at us in the rear-view mirror. As we got off at the next-to-last stop, the driver mumbled, "Good riddance, you noisy kids."

Jenny and I looked at each other and burst out laughing. "Fuck him anyway." She grabbed my hand. "Come on." She pulled me down York Street to one door past the movie theater where we climbed the stairs to the second-floor office. We opened the door on a buzzing beehive of college aged guys and gals, their cheerful voices droning at innumerable phone lines at workstations that filled tables around the room.

A burly fortyish man rose from a desk and confronted us. "Well-well, what do we have here, Jenny? Some fresh talent?"

She giggled and pushed me forward. "This is Ron. He's a good talker and needs a job. Wanna give him a try?"

"Let's see how he does." He handed me a script. "Read this with gobs of feeling, like you just won a million dollars and want to tell the world about it."

I gulped and cleared my throat. "Hello, there! I'm working to raise money to fund community projects to help the young people in your neighborhood by selling subscriptions to popular newspapers and magazines..."

"Louder," the boss said. "Put more umph into it." I began again, and he nodded. "That's much better. Practice it a few more times with enthusiasm."

"What youth work do we fund?" Both Jenny and her boss giggled at my naïve question.

"None," he said, beaming. "Technically, it's not a lie, because it's supporting you, the young telephone solicitor, and the paper boy, too!"

This job would require muzzling my idealism in service to the almighty dollar, but I told myself that I wasn't selling my soul, only investigating the capitalist realm.

The boss smiled like a well-fed fat cat. "Young man, you have an excellent voice for telephone sales. We pay commission, and you'll make a lot more than you would grinding away like a slave for an hourly wage. Isn't that right Jenny?"

"Sure thing." She winked and squeezed my hand. "Don't worry, Ron, you'll do great. I'm gonna get busy and start my calls now. Okay? See you afterward." She sat, picked up the receiver and added her voice to the lulling background sound.

The boss laid his hand on my shoulder. "Heed my advice and you'll pull in dough hand over fist. Otherwise, if you blow too many sales, I'll let you go. Understood?"

His eyes bore into mine and I blinked. "For example, if someone tells you they don't read the newspaper, you say, 'That's okay, because I don't either!' You'll get 'em to laugh with you and they'll let their guard down, feeling like you're a friend. Then you say, 'I use it to line my bird cage,' more laughter, then you jump in with, 'the important thing is to help our young people, so please sign up and fund our youth work.' Bang! You'll convince them that it'll be a charitable donation and they'll feel too guilty to say no."

His voice took on a menacing, hard edge. "There's another thing I insist that you keep in mind here. If they sound black, hang up." I blinked in surprise at that worn out raciest stereotype which I assumed would self-limit his pool of customers. "Why, you might ask." I shrugged, unsure of what to say. "Because in my experience, black folks never pay up! Believe me, I've been through it a million times and had enough. To make your pay, you can't afford to waste your time and mine on deadbeat darkies. Got that?"

I could only nod in mute agreement, for I was undercover, deep in the dark heart of this capitalist society, the "Belly of the Beast," as the Weathermen called it, and I sure didn't need to get fired before I started. Anyway, I reasoned, why should I sucker blacks into buying this consumer fraud?

"Here." He handed me several pages of phone numbers and I threw myself into dialing one after another. Using my best upbeat salesman's voice, I tried to sucker in whoever answered. If there was no answer, I'd call them back later. All around me, celebrations broke out as my fellow callers closed deal after deal, but my best wasn't enough. The boss, listening in on my line from his desk, even jumped in a few times to nail down a sale, in which case he took the commission. By the time Jenny signaled that she, flush with success, was ready to leave, I'd achieved nothing but disappointment.

"You'll get the hang of it tomorrow," the boss said by way of encouragement.

As I followed Jenny out into the cold fresh air of late afternoon, she gripped my hand tight, making her desire clear, while her words tumbled out at a mile a minute as we waited at the bus stop.

"I just moved into a place with two cool roommates. They had dibs on the two bedrooms because they pay most of the rent, so I crashed into my sleeping bag on the living room floor. It's comfy enough, ain't too bad, anyway."

She ducked her head to look up at me with eager eyes. "When I've got more savings and find some, you know, a guy maybe like you, we'll get someplace bigger."

We got off the bus in Oak Park, rounded the corner, and climbed a wooden flight of stairs at the back of her building. The smell of herbs and tomato sauce greeted our entry through the open kitchen door, where a trim brunette stood stirring a huge pot of spaghetti.

"Jenny!" She wiped her hands on her apron and reached out. "You've brought home a guy? Terrific! We're having a housewarming party tonight." She grabbed my wrist, her touch and the clean musky sweat of her body aroused me. "You'll stay, won't you?"

"Sure thing." I clamped down hard on my sphincter in a vain attempt to restrain my instant erection for this more desirable lady. "I'll just call the people I'm staying with and tell 'em I won't be back for dinner." I'd much rather be there if only to bask in the glory of Jenny's sexy roommate.

"Carol." Jenny stepped between us. "This is Ron. We met on the bus, and I got him a job where I work."

"Wow, Jenny. He's quite a catch, ain't he? Meg will be here soon. She's with both our guys and they're bringing wine." Her lips curled into a sideways leer as she winked at Jenny. "After all, wine makes a fellow mellow." She shot me a knowing wink too and added. "There's nothing a chick likes more than a mellow fellow. Right Jenny?"

Jenny giggled, and I blushed, wishing it was this delightful Carol instead of her I would be mellowing with, but I pushed that thought away as unbecoming a man of honor, much less a bodhisattva. This girl needed me, and I wouldn't be so selfish as to disappoint her.

Jenny and I finished setting the table by the time Meg, as alluring as Carol, with long blonde hair streaming over her shoulders, barged in, shouting congratulatory greetings on this auspicious occasion. Two strapping guys in casual dress, whose names I didn't catch, followed bearing armloads of long French bread and several bottles of red wine.

One of the men pulled out a baggy of rolled joints. "Let's stimulate our appetite." After a couple of tokes, I begged off. Pot began to affect my memory and reaction time and made me uncomfortable.

Later I learned that THC built up in your body over time, but I had to take a couple of hits just to be sociable and prove I wasn't a narc.

"Let's eat!" Carol called from the kitchen, and we dug into a well-lubricated feast. Besides the reefer, the wine mellowed us all into an amorous state. The slurping sounds of her tipsy roommates' wet kisses encouraged Jenny to fling herself on me. Her lust, combined with the vision of her excited roommates, overwhelmed my useless pity. I'd learned to love the one I was with since I couldn't be with who I wanted.

After some minutes Meg rose and, giggling like a naughty school-girl, she pulled her man to his feet and maneuvered him to her room. Carol took that as her cue and pushed off her paramour, who was nuzzling her neck and stumbled away with him before turning to flash her pearly whites at Jenny and me.

"Are you two going to be all right out here?"

Jenny broke from my lips to leer up at me. "What do you think, Ron? Are we going to be all right?"

I'd be pushing my luck to suggest an orgy, so I nodded my okay and Carol vanished behind a door with her man.

Jenny spread two blankets as a makeshift mattress on the carpeted floor and rolled out her sleeping bag, all the while rattling on about something or other until I slid my hand down her pants, fingering her dripping wet pussy which cut off her stream of words. She gasped, then moaned as I wrenched up her top to find disap-pointment in her flat sagging tits. Undaunted, I nuzzled them as if they were the pert globes I craved, while she unzipped and squeezed my ready rod. She gasped and writhed as I pushed aside all tender-ness and rammed into her mushy wetness with almost hateful energy, allowing my brutal passion full reign. She arched her back and gasped with teary eyes. *Oh, GOD, yes-yes*, encouragement that inflamed me even more until I finished pumping her full of my white-hot fury and rolled over. A wave of tender feelings then washed over me as my mad lust subsided.

"Thanks, Ron." She nuzzled into my sweaty chest. "God, I needed that."

"So did I, Jenny, groovy that you like it as rough as I do."

Her gratitude eased my conscience at using her like a toy. I didn't want to be too sweet a lover, lest I hurt her feelings even more when I vanished, as I knew I must. Did that make me evil? We were equal partners in healthy lust, using each other in lieu of a better suited lover.

In my dreams it was Sue and Marge I embraced. I awoke to find Jenny in their place and my cock hard and ready. Without a shred of ceremony or remorse, I plowed into this sweet surrogate for the women I'd rather have, and she responded, eager, pulling me in into her with each thrust until we both collapsed into utter exhaustion. She kept a grip on my softened cock, holding it tight within her pussy with her legs still embracing me as I drifted beyond consciousness.

Our friends left early in the morning, some for work and others for university classes. Jenny and I waved our goodbyes from our nest on the floor. Our job started later in the day.

We finally roused ourselves to linger over a leisurely brunch before heading out. Entering the office, the radio blared a popular song.

> Ride, ride, ride, hitching a ride.
> Gonna get back home... to my baby's side...

The lyrics pulled me back to the open road where I belonged and seemed to accuse me of becoming a spiritual sell out, pushing unwanted merchandise on people because I needed the almighty dollar. All I could do was grit my teeth and push on in a struggle for ill-gotten loot. Script in hand, I dialed numbers and read my lines with as much feeling as I could muster, yet I couldn't close the first or second sale.

With a frown on his face, the boss came to stand over me. "Slow down, son. Put more bubbly joy in your tone." I tried as best I could on the next call. His eyes bored into me as he listened in, searching for flaws in my delivery.

"That's a little better, but you're still not pushy enough. Try again. No sale means no money in your pocket."

"Well, maybe my list is no good."

The boss grabbed my call sheet and handed it to another guy. "Watch him nail a fast couple of sales!" With growing desperation, I listened with exasperation as his two out of three calls closed successful sales within five minutes. The boss threw the list back to me, with a gruff. "Now you do it."

I gave it my all, but six calls later, success still eluded me. The boss waved me over to his desk. "Look, kid," he said, his voice dead-pan. "You're just not getting the hang of this, and I can't waste my valuable time on you, sorry. Goodbye, you're through."

All my desperate efforts hadn't earned a single penny. Jenny broke off the call she was on and hurried over.

"Don't let this bum you out Ron, not everyone can do it. There are better things in store for you." She drew close and whispered, "It's Friday. Come spend the weekend with me. Okay?"

"Okay." I nodded, feeling a bit more cheerful. A couple of hours later, I met up with her at the bus stop for the ride back. We needed each other's healing magic, whether for the long or the short term, and that's all anyone could hope for in this transient world.

Maxwell Street

J enny rose over me on her elbow, sweeping her long stringy hail over my naked chest. "Wake up, lover-boy. It's Saturday and my roomies are driving to meet a friend. Wanna come?"

"Sure, I've got no plans." I sat up and stretched. Thanks to Jenny, I had a regular sex life again and felt healthier and more in the groove, in tune with the universe. After eggs and bacon, we jumped into Carol's station wagon and headed to the city.

"You'll like Carl, Ron," Meg said as we pulled into a school parking lot. "He's a teacher here."

Carol laughed. "But he's not at all straight, no way! He's an old be-bopping jazz-loving beatnik, nothing like Maynard G. Krebs. Remember him from *The Life and Loves of Doby Gillis?*"

"Yeah," I said. "I was nine years old. He was the first beatnik I ever saw, a silly stereotype of course.

"Come on," Carol said, getting out of the car and opening the back. "Carl finagled this school kitchen for the day, grab one of these grocery bags and come in.

As we loaded up and followed her roommates Jenny said, "I

forgot to tell you, Ron," "We'll be cooking up a batch of chili from scratch. Carl sets up a stand to sell it on Maxwell Street. Ever been there?"

"No, but I heard that's where Muddy Waters and the Chicago Blues got started."

"It used to be a Jewish community," Carol said. "They still own most of the shops, but it's now mostly black, a skid row ghetto."

A guy chopping meat on the counter smiled as we walked into the large kitchen. He raised his bloody hands at me. "Hi, I'm Carl. You must be Ron. Carol told me you're Jenny's new squeeze. Grab a knife and start cutting up those vegetables you brought in." With his long salt and pepper hair tied in a bun under his beret and a scraggly beard, he looked a lot like Allen Ginsberg. He washed his hands. "Are you going to brave the cold and come with us tomorrow, Ron?"

"Sure, I'm curious about it."

"Every Sunday Maxwell Street becomes a grand bazaar. People set up stalls full of obscure treasures and junk of every sort at bargain prices."

Long before the sun rose on the next day, I rode with the gals to pick up Carl and the huge kettle of chili. There were only a few other hardy souls about when we pulled up to our designated spot to unload on Maxwell Street. The harsh wind whipped up icy snow that stung us as we unloaded the folding table, gas burner and disposable cups and spoons from the station wagon and set up our stand on the dark street.

Despite his heavy coat and earmuffs, Carl moaned his lament. "It's cold as a witch's tit out here."

I hadn't heard that quip before and it cracked me up. I nudged Jenny. "Well, all the witches I know have nice hot tits!" Weak laughter was all any of us could muster through our chattering teeth.

The girls got back in the empty car and Jenny called out, "We'll be back later. You don't mind waiting with Carl, do you, Ron?"

I shrugged my shoulders. "I guess not. See you then."

Carl lit the camp stove to keep our chili and hands warm. Soon, other stalls set up beside us and became our first customers. After a weak glow spread across the eastern sky, I could better make out the hardscrabble storefronts, with assortments of old furniture and hardware displayed in the windows. Another hour passed before a few well bundled strollers made their appearance, Looky-loos, who didn't buy on their first pass, but coming back around, some of them heeded Carl's sales pitch.

"Hot homemade chili, folks. Fifty cents a cup and a dollar a bowl."

We served it in Styrofoam cups with plastic spoons and warmed our own bellies with this delightful breakfast fare. By noon, the trickle of window shoppers grew into a crowd, which surprised me on such a day. Whatever they were in the market for, whether used tires, old books, clothing, antique jewelry, or furniture, or just to brave the cold for the atmosphere, a bowl of hot chili was the perfect meal on such a freezing day.

The ladies came back, and each of us took turns hawking the chili and stirring the pot so the others could explore this run down, yet picturesque, skid row area of Chicago, replete with well bundled men huddled in doorways, swigging the inevitable bottle of rotgut or fortified wine. Most of the Winos were black with some ruddy-faced whites thrown in.

Jenny said, "You've got to come here in the summertime, Ron. That's when it's really happening here. People swarm in to hear live blues music, share dope and good vibes. It's too damn cold for that now."

"Yeah." I took off my gloves and blew on my hands. "I'm surprised anyone comes here in the winter. Chicagoans are a tough bunch."

"I'd better get back to help Carl," Jenny said. "You should look around some more."

She no sooner left than a voice hailed me. "Hey Ron!" I turned around to see a guy with a guitar slung around his shoulders. I knew him from the Down Under coffeehouse, where he sang gospel and folk songs. With his trim black hair and goatee, he resembled Mitch Miller, from the mid-sixties TV show *Sing Along with Mitch*. He was also a proselytizing Christian, a fisher of men, but I was in an expansive mood, and answered him. "What's up, man?"

"I haven't seen you at the Down Under in a long time, Ron. What gives?"

"Well, I've been out of town the past year or so."

"Are you free tonight? We're having a big party. Should be chicks there." He'd said the magic word, chicks!

"Sure, can you give me a ride home afterward?"

"Sure thing."

"Great, I'll be over at the chili stand when you're ready to go." I waved my hand in the general direction.

Jenny was serving a customer when I told her I was leaving to see some old friends.

"Ok," she glanced up at me, then lowered her voice. "Are you coming back?"

"Well," I hesitated. "I don't want to wake your roommates. It might be at some ungodly hour."

She flashed a wink and gave my hand a squeeze. "Come back as late as you want. Just knock softly, dear. I'll be sleeping right at the door." She turned away to stir the chili, and I slipped away to find Mitch.

It was an okay party, although the delicious-looking chicks all had steady guys in tow. A few gave me flirtatious glances that raised my pulse, and I made a note to swing by the Down Under some time with Bob Brady at the wheel. Who knew what could happen?

Mitch clapped me on the shoulder. "Time to go, Ron. Still want that ride?"

"Sure, I'm staying with friends in Oak Park."

He squinted at me. "Friends, huh? I bet they are pot smokers."

"Come on, man, everybody smokes pot."

In the car, he took a deep breath and launched into his missionary spiel. "Are you sure you don't want me to drop you at your folks in Wood Dale? They must be worried sick about you, and I'm worried that you're mixing with immoral company."

"Some of them are college students from wealthy families."

"*Harumph!* Servants of Satan come from all classes. I too, was once a rootless young man like you, intoxicating myself with pot and seeking salvation in the idolatry of pagan religions. When I met Christ, he revolutionized my life, and you too will profit from a personal encounter with the one true god."

I'd been trying to be polite, but I'd grown weary of conversations with bigoted Christians who refused to open their eyes and hearts. "Look, man, I'm not opposed to your Christ, who quoted some of Buddha's teachings, just that Christianity became too narrow minded and hidebound. There is far more spiritual sustenance in the religions of the East."

We arrived at Jenny's place. Mitch grabbed my sleeve as I opened the car door. "Wait, Ron. I'll ask you one more time. Wouldn't you rather go home to your parent's tonight?" I shook my head no. "Then pray with me a moment for the salvation of your soul."

I held my breath and my tongue until he finished, but he followed me like a chaperone upstairs to the apartment door. "Okay, I'm here now. Thanks for the ride."

"I insist on seeing you safely inside."

I knocked, and the door opened wide, revealing a disheveled Jenny, her hair undone and tussled like a madwoman, gripping a sheet around her middle that left one of her tits exposed.

"Hi, lover-boy, I..." She looked over my shoulder at Mitch and her eyes bugged open. Before I could explain or introduce him, Mitch exploded.

"I knew it!" he shouted in triumph, having discovered my hidden sin. "I knew you were up to something, cohabiting with shameless, immoral girls."

She took a step back, and I rushed her inside, then slammed and locked the door behind us. Poor Jenny. How could this Christian be so unchivalrous and cruel? I hoped the commotion didn't wake her roommates.

"Whew, sorry about that, Jenny. This born-again guy gave me a ride and insisted on seeing me to the door, but I never expected him to be such a nutty fanatic." A nervous laugh escaped me. "It's funny, though. He must think this is a brothel!"

She blinked. "A what?"

"You know, a bawdy house, a house of ill-repute, commonly called a whorehouse."

She stared up at me, doe eyed, half asleep, and oh so vulnerable. Her sheet slipped farther down her body, exposing her warm naked flesh to my caressing touch, which aroused my steed to stand tall as I walked her backwards to our bed, where we collapsed.

"My god, Jenny, you look sexy tonight." I kissed her, roughing my lips back and forth over her face, and nibbled her lip. "Maybe the crazy Christian was right. Maybe you, my dear, are a fallen woman, a harlot, dragging innocent me down into the Pit of debauchery. Sounds delightful, don't you think?"

She moaned. "Shit, Ron, I don't know what the fuck a harlot is or what you're talking about but keep doing what you're doing. It turns me on."

My childhood Bible reading had imbued words like harlot and whore with a heightened erotic appeal and I'd sworn off 'nice girls,' vowing to only love depraved and forbidden women. But of course, these are only stereotypes and all real women, like men, are imbued with the same secret fantasies and drives. After the wild drama the Christian gave us, my warm feelings for Jenny grew exponentially. Without much effort, I lasted long, riding her saddle until we orgasmed together.

Poor Jenny, with her sunken chest, she wasn't as attractive as Sue or Marge, both of whom remained heavy on my mind, but she'd risen in my esteem. As painful as it was for me to admit it, I was using her for my selfish lust, but ugly girls need love too, and that thought helped me overcome my useless guilt. There was no reason to let my feelings get in the way of our mutual pleasure. Satisfying each other's needs was good karma all around.

A Phone Call

My grandparents drove in from Chicago most Saturdays and I trekked up from the West End to visit my family over coffee and cake. When I walked in one day, Mom winked and said, "Some girl has been calling for you."

"Really?" My heart leaped. I hadn't given out my folks' number to anyone. Whoever it was, must have done some detective work to find me. "Did she leave her name?"

"No." Mom searched my face for any reaction because I never discussed my love life. "But I told her you were supposed to swing by today. Maybe she'll call back in a bit."

I evoked the faces of my lost loves. Karen, Marge, and Rochelle, my beautiful black nurse, Valerie who'd rung in the New Year with me and finally Sue who'd given me her sexy Satanic body. The caller could even be Bonnie, who'd enticed me to New York last fall to join her radical collective. That episode seemed like a lifetime ago, although only six months had passed. I missed them all. Each of them brought me enough joy to keep me going, but mere memories alone weren't enough. I needed someone's warm body close to mine.

"Hi Buck." Grandpa greeted me with my nickname as he

walked in the door. Mom gave him a hug. "Ronnie." She turned to me. "Pour us all some coffee. You still remember where the cups are, right?"

We chatted over frivolous topics, avoiding those that mattered most in any of our lives. The whole time I kept one ear cocked, listening for the expected phone call. Dad came in for his share of the coffeecake, but he could never sit still for long and went back out to fiddle with his old Packard that he hoped would be a collectable someday.

The dreary hours passed, my Grandparents had long since gone, yet still I waited, growing ever more exasperated. Finally, I rose to face the long two mile walk back to the West End. With my hand on the doorknob, the phone finally rang.

"It's probably just a sales call," I said, stifling my anticipation. I'd already been disappointed so many times.

"Oh, I'll get it," Mom said, leaving the kitchen table for the wall phone.

"Yes, who is this?" Her high-pitched sugary telephone voice sounded so different from her everyday tone. "Okay, he's right here." She held out the receiver. "It's Sue."

A rushing torrent pounded in my head. I stumbled across the room. "Hello Sue!" I didn't even try to hold back my enthusiasm. "I'm so glad you called."

"Did you get the message I sent you in Riveredge?"

I lowered my voice. "You mean about being pregnant? I wasn't sure if it really came from you. Is it's true?"

"Yeah, Ron. It was true, all right."

"Wow, that's great news, Sue. I didn't realize they could tell if you're pregnant after only a few days. They wouldn't tell me where they sent you or let me get in touch."

"The fuckers sent me to another hospital and said I couldn't ever see you again."

"Well, I'm glad you found my parent's number. Are you at home now?"

"Yeah." She hesitated, and a muffled female voice said something in the background before she continued. "It was a boy, you know."

"A boy! Great!" Words spilled out of me, unconcerned if my watching mother heard. This was our chance to right the wrongs of the earlier generations. I wouldn't make the same mistakes my dad and too many other men did with women. "You should be two months along by now, Sue. Do you have any names picked out? I kind of like Carl."

She coughed. "I *was* pregnant, but..." Another pause, more whispering in the background. "Does that make you feel like a big man?" Her disembodied voice sounded cold, hostile, as she was Satan herself. "It doesn't need a name now."

"What do you mean?"

"You *had* a son, Pappa, but my parents made me get rid of it."

My excitement crashed. It took a moment for me to respond.

"Abortion? Why?" The other woman began chuckling in the background, but I ignored her. "I thought you wanted a baby and abortions are illegal in Illinois. Would your parents make you have an illegal one? You told me they were *stone fucking* Catholics."

"It's true, Ron, I was *PG,* alright, with a boy. My parents took me to Indiana, where it's legal. Shit! You better goddamn well believe it wasn't my idea!"

"Okay, Babe. Calm down, I believe you. Where are you at? We need to talk in person. Who is listening in with you?"

"Ah, a friend."

"Can I talk to her? Is she telling you what to say?"

One of her Satanist friends could be coaching her. Maybe they had this planned from the beginning, but I couldn't accept that Sue would turn on me. Our moment of naked passion in the snow had been so honest and giving, talking on the phone felt too impersonal. I needed to watch her face as she spoke. Then I could rouse her creative lust and become her Satanic Majesty again, a role vital to us both. I had to keep cool and manage this situation step by step.

"Look, Ron. I told you not to get involved with me. What I called for... I mean..." She took a deep breath, and I heard intense whispering in the background. "All I want from you is some money to pay for it. That's all."

"Money, huh?" I couldn't tell whether she was speaking for herself, or the other woman was pulling her strings. "You wanted the baby. Right? They made the choice to cut it out."

"My parents paid, but my mom wants you to pay them back because you knocked me up. Right, Daddy?" Her calling me Daddy after aborting my son felt like a knife in my heart.

"Look, Sue, I didn't have any say in that abortion, and would have been happy to help raise the kid. We need to talk in person before I fork anything over. I don't have any bread right now, but I'm not stingy. If we get together and talk, I can work something out."

"When they pulled it out, you know, the fetus? They could already tell it was a boy. So, like, congratulations, stud, you had a son! I bet you're happy about that."

She'd upped the ante, twisting the knife in my guts, but I had five sisters and an alcoholic mother. I knew something about crazy, *mindless* women. Maybe that was part of her charm. I still wanted her, crazy and satanic as she was. If I got the chance, I'd fill her belly with new life. Hell, I'd even cut my hair, which was against my principals, and get a straight job to support her, support us. I kept trying to talk sense through the telephone.

"Take it easy Sue. I'm super glad to hear your voice. I've been thinking about you a lot."

"Really?" She used that sarcastic mock surprised voice like Mom used on Dad. "Do you miss me, Hon? Me too. Does that make you feel better, dude?"

"Yes, really, it does. Let's meet somewhere and talk about this in person. You can even bring your friend. I'd like to meet her."

"Well, I, uh, you can't come over here, man. My Dad has a shotgun, he'll kill you."

"I'll chance it. Where do you live?"

"On Winchester Street in Chicago, but don't you ever come over here. Just send me the money by check." She never gave me her phone number, but Tinin was a rare name, with only three listings in the phone book and only one on Winchester, a short street on the South side. I tried calling, but whoever answered told me Sue was not accepting calls. I debated going. If it was on the Northside, I wouldn't hesitate, but the Southside was unfamiliar turf. Without Sue's active help, even if her dad didn't shoot me, it wouldn't end well.

She called me back a week later, but this time she had me talk to her mother. At least, that's who she said it was, although she sounded too young. I insisted that I needed to come face to face with them both, but she refused, insisting that I *owed* them money for the abortion, but I couldn't see them first. "How much?"

She said a hundred at first, then settled on fifty bucks, or whatever I could get 'right away.' My doubts rose. The other woman, whether she was her mother, or her Satanist girlfriend was manipulating Sue, playing a cruel game on me. I couldn't even be sure that Sue was ever pregnant. I wanted to believe that I fathered a son, such joy ran through me when she told me that, but then to hear that he was dead, yanked out of her womb, hurt me to my core.

Such is Samsara, the intrinsic suffering we all experience on the revolving wheel of life and death. Only Buddhism could comfort me. Meditation helped me to plumb the cosmic truths to escape the wheel, but I needed to bring her and all my lovers with me. That's what the Mahayana is all about. There is no real salvation for oneself alone. It's still hell to watch your loved ones suffer from a safe distance.

March 26, my birthday, was fast approaching. I'd be eighteen and liable to be drafted into the military. There was nothing I could do about Sue, and she slid into the back of my mind as I, and all young men my age, confronted our life and death choices. We were all pawns manipulated by historical forces. We'd either end up fighting in the jungles of Vietnam for Uncle Sam's Army or fighting against it in the streets with the anti-war movement.

The Feds Pay a Visit

As the sun rose higher, I peeled off my heavy coat to bask in the celestial rays on my two-mile cross-country hike to my folk's place. It was mid-March, and the occasional sleet and snowstorm still blew over Chicagoland. With better traveling weather in a month or two, I looked forward to slipping away, spreading my wings back on the road as soon as I could.

Mom, less tipsy than usual by noon, met me at the back door with a hug. "Grandpa and Grandma will be here soon, Ronnie, and your father's taking an hour off from work."

She always referred to Dad as 'your father' to us kids, but she called him Jimmy when speaking to our grandparents. They drove in from the north side of Chicago most Saturdays, but this day was special. It was Wednesday, March twenty-fifth, 1970, the day before my eighteenth birthday, and we planned a serious conversation, which could turn nasty. My five sisters would be in school. They didn't need to be around for that.

The Cold War heated up in Southeast Asia. Our nation needed manpower, so when a guy turned eighteen, he had to register for the draft, a mandatory rite of passage into manhood. We still couldn't vote or drink alcohol, legally that is, but our leaders used us to enforce Pax Americana on the rebellious Third World.

For some years, I hadn't known how to act out birthdays with my folks. Our parents see us as the kids we once were, cute but stupid, not the savvy adults we believe ourselves to be. They can't help embarrassing us with diminutive endearments more befitting our ancient tadpole stage of development, but I'd changed into a frog. Tension built up between Dad and me even before my arrest in the SDS riot in October. He couldn't understand how I'd transformed from an obedient boy into a Leftwing radical, a Commie. If I'd robbed a bank, he might have felt less shame, or even nursed a secret pride in me, his only son.

I helped Mom make coffee and a pile of sandwiches. We finished setting the table just as Grandma walked in and gave me a wet smooch on my cheek.

"Happy birthday, Ronnie! We can't make it tomorrow, ya know, so we'll celebrate your birthday today."

Grandpa came right behind her. "Happy birthday, Buck!" He grabbed my hand in a vise grip before pulling me in for a bearhug. Emphysema was taking its toll, making him stop for breath every other step on a flight of stairs, but he still drove his well-kept Buick the twenty miles out to see us. I'd caught him sneaking cigarettes from secret stashes around our property but didn't have the heart to take away his guilty pleasure. Abstaining wouldn't delay his inevitable end, not after a lifetime of two-packs a day.

Dad gave me a sober nod and a brisk handshake when he walked in. We all sat down for a quick lunch, after which Mom carried in the cake. Instead of eighteen individual candles, a big blue One and a white Eight sat in the middle of the medium sized chocolate frosted strawberry cake and we sang the time-honored, happy birthday song.

"Make a wish," Grandma said.

"Do I have to keep it secret?"

She stifled a giggle. "It won't come true otherwise,"

I blew out the candles. It was almost like all my other birthdays, but time had marched on and so must we. Dad cleared his throat to address the issue at hand.

"Now that you're turning eighteen, Ronnie, we'll have to pick a day to drive out to Wheaton and register you for the draft."

"Why Wheaton? That's kind of far."

"Because it's the DuPage County seat. How about Mom and I take you next Thursday, a week from tomorrow?"

"Sure, I've got nothing planned."

Dad twisted his face like he'd bitten a lemon. "Still no job, huh? Why don't you cut your hair, Ronnie? Life would get a lot easier for you." He zeroed in on me. "It's about time you bucked down. Too bad you dropped out of school, you could have gone to college, gotten a deferment from the draft. Who knows what you could have made of your life?"

"But, Dad, you always complain about those arrogant college boys at work. I thought you hated them for stealing your promotions?"

"Well..." He cleared his throat. "I was drafted as soon as I graduated from high school. In my day, we had to protect our shores from the Japanese, and your generation now faces a similar threat from Asia."

I rose to the bait. "No, Dad. You fought against the Japanese Empire. That was noble, but the Vietnamese were fighting to free themselves from both the Japanese and the French Empires. We sold them out to the French before they gave up and now, we've taken over the from them. They're still struggling to free themselves from the dictator the French left in their place. It's a new form of imperialism that we support."

"What the heck is wrong with imperialism anyway?"

"Huh?" I dropped my fork with a clunk and looked up at the ceiling, exasperated. "I can't believe you said that. We fought British imperialism to become an independent country. Other nations, including France, followed our lead to democracy."

"Well, Ronnie, that was a long time ago. Those people in miserable backward countries need to accept American progress. That's what's showing them the way to a better life, to be modern and sanitary. Today's industry, you know, is looking to the future."

It was useless to keep trying to explain my position. I reached for the pot and poured myself more coffee. Mom glanced up at the wall clock. "Jimmy, keep track of the time."

Dad had a twenty-minute drive back to his office job in Schiller Park and was still bucking for that illusive promotion and raise, which always seemed to go to those upstart college boys.

"Okay." He pushed away from the table with a sigh. "Don't forget, young man. We'll see you here early Thursday, April second. A week from tomorrow."

I nodded agreement, and he left. Mom and I cleared the table and then we retired with my grandparents to the recreation room, where the drone of small talk eased the tension. Mom and my grandparents seemed comfortable, chatting, and relaxed, but I felt uneasy. My mind was far away, and I couldn't think of much to say to them.

Probation wasn't too bad. I was lucky to avoid a longer sentence in Cook County Jail. I only had to fill out and mail in forms about my employment or lack thereof every three months, but I ached to get back to my real life on the road and in the counterculture, even though the judge forbad me from leaving the State of Illinois. After long soul searching, I decided against trying to go underground like the Weatherman. I'd find a way to mail in my forms with an Illinois postmark while on the road.

Finally, it was time to go. I looked forward to the leisurely stroll back through the countryside to the more congenial Delmonte home on that sunny day. An eerie prickly feeling raised the hairs on the back of my neck, maybe destiny was calling me, because for some reason I walked out the front door rather than the back, as I almost always did.

Instead of cutting through the back fields and empty lots to pass through the forest preserve, I'd walk along Addison Road. But closing the door behind me, my attention became riveted on a slow-moving car driving south. There was nothing unusual about it until it turned into our driveway. An apprehensive instinct told me to flee back inside and run out the back door. I could have lost them, but I swallowed hard and kept walking to meet whoever was halfway up the drive.

The driver, with short dark hair, arched his eyebrows at me, as if comparing my features to a photo he'd studied. Despite his plain-clothes suit and tie, he looked like a cop.

"Are you Ronald Schulz?"

I fought down a fresh rush of panic, wondering if they'd come to haul me off. Maybe I should say no, bluff him and get away. This could be my only chance, but I decided to play it straight.

"Yeah." I took a deep breath and steadied my voice. "I'm Ron Schulz."

A younger, smiling crewcut blond stepped out from the passenger side and came around to me as the driver got out, putting me between them. It was too late to run, and my mind raced with adrenaline as I tried to stay calm.

These trim bodied men in suits looked to be in their mid-twenties, not at all like the beefy uniformed thugs I'd often seen. Maybe they were with the Red Squad, Chicago's own anti-radical intelligence unit, or even from the vigilante Legion of Justice, Sutton's Storm Troopers, an irregular force who beat and terrorized movement people. Thomas Sutton, a shaven headed attorney who'd run for governor of Illinois in the Republican primary of 1968, was far to the right of even Republican party conservatives. His Legion did the Red Squad's dirty work with an extra-legal flourish.

The serious one pulled out his wallet. "Federal Bureau of Investigation." He flashed his badge at me, like in the movies. I'd never seen an actual FBI badge and didn't know how to tell if it was a fake, so I grabbed his hand to study it before he pulled it back. He pursed his lips in irritation, but the blond, still smiling as if the whole thing was a joke, presented his badge too. I nodded, as if satisfied the badges were in order, and they put them away. I hoped the Feds would be less of a threat than the Legion.

The serious guy took the lead. "Mr. Schulz, we'd like to ask you a few questions."

"Yeah, okay." I remained guarded. "I guess that depends on what you want to know." I decided it was wisest to play along without saying much.

The blond opened the rear door. "Have a seat, Mr. Schulz."

"No, that's okay, I'll stand." I was leery of going on a one-way ride with them and hoped my family members inside were watching. I needed witnesses.

The serious guy referred to his notebook. "You were arrested last year on October eleven, 1969, during the Weatherman demonstration at the Federal Building in Chicago. Isn't that true?"

"Yeah," I answered, although it wasn't the Federal building but the downtown Loop. I wouldn't correct their mistakes.

The smiling blond took over. "Mr. Schulz, are you aware of the fugitive status of the Weatherman leadership? They've jumped bail and are on the run."

"Yeah, I heard about it on the news."

"Mr. Schulz." The serious guy again. "We are trying to locate..." He rattled off a list of names.

"No." I was familiar with Mark Rudd and Bernadine Dorn, not the others, but I didn't want to aid their investigation even by admitting that I knew almost nothing.

"Are you sure?" The serious guy riveted me with his steel blue eyes. "You could help your situation by aiding our investigation."

"Yeah, I haven't seen anyone since I got out of jail."

The blond chuckled. "Well, thank you for your time. We appreciate your courtesy. At least you talked with us. None of the others we've questioned even agreed to that."

That made me worry that I might have given away something. They seemed like pleasant enough chaps, and shook my hand as if we were compatriots, but we stood on opposite sides of the political land-scape. I watched them back out and disappear down the road.

The whole experience felt unreal, like a desert mirage. To have run into the Feds on my one-and-only time going out of the house by the front door, at the exact moment they arrived, was spooky. Maybe it was a cosmic synchronicity, part of the karma I needed to let play out.

In the past year, I'd been practicing Dream Yoga and achieved some success in manipulating my dreams. It took a lot of practice and didn't always work. In my recent dreams, the FBI had figured promi-nently as attacking enemies. I learned to remain calm as they shot at me, which caused them to dissolve as I flew into the sky or passed through them without harm. Maybe this *in the flesh* experience was an unrecognized dream. I ran back inside to find my family sitting in the living room as I'd left them.

"The FBI was just here. Did you see them?"

All three of them stared at me with blank faces and said nothing. They hadn't looked out the window, and that sort of thing didn't happen in their world. Even if I told them I spoke with little green men from Mars, they wouldn't be any more surprised. My stint in the mental hospital had convinced them I was *not well* in the head. The shrink told them I was a schizophrenic who hallucinated, and for a moment I too doubted my sanity. There was nothing more to say. I turned and went back to the West End, the people who understood me.

Confirmation came much later. In June 1996, via my Freedom of Information request #397447, marked CONFIDENTIAL, with a penciled X over it.

The following investigation was conducted by SA (name blacked out) on March 25, 1970: Investigation regarding the location of (Names redacted).

RONALD J. SCHULTZ, (sic) 291 North Addison Road, Wood Dale, Illinois, advised the Chicago Police Department arrested him during his participation in a demonstration at the Federal Building in

Chicago. SCHULTZ (sic) stated he was aware of the fugitive status of the SDS leaders and advised he had very limited contact with the Weatherman faction of SDS. He advised he did not know the current whereabouts of the fugitives. He stated he met (Names redacted). He stated he would not cooperate with the FBI, although he does not agree with the Weathermen.

April Fool

So, are you experienced?
Have you ever been experienced?
Well, I have...

J immy Hendricks' lyrics on the stereo lifted my spirits as I descended into the dark, womblike basement of our coffeehouse. In the morning I'd be going to register for the draft, and I'd come seeking music and the companionship of friends on that Wednesday, the first day of April.

Jeff Janacek called out. "April Fool's Day, Sucker!" His discordant greeting put me on guard. Everything I heard that evening could be just a tiresome prank that tried my patience, so I found a quiet corner. Eva Delmonte came over grinning and sat beside me, something she'd never done before, but she was thirteen, and navigating her way into our older crowd.

Over the past three years, I'd watched her grow up. In days gone by, she'd smile and call out a welcome as I passed where she sat out on the lawn during nice summer days. She'd wear her mother's oversized dresses and shoes, hosting pretend tea parties with her dolls and friends, a mere child. With my face frozen into an older boy's pretense of indifference, I only asked for her brother's whereabouts. Nothing else had ever passed between us and we'd remained strangers, but in the ebbing winter and faltering Spring of 1970, I'd been welcomed into her family home, making her almost my sister.

"Ron!" She clutched my forearm for full attention. "You meditate. You're a spiritual guy, right?"

"Uh, yeah, sure. Wanna learn?" April Fools be damned. I took my spiritual obligations seriously and began my usual explanation. "Sit up straight, breathe in deep and exhale slow, let your mind follow your breathing..."

She rolled her eyes at me, so I didn't launch into the altruistic affirmations of a bodhisattva. It would take time to explain interdependence and the compassionate motivation to her. She tightened her grip on my arm.

"Did John Borley ever say anything to you about me?"

"John? No, about what?" She spoke his name with reverence, but I didn't connect the dots right away. Then it dawned on me. John, of all guys, was on her romantic radar. He'd almost gotten her brother Chris busted, after that near fiasco, Chris told me the best way to sabotage the American War Machine was to get John to join the Army.

"No, Eva, I haven't talked to him in weeks. Ah, do you like him?" I decided not to ask if he'd broken her cherry. I tried to see him through her eyes. If he kept his mouth shut, John was good-looking, and in her narrow world, there were too few candidates to choose from. Jeffery was too short. The Rockwood twins were too preppy and self-absorbed. But who was I to judge any of them?

"Where do we go there when we die?" She'd flipped the topic again. "Do you believe in heaven? What about hell, is it a real place?"

"That depends. Heaven and hell aren't permanent. We've got to develop spiritually to free ourselves from the cycle of birth and death." Eva wrinkled her brow, so I elaborated. "It's not up to some jealous god on a cloud. Our good and bad thoughts and actions create both heaven and hell. We need to take responsibility for our own salvation."

"Get to the point, Ron. What I really want to know is what happens right after death?"

My ready answer came from the Tibetan Book of the Dead. "We enter a kind of dreamlike or nightmarish dimension called the Bardo, in between our death and rebirth. Depending on how we react to that confusing or terrifying experience, propels us to reincarnate into new bodies in this or other realms like heaven and hell. None of these states are forever, like the Christian concept of eternal reward or punishment. The cycle of our birth and death continues..."

She squeezed my arm harder. "How does it feel to die?" She blinked and drilled me with an intense gaze. "Tell me, because I wanna die soon."

"No, Eva, don't talk like that." She wasn't laughing and stared me down, too serious for it to be an April Fool's joke. "You're young and inexperienced, Eva. You don't know what you're in for, and death is no escape. You have way too much to live for and should create much more good karma and prepare your mind with meditation before you go jumping into death."

"I mean it, Ron. I don't want to live anymore. Maybe I'll kill myself."

Here it was again. The death lust I'd seen at Riveredge that beguiled so many of my stressed-out peers. But her life couldn't be as messed up as theirs. Or could it? I too, had flirted with suicide during my school years and maybe, without the insight I'd gained from meditation, I too would have given up and tried to end it. Eva needed my advice; with a lungful of fresh air and determination I jumped in to save my almost sister.

"Do they bully you at school, call you names and laugh? I got that too, but soon you can drop out like I did. That gave me the confidence to survive. Dying is no solution, Eva, no matter how bad it seems right now." I thought about all she'd said and switched gears. "Don't kill yourself over John, or any guy. Sure, love hurts, believe me, I know.

People can be stupid dipshits. They're lost and confused, creating karma they'll regret someday. There are other, better guys out there in this big crazy world. Give it a chance."

Then I shut my trap and let her rap, listening as she unloaded all her anxieties, the normal fears of every girl entering womanhood. She worried about her looks. *Am I pretty?* Her hair. *Is it too frizzy?* Her figure. *Are my boobs too small?* All the things that can make or break a woman's fortune, that can bring her the attention and love she craves from a shining knight who will save her from herself, or leave her to sulk in desperate loneliness, all because she was trained to be passive, rather than an active agent in her life.

"You're pretty enough, sure," I told her, but like most girls I knew, she wanted to hear ever more assurance. Should I tell her she was drop dead gorgeous? Maybe, but I didn't want to overdo it. Despite my discomfort at doing so, I tried to appraise this little sister from a guy's perspective. She was slim, not at all fat, but not yet curvaceous or endowed in the breast department. That would come. Her features held promise, all anyone could hope for at her age. Attitude counted for much more.

"Looks aren't everything, Eva. Your personality..."

"I'm so sick and tired of hearing that personality shit, Ron. I'm an ugly duckling."

"You're not ugly, kid. That's something to be glad about."

Sweet, plain faced, and scarecrow thin Jenny popped into my mind, and a pang of guilt shot through me. Yes, superficial looks can make or break a chick's future, more so than it can for a dude. All some ugly guys needed was a roll of money or a flashy car. Life isn't fair.

The coffeehouse was closing, and icy sleet rained down, making the roads slick. We joined a group heading our way along Lake Street, all of us in dark clothes. There were no sidewalks, and the gravel shoulders weren't pedestrian friendly, with big deep puddles and washed-out drop-offs that we had to step onto the road to avoid.

Cars whizzed by too fast and close. A driver could skid out of control on the slick road if he hit the brakes too hard.

In a flash, Eva jumped out into the headlights of a car, catching me off guard. I hauled her back in as the car swerved, fishtailing, and blasting its horn.

"Damn it, Eva! Be cool."

"I told you I want to die, Ron. Believe me now?"

Her face glistened with icy sleet, eerie and beautiful, as if from another world. As the next car approached, she charged back onto the street, but I was ready, yanked her in and kept a grip on her arm.

"Don't be fucking crazy, Eva! If you kill yourself now, your next life will be worse." I held her shoulders, steering her in front of me as we skirted a drop-off on the shoulder.

"Let her go," one of the smart-ass guys with us said. "She just wants attention, man. Ignore her and she'll stop!" That was just some behavioral modification bullshit they were slinging. This was no time for games when death lies in wait.

Waking through the front door, Eva smiled and giggled, like it was all a big joke.

"Goodnight and sleep tight, Ron. Oh, yeah, you're getting your draft card tomorrow. Maybe they'll send you to Vietnam like my older brother, Ricky."

Death and a Draft Card

My parents and I climbed the steps to the DuPage County Courthouse in Wheaton, where they thought I needed to register for the Draft.

"Not here," the clerk said. "You need to go over to the Post Office."

Lucky for us, the staff there weren't busy. A lady clerk waved us to a counter and pulled up a form. She pushed her glasses down on her nose and began typing our answers to the questions.

"Do you have any personal marks or recognizable scars on you?"

"Sure, one on my right knee." I volunteered the information before realizing it marked me for the G-Men to identify if I went on the lam.

Dad chipped in. "You have that hernia scar too, remember Ronnie?" At least we'd kept mum about the scar above my left eye, my souvenir of the police clubs last October. The lady handed over my completed draft card.

SELECTIVE SERVICE SYSTEM
REGISTRATION CERTIFICATE

This is to certify that in accordance with the selective service law Ronald James Schulz Selective Service Number 11 122 52 475 date of birth March 26, 1952. Place of birth Chicago, Illinois eyes Blue color hair Brown height 6 ft. 2 in. weight 155. Special physical characteristics. Hernia scar, scar on right knee. Registered for the Selective Service this 2d day of April 70.

The lady signed it with flowery loops, making it official. No photo attached, only a few states had pictures on driver licenses then. The other side of the card gave the rules. I had to keep this card in my "personal possession at all times and to surrender it upon entering active duty in the Armed Forces." I was to notify them in writing within ten days of any change in my address, change in "physical condition or occupational (including student), marital, filial, dependency or military status.... Any person who alters... or mutilates... for the purpose of false identification... delivering to another... may be fined not to exceed $10,000 or imprisoned for not more than three years or both..."

It was official. I'd registered to serve my country and would do so *selectively*. Burning draft cards at antiwar rallies was a popular protest. But every time cops stopped a freak, and they stopped long-haired guys like me all the time, they demanded to see their draft card. now that I was eighteen, they could arrest me without it, and I didn't need that extra hassle.

The Underground Railroad took escaped slaves to Canada in the days before the Civil War, and once again, it became the destination for draft dodgers and military deserters from our *free* country. Whether to burn my card, run off to Canada, or just not report for duty if called, was a question I'd decide later.

It was already dark when my folks dropped me off in front of the Delmonte house. I bounced in the front door, eager to discuss the events of the day with my companions. Steve was wielding a broom in the otherwise silent and empty house, a rare sight. The floor was immaculate, and I was about to compliment him on his work when Steve rushed toward me with his forefinger to his lips.

"Shush! Don't say anything happy."

"What's up?"

"My little sister just got killed."

"Little sister?" It was too late to be an April Fool's joke. I took inventory, thinking of the littlest one first. "Was it Madeline?" He couldn't mean Mary; she was the oldest.

"Eva's dead." His voice was steady, betraying no emotion. "She got hit by a car."

Except for the sound of his sweeping, the house was dead silent, like a weird dream. I retreated to the bedroom, where the other brothers painted in the details with subdued voices. Two cars hit Eva, one after the other. She must have died instantly, although the ambulance took her to Elmhurst Memorial Hospital, where the doctor pronounced her dead. She'd been walking with her girlfriends under that new overpass built over Route 83, where it intersects Lake Street, not far from where I'd pulled her off the road the night before.

"Teenagers drove both cars," Mike said.

"Were they greasers?" I asked. "I've seen greasers swerve off the road to scare pedestrians."

"Who the fuck knows?" Chris answered. "But it wasn't hit and run. I don't think they hit her on purpose."

The guys, eighteen and nineteen years old, were from Lombard and Villa Park. They'd remained at the scene, offering what help they could, and the police insisted they weren't to blame, refusing Father Bruno's demand to press charges against them. Eventually, he resigned himself to the uncomfortable fact that no one would or could *pay* for his daughter's death.

Later that black evening, the boys and I stood outside with Mrs. D, who was red-eyed from crying, waiting for her mother in the darkness outside her home. Her boys had shot out the streetlight on the corner so many times that the county stopped replacing it.

"Those young hooligans murdered my Eva," she wailed. "What

kind of country is this when young punks can run over your child and get away with it? She'd always been such a happy, vibrant girl."

Her eyes fell on me, my cue to say something more meaningful than the sweet, deceiving lies people usually say in these situations.

"Jesus said the truth will set you free. Right?" I thought mentioning a Christian theme to this staunch Catholic lady would help her face the facts. She nodded, her red, teary eyes on me to say more. I gave it to her straight.

"Last night, Eva told me she wanted to die. On the way home from The Place, she kept running into the traffic. If I hadn't been there, she would have died then."

"What?" Mrs. D blinked and stared openmouthed at me in a moment of suspended animation. Then the most horrifying shriek I'd ever heard burst out of her and she continued wailing with vehemence. Too late, I realized I should have kept my trap shut.

"Nice going," Chris hissed behind me. "You sure as fuck didn't have to say that."

Mrs. D's mother drove up, and she climbed into the car, putting her head on her mother's lap. With choking sobs, she wailed, *Oh, mommy, mommy...* The grieving mother became an infantile child.

Chris pulled me into our room and closed the door. "She's been through an awful lot, ya know. Two miscarriages, nervous breakdowns, now this. She's been like this before, but she'll come out of it."

The leaden weight of my guilt for shooting off my mouth weighed on me, but I too had to carry-on, there was no going back.

The Inside Scoop

Bob Brady and Eva's girlfriend Janet filled me in on her last day of life. Bob was at the Borley household to see John's sister, Sue, for whom he had the hots, when Eva, with her friends, Sue, and Janet, arrived from school.

"It was just a typical day," Bob said. "Eva was swigging her usual codeine cough syrup, and we passed around a joint, but she only had a few tokes off that. Everyone was feeling mellow, kicking back. Eva smiled at me and pulled out her wallet. 'Look at this, Bob.'

"She had a finder's card that read in case of emergency contact John Borley, with his address and phone number. That's when I learned she liked him. Then she handed me a fresh joint. 'Keep this for later,' she said, like it had some special significance. She stared at me a moment before adding, 'Bob, you're a nice person.'

"That blew me away. I didn't know what the hell to say. She was high, sure, but she'd never said anything like that to me before.

"She was just a kid, they all are. Janet is fifteen and Sue is fourteen. Eva was carrying a cheap suitcase packed with a big bag of weed and her potent bottle of cough syrup, buried under some clothes in case somebody searched it. Then she and her two friends took off for the West End. I never expected it would be the last time I'd see her. It's like she vanished into the great beyond. Wild, huh?"

"You bet, Bob," I said. "The night before, Eva kept waltzing into the traffic and I had to drag her back. She was suicidal, saying she wanted to die."

Janet shook her head. "No, Ron, she was happy. I know my best friend. I cannot believe she'd deliberately try to kill herself without talking to me first. It must be an accident. You know how dangerous walking on narrow shoulders is since they started all that construction. The traffic came at us from behind. Eva was walking right behind me, just like every other day. Then *wham*! Before I turned around, I heard another *wham* and saw her lying in the middle of the road. Both cars stopped. They tried to help, but I didn't want us to get in trouble if the cops found the pot, so I grabbed her suitcase and ran home for help and stashed it. The cops came with the ambulance."

Because of the card in her wallet, the hospital called the Borley residence, not her parents. Bob and Sue Borley picked up the call and raced out to his car to drive to the hospital.

"This is where it gets spooky," Bob said. "I fired up the engine just in time to hear the radio blare the opening line of *Spirit in the Sky*.

"Yeah," I said. "I know those lyrics by Norman Greenbaum."

> When I die and they lay me to rest
> Gonna go to the place that's the best
> When they lay me down to die
> Goin' up to the spirit in the sky...

Bob went on. "I mean, what are the chances of those lyrics coming on at that exact moment? Sue and I sat listening to the complete song before either of us could react. Then, stoned as we were, we felt heavy vibes of cosmic synchronicity, man, as if Eva was hailing us from the far shore. Dig? Soon after we arrived at the hospital, John Borley showed up and began lecturing us on traffic safety, of all things. Jeez, like he didn't even know that Eva was nuts about him. Do you think he felt at all responsible for what Eva did?"

"Maybe he is in denial," I said, feeling a sudden sympathy for John. I doubted he'd broken her heart on purpose, but it's almost impossible to live a blameless life and there's no benefit in drowning ourselves in shame when shit happens, which only turns into immobilizing self-pity. Yes, I too carried an unquenchable shame. We can only try to learn from our mistakes and move on or we die inside.

"It really doesn't matter how she died," Bob said. "Whether it was a careless accident or suicide, she's fucking gone, and we miss her."

"Yeah, Bob. I'd tried to help Eva, but if she was determined to die, nothing I could do could keep her alive. I hope that what little I told her about the Bardo helped her wandering in the after-death state. Whatever troubles she left behind, she'd encounter new ones wherever she was going in such a hurry.

At Riveredge I was surrounded by people with suicidal tendencies, yet I still have a tough time understanding why a girl of thirteen, just beginning to blossom into womanhood, would want to kill herself. From listening to her friends and siblings, I only got a partial answer.

So many things become overlooked in a big family like the Delmonte's and one of them was Eva. Maybe no one ever told her she was drop dead beautiful, something every girl longs to hear. She could only afford to wear the patched and faded blue jeans that were only then becoming trendy, but not at her school. Some days she'd come home in tears from the ridicule that malicious classmates heaped on her shabby wardrobe.

Her father held a good-paying job at the railroad, or it would have been if only he didn't have so many mouths to feed. Thirteen total children made for a large brood, even by Catholic standards. Bruno had done his duty by the divine command to "go forth and multiply." The church didn't consider the financial burden that bringing so many children into the world would impose. He had to spread it thin just to care for the basics.

Eva's clothes came from the donated sacks of used clothing brought over by Catholic charities and dumped into a great pile on the concrete floor in the utility room. The kids and their mother went through them for whatever fit or caught someone's fancy. Those that entered neither category became soaking wet when the washer overflowed before that over worked machine finally conked out and in time, mildew turned the clothes to rot.

The rusting Volkswagen Beetle still sat parked in the yard, crammed with another massive pile of clothes that were on their way to a laundromat when it refused to start. There it remained, mildewing, rotting as the months and then years went by. A visual monument to the futility of managing a huge family. Goodbye Eva, we miss you, but never really knew you.

The Warrior Returns

Still teary eyed, but more subdued the next day, Mrs. D turned to me. "Ron, I'd like you to be one of the pallbearers at Eva's funeral." She'd either forgotten or forgiven what I'd told her about Eva acting suicidal the night before her death.

"I'd be honored, Mrs. D., Eva was a wonderful girl and I really appreciate how you've made me feel like a member of the family."

She sighed. "You've been pretty helpful around the house." She put a hand to her forehead. "You can stand opposite Ricky at the front of the casket."

"Ricky? I thought he was in Vietnam."

"Well, some good news came out of this. Ricky is coming home from Vietnam for Eva's funeral."

Modern passenger jets flew guys straight home from combat zones in hours.

Chris pulled me aside. "Watch your mouth, Ron. I heard guys coming back from Vietnam don't like to talk about the war."

"Come on, Chris. He'll only be around for a few days before he's gotta go back. This may be our last chance to find out what it's like

271

over there. I'm bursting with questions about the war. Aren't you? We'll end up there too if we don't run off to Canada soon."

Chris fixed me with a piercing gaze. "Just be cool with him. Remember, you're sleeping in his bed."

I hadn't thought about where Ricky would sleep. My mouth had already gotten me into enough trouble, but it seemed like a crime to be silent about something so crucial to our lives. I'd read so much but needed to hear the straight scoop.

John Wayne Heaps was the first guy I knew sent to Vietnam, but we weren't friends, quite the opposite. As a freshman in high school, I expected hazing from the older students, but for some reason, he singled me out and directed exceptional hate toward me for the brief time I knew him. He dropped out and joined the Marines to be killed in action on September 14, 1968, after less than three months in the Country. Despite our being enemies, I stood in the back at his closed casket funeral and heard the laudatory eulogies. Even our enemies have people who love and honor them.

Ricky's return, whole and uninjured, was more of a somber than joyous occasion. While I was tight with his younger brothers, I'd never even had a casual conversation with Ricky. He stood in the living room with his brothers and me, looking around as if trying to remember his surroundings. "I only have a couple of weeks' leave before I've got to fly back and finish my tour of duty."

His brothers nodded and seemed at a loss for words, so I jumped in, trying to speak in a faint whisper. "Hey Ricky, how is the war? I mean really." He glanced at me but didn't say anything, so I added. "Did you kill anyone in Nam?" I tried to keep a casual, jocular tone, to break through the gloom, but it came out sounding like sarcasm.

His mouth twisted into a grimace, and he looked into my eyes. "Promise me you won't join up."

"Aw, hell no, I won't go!" I paraphrased the Anti-War slogan and laughed still trying to lighten the moment, but Ricky wasn't laughing. His sister was dead, and he'd be going back into the war zone soon enough. It wasn't the right time for this conversation, and maybe there's never a right time, but I'd never get another chance.

Ricky spent the nights with friends rather than kick me out of his bed. On Monday, April 6, I suited up at my parent's house. With his unusual patience, Dad tried to teach me how to tie a necktie. He finally gave up and left it looped so I could pull it tight to my Adam's apple. That item of masculine apparel felt like a garrote to throttle me into submission to conformity. On this occasion, however, I donned it to honor the feelings of others.

I stood by Eva's casket, gazing at her stiff thirteen-year-old corpse. They had dressed her up in fancy clothes and rouged her face, as if she was going to the Prom. The sight was déjà vu for me. The previous July I'd been standing over the stiff body of my thirteen-year-old cousin Carolyn, felled by heart cancer. Both pretty young ladies had only begun to live before death struck them down at the same age, proof that we are never too young to die.

As I had with Cousin Carolyn, I prayed, channeling psychic energy to her spirit, which I imagined was still hovering about her abandoned body. Whenever her grieving relatives weren't close by, so as not to disturb their Catholic sensibilities, I whispered for her to recognize her dreamlike situation in the Bardo, as recommended in the *Tibetan Book of the Dead*. She needed to take charge of her confused wandering between dying and being reborn, to move on into a better rebirth, or even an enlightened state of mind.

Several times, I thought I saw her body quiver. Whether it was my imagination or just the motor reflexes of an empty corpse. I wondered if Eva was trying to come back into her abandoned shell of a body. But of course, the funeral home had pumped out her blood and replaced it with poisonous embalming fluid, yet another unnatural custom I disliked.

Eva's Mass began at 10:00 a.m., at St. Alexis Catholic church in Bensenville. I'd attended many funerals, but this was my first time as a pallbearer. After the mass and tearful eulogies, I took my place opposite Ricky, the rest of the brothers behind us, but instead of lifting and carrying the casket, as I'd seen in movies, we glided it with ease on a wheeled trolly to the hearse. Without speaking, we sat together in the car and rode in the long bumper to bumper funeral parade. It took us east on Grand, across the DesPlaines River and deep into the winding paths of St. Joseph's cemetery. Eva's final home was six miles due north along the river from Riveredge hospital.

The priest used his silver scepter to sprinkle holy water over the coffin before ropes lowered it into the dark pit. Her mortal remains lay filed away into mother earth, as all of ours' will be in time. Our memory of her too will pass unless we leave some record of her short, troubled life.

Ricky swung by the house from time to time. A week went by and then another. I asked him how much leave he'd gotten, but he shrugged it off. One day a government car pulled up, looking for him. He'd gone AWOL, absent without leave. We soon learned that he was safe in Canada where he remained for some years, one less cog in the war machine. I respected him for that.

With the conclusion of the Vietnam War, the United States reverted to an all-volunteer army. Draft cards became outdated. After more than fifty years, I still have my unlaminated draft card, worn and faded from going through the washer a few times, but still legible. It's a rare memento of those turbulent bygone times.

Aftershock

For a couple months after my release, I dropped by Riveredge for my perfunctory sessions with Doctor Ghattas, then I'd waltz down into the cafeteria at lunchtime to see any of my acquaintances who were still around and grab a free hot meal with them. My face was still familiar to the staff, who assumed I was still a paid resident. That worked until one day Ghattas came and saw me. He scolded me and put the staff on notice. No more free lunches for me.

Marge had burrowed deep into my head and heart, and I realized how much I needed someone like her at my side. Desperate to reconnect, I returned a final time to Riveredge. Whether she was still with Rick or anyone else, I'd pour out my heart to her, and if she reciprocated, I'd pop the question and propose marriage right there on the spot, no matter who or what stood in our way. She'd been released or transferred but a sort of mental hospital subculture had evolved from the core of patients who kept in touch. They'd be out, only to wind up back at the Edge after yet another overdose or suicide attempt. I counted on that grapevine to get in touch with Marge.

I approached an anemic looking girl I recognized but hadn't

gotten to know very well. She'd been a shy wallflower, too preoccupied with her interior life for us to become acquainted.

"Hi. Cindy? Remember me?" She fixed me with her usual deadpan stare. I remembered that she drowned her emotions with downers and expressed little joy in her life.

"Ron, is it? You grew your hair, looks nice."

"That's me, all right. Is Marge around? Have you heard anything from her?"

"Marge is dead."

"What? No! You must be thinking of another Marge. Her last name was, ah... it begins with a W. Oh yeah, Weiselman, that's it."

"Yes, that's her. She took a big handful of Valium and slit her writs."

A funeral dirge began playing in my head, but I shook it off. It couldn't be her.

"Marge would never go out like that."

Cindy stared at me with no change in her expression. "Marge was very unhappy with her controlling mother. We had that much in common."

"Look," I said. "I know she'd cut herself in the past, but she'd gotten tougher, stronger. She's a survivor."

Unwilling to accept her death until I found verification, I asked around, but the staff either didn't know or wouldn't tell, citing privacy concerns. Decades later, after computers and social media made sleuthing easier, I rediscovered another long-lost valentine. Valerie, whose sweet tobacco flavored kisses had helped me ring in 1970, she filled me in by email.

I don't think most of us deserved to be in institutions, Ron. I'd been in another institution for a year prior to the Edge but didn't live on Two South until my last two months there. I'm certain I was allowed 'group activities' only. I spent an inordinate amount of time in ICU, but I didn't attempt suicide, hadn't committed crimes. I wasn't the craziest person around, but they really didn't know where to put me.

Marge became a very dear, well, my best friend. She was actually very sweet, but like many of my friends from that time, she died by suicide. She lived in Elmwood Park with her parents and her big brother. Her mom gave her one hundred three-grain Tuinal caps as a 'hush' gift, not to mention Mom's hidden vodka bottles. She was going to pick me up the next day but said she didn't want to become eighteen and died that night before her birthday in September 1970.

Except for psychedelics, drugs were never my thing. I don't know much about them, so I looked on-line to learn that from the nineteen-sixties through the eighties Tuinal, under the street names "double trouble," and "blue tips," saw widespread abuse as a recreational drug. Like other barbiturates, there was an elevated risk of dependency and overdose, so manufacturers discontinued it by the late nineteen-nineties. Marge joined celebrities like Arthur Koestler and his wife Cynthia, who committed suicide by Tuinal on March 1, 1983. Singer Phyllis Hyman also committed suicide by Tuinal and vodka only hours before she was scheduled to perform at the Apollo Theater on June 30, 1995. Stage fright can be a real killer.

Valerie had more information about our other friends too.

Remember Marianne Calvi? She was married a few times, I think. She had the first gastric bypass I'd ever heard of, because she didn't like dieting. She cut herself another time too, just so her father would bring her fast food or better Italian food. She was quite the criminal. When I was younger, I was rather amazed by her stories. She loved pouring liquid on the floors at department stores, then lying in the mess, crying for help. She said it was almost always good for a fast $50-$500 from the store. I didn't find that funny, just criminal. She had an affair with a man who escaped from Madden Mental Health Center in Hines, Illinois. He'd cut his wife up after he killed her, sent different parts to different folks. He even sent her head in a box to her parents. Marianne just ignored all that and said he made her wear stilettos in bed.

As for me, I served about five years, then I took myself out on a long pass, got a job in a law firm downtown, found an apartment, and called to say I wasn't coming back. Life has been good to me since I'd left Riveredge. I'm married, no kids...

In the spring of 1998, I tried to re-connect with my old friend Pete Fischetti, sending a letter to an address I found in Chicago. Months later, my telephone rang rousing me from deep sleep and a woman's voice asked, "Is this Ron Schulz?"

"Yes."

"Your letter to Pete Fischetti got forwarded to our new address." She coughed and took a deep breath, and I held mine as my heart raced. "I'm his widow, I'm afraid you're too late to talk to him. He died of a stroke back in April." She sighed, and I heard my clock ticking while I tried to shake a response out of my half-awake brain.

"I'm deeply sorry to hear that. He was such a vibrant, generous guy."

"Yes, he was. Now he's gone, and I miss him terribly. Pete often spoke about the times he shared with you in Cook County jail and the mental hospital. He'd been writing a book when he passed away and we're going to publish it posthumously."

"Um, a book? Wow, I'd love to read it, and I'd like to keep in touch. What's your new address and phone number?"

"Well..." She smacked her lips. "No, that's okay. I'll call you back with details about the book's publication. His father had a book out too. Did you know?" I heard her rummaging around before she got back to me. "Pete's father, John Fischetti, wrote *Zinga Zinga Za: From Little Italy to the Pulitzer Prize*. It tells his life story with a collection of his political cartoons that he published in the Tribune and Chicago Daily News."

"Thanks, I'll have to check it out. I only met his dad briefly, but he seemed like a great guy."

"Goodbye, Ron." She hung up before I could say anything more and I collapsed back on my bed.

After all our pot smoking while rambling through cemeteries, Pete left his own mortal coil far too soon. I found him listed in the Social Security Death Index:

Peter FISCHETTI Birth Date: 22 Jul 1950. Death Date: 18 Apr 1998.

He was only 47, but age is no predictor of death.

Despite her promise, Pete's widow never got back to me. Over the years, I kept searching for his name among author lists without success, but unless you're a media star like his papa was, it can be difficult to get a book published before our time on earth runs out. In time, all of us, once young and bursting with vitality, become as old and gray as our parents and grandparents were when we set out to change the world.

As youths, we charged into this world with fresh arrogance, eager to make our stamp on this ancient world before passing the torch to descendants yet unborn. We too ought not to dismiss the new young as many of our elders did us. They need more encouragement than admonishment. What insight can we impart to the next crop of humanity?

Lest our shared experience vanish into the great maw of unrecorded history, I'm driven to celebrate those heady events and my feelings about them. If I can ignite a spark to amuse and remind the reader of who we once were and will be again as we cycle back through the cosmos, my efforts will have paid dividends. Blessings upon all who read or hear this. Om-ah-hum!

Discharge Record

RIVEREDGE HOSPITAL
Forest Park, Illinois

SCHULZ, RONALD Age: 17
Adm: 10/20/69 Marital Status: Single
Dischg: 2/19/70 Occupation: Student
<u>Diagnosis</u>: Schizophrenia (Unspecified)

<u>EPS</u>: The patient was referred to the undersigned by Mrs. Austin, school psychologist at Fenton High School. The patient was brought to the hospital after he and his parents had seen Dr. Ghattas. The patient had become psychotic when in Cook County jail after having been arrested for being in a protest demonstration as a member of the Students for Democratic Society. He was arrested for fighting with a police officer, and it was reported that he was trying to protect another member who was being hit over the head by police. When his father visited him in jail, the patient seemed so different from how they had known him; he rambled and cussed. The parents tried keeping him at home... but he would get on his

soapbox and was also hallucinating and was subsequently admitted
to the hospital.

PP: The patient is a 17-year-old single male, oldest in a sibling ship of
six, having five younger sisters. His parents described him as being a
very passive boy who never fought and used his fear of fighting as a
reason for dropping out of school in his junior year. He ran away
from home when he was a freshman and spent three weeks in New
Orleans. Since dropping out of school, he has been roving and
worked some. He has been isolated from the family, has few friends,
and has been a withdrawn, unhappy, and below moderately func-
tioning boy for a long period of time. He is described as having a good
relationship with his sisters, does not seem to have had much of a
relationship with his mother, and has practically had no relationship
with his father.

INCAPACITY: Severe for social and vocational adjustment. The
patient was admitted with the complaint of severe agitation, delusions of trying to conquer the world, and several ideas of having rebel-
lions. He gave a history of having been excited over the past few
weeks and seemed to feel that he had no goal in life. History indicates
that he has always been a loner, unable to accept responsibility, and
seemed to feel inadequate. At the time of admission, he was quite
confused with some persecutory delusions. No hallucinations were
evident. Memory was good for recent and past events.

Dr. Ghattas saw regularly the patient in psychotherapy interviews
during his hospital stay. He seemed to feel very inadequate and
talked about his feelings of isolation. His sense of denial seemed to be
mild. He talked about his relationship with his parents and his fear of
being able to relate to them. He seemed very anxious and rebellious,
but by 11/24 was more verbal and more communicative. In early
December he still seemed to be worried and talked about his fears of
accepting responsibility. He was very uncertain and fearful about any

limits and seemed to feel very restless. He seemed to feel very scared about the outcome of his court case. He gradually improved and became more responsive and more aware of himself and his rebellious feelings. Improvement continued and he was discharged on 2/19/70 to be followed in outpatient care.

COND ON DISCH: Improved. ...

Dictated & Typed: 2/27/70 Subhail Ghattas, M.D.

D r. Ghattas' assessment amused me when I read it decades later. My "delusions of trying to conquer the world," makes me out to be a fascist or narcissist, not at all how I saw myself. Yes, I "rambled and cussed" got on my "soapbox" to exhort the Revolution, but I wasn't "hallucinating," unless this refers to the cosmic vision I had on LSD and my out-of-body experience when I was three years old, which I should never have mentioned to him. True, I sometimes withdrew from what I saw as negative social situations, hoping to live to fight another day, but I take issue with the claim that I had "few friends" and was "unable to accept responsibility."

Maybe I was too hard on Dr. Ghattas. None of us, hip or straight, fit the tight mold of our class and social expectation. It was difficult for me to bridge the gap between us. I saw him as a representative of the status quo, trying to brainwash me back into the obedient role our capitalist, consumer society demanded, not as a man, an immigrant, struggling to do his best to raise a family and achieve success in his new American world.

The last two sentences, *No hallucinations were evident. Memory was good for recent and past events,* seem to contradict everything above and helped advocate for my release. I was free at last and ready for the next chapter of my life. The new American Revolution was just getting started, and I needed to find my place in it.

About the Author

RONALD SCHULZ was born in the nineteen-fifties in Chicago. He dropped out to explore the Sixties radical counterculture before hitchhiking across Europe and Africa on a roundabout Buddhist pilgrimage to Nepal. Now a semi-retired hobo, and a new author writing his honest history of those tumultuous times, he hopes to honor the memory of departed friends before he too vanishes from this planet. He has taken advanced writing classes at the University of Washington and Hugo House. Ronald is a father of two, grandfather of three, who believes in living life to the fullest, regardless of circumstances.

Thank You

Thank you for purchasing and reading this work.

If you enjoyed this book, please take the time to leave a review on Goodreads and the site you purchased the work on. Reviews allow others to discover the work and entices the author to continue writing.

www.ingramcontent.com/pod-product-compliance
Lightning Source LLC
Chambersburg PA
CBHW070910120626
46546CB00001B/210